CRITICAL SURVEY OF POETRY
War Poets

Editor

Rosemary M. Canfield Reisman
Charleston Southern University

SALEM PRESS
A Division of EBSCO Publishing, Ipswich, Massachusetts

Cover photo:
Chinua Achebe (© Ralph Orlowski/Reuters/Corbis)

Copyright © 2012, by Salem Press, A Division of EBSCO Publishing, Inc.
All rights in this book are reserved. No part of this work may be used or reproduced in any manner whatsoever or transmitted in any form or by any means, electronic or mechanical, including photocopy, recording, or any information storage and retrieval system, without written permission from the copyright owner except in the case of brief quotations embodied in critical articles and reviews or in the copying of images deemed to be freely licensed or in the public domain. For information address the publisher, Salem Press, at csr@salempress.com.

ISBN: 978-1-42983-653-1

CONTENTS

Contributors iv

War Poets 1

Chinua Achebe 4
Endre Ady 8
Rafael Alberti 17
Guillaume Apollinaire 26
Louis Aragon 37
John Balaban 48
Edmund Blunden 55
Bertolt Brecht 63
Rupert Brooke 74
W. D. Ehrhart 83
Philip Freneau 91
Roy Fuller 102
Ivor Gurney 109
David Jones 118
Christopher Logue 123
Walt McDonald 129
Wilfred Owen 138
Sándor Petőfi 147
Pierre Reverdy 166
Isaac Rosenberg 176
Siegfried Sassoon 183
Alan Seeger 194
Louis Simpson 199
Edward Thomas 212
Bruce Weigl 219

Checklist for Explicating a Poem 228
Bibliography 231
Guide to Online Resources 234
Geographical Index 238
Category Index 239
Subject Index 241

CONTRIBUTORS

Peter Baker
Southern Connecticut State University

David Barratt
Montreat College

Enikő Molnár Basa
Library of Congress

Carole A. Champagne
University of Maryland-Eastern Shore

Anita Price Davis
Converse College

Lillian Doherty
University of Maryland

Theresa E. Dozier
Prince George's Community College

Robert Edward Graalman, Jr.
Oklahoma State University

Sarah Hilbert
Pasadena, California

David Harrison Horton
Patten College

Ramona L. Hyman
Loma Linda University

Jeffry Jensen
Pasadena, California

William Jolliff
George Fox University

Irma M. Kashuba
Chestnut Hill College

Philip Krummrich
University of Georgia

Mary Lang
Wharton County Junior College

Michael R. Meyers
Pfeiffer University

Michael D. Moore
Wilfrid Laurier University

Bernard E. Morris
Modesto, California

Edward F. Palm
Maryville University of St. Louis

Jay Ruud
Northern State University

John C. Shields
Illinois State University

Richard Spuler
Rice University

Vivien Stableford
Reading, United Kingdom

Stefan Stoenescu
Ithaca, New York

Ryan D. Stryffeler
Ivy Tech Community College

Martha Modena Vertreace-Doody
Kennedy-King College

WAR POETS

Throughout history, war has had a brutalizing effect on the human condition, and the carnage has seemingly become more horrific over time. Technological advancements have led to even more efficient ways to slaughter enemies and terrify the citizenry. Many poets have written about wars of which they have had no direct experience; it is the "soldier-poet" who has the firsthand knowledge of what war can do, not only to the body but also to the psyche. One of the classic poems about war is Homer's *Iliad*, which dates back to c. 800 B.C.E. (English translation, 1616) and traces the course of the Trojan War.

While the *Iliad* is an important example from the Greek heroic tradition, there are several examples from other, even older civilizations that speak to both the glorious nature of battle and its brutal consequences. Ancient poets wrote about legendary warriors in order to focus on a bravery that is at the core of the heroic ideal. Poetry from this ancient heroic age served to bolster people and civilizations with the best qualities that it had to offer. A willingness to make the ultimate sacrifice for one's country or cause became the desired attribute for which all warriors should strive.

As warfare changed over the centuries, this heroic ideal began to lose its impact. Following the invention of new, more barbaric methods of slaughter, it became harder for poets to recount the legends with the same fervor. While the Middle Ages had its chivalry, the valorous conduct of warring sides had dramatically changed by the seventeenth century. Scholars have argued that the invention of gunpowder not only altered the way in which wars were fought but also made it impossible for poets to write about warfare with as much enthusiasm, given that the combatants were now being blown apart.

As the nature of warfare changed, so poets' encounters with the consequences of battle became more prominent in their work. By the nineteenth century, even more horrendous weaponry was available for armies to exploit. The technology of warfare seemed to be outpacing medical advancements, resulting in thousands of wounded soldiers who were doomed to agonizing deaths. Lord Tennyson wrote his famous 1854 poem "The Charge of the Light Brigade" in response to the tragic charge of British cavalry toward Russian artillery during the Crimean War. He depicted the event as a heroic act on the part of the British, which seemed to be what the British public wanted to believe. Tennyson, though, was far removed from the front lines of the war. While his approach turned a reckless episode into a heroic act, this was not how all poets approached to the subject of war. The poetry of Walt Whitman and Stephen Crane, for example, bluntly exposes the grief and heartache that came out of the American Civil War. By the turn of the century, it was obvious that war, skirmishes, border disputes, and other conflicts were taking a heavy toll on the general population.

Poetry Responds to a World War

During World War I, every able-bodied man was expected to put on a uniform and fight for his country. The soldier-poet also was thrown into the trenches. Some of the most memorable poetry about real war by real men in uniform came from the English poets who fought in that war. Men such as Wilfred Owen, Rupert Brooke, Isaac Rosenberg, Edward Thomas, David Jones, Ivor Gurney, and Siegfried Sassoon wrote about what they experienced firsthand. Of these seven, only Sassoon, Gurney, and Jones survived the war. The poetry these men left behind serves as a gut-wrenching reminder of what war truly is for those who are combatants. During World War I, soldiers were subjected to trench warfare and mustard gas. For them, the experience was not an abstract concept, or a political exercise for the greater good. It was a terrifying everyday event that the soldier-poet found a way to transform into poetry. In the heartbreaking poem "Dulce et Decorum Est," Owen speaks of his experience at the front; the opening stanza paints a grim picture of a soldier's dire situation:

> Bent double, like beggars under sacks,
> Knock-kneed, coughing like hags, we cursed through sludge,
> Till on the haunting flares we turned our backs
> And towards our distant rest began to trudge.
> Men marched asleep. Many had lost their boots
> But limped on, blood-shod. All went lame; all blind;
> Drunk with fatigue; deaf even to the hoots
> Of tired, outstripped Five-Nines that dropped behind.

The title of the poem is taken from one of Horace's *Odes* (23 B.C.E., 13 B.C.E.; English translation, 1621) and can be translated as "sweet and fitting it is to die for one's country."

Having poets put their experiences into poetry helped to educate the public about war and added a powerful voice to the public discourse. These poets served as representatives of what could happen to all soldiers. The British soldier-poets were not the only ones to produce haunting poetry; the French poet Guillaume Apollinaire died in the war, and his collection *Calligrammes* (English translation, 1980) was published after his death in 1918. The collection includes poems that deal with his terrible experiences in the war. The war poems of the Russian poet Nikolay Gumilyov were published in his 1916 collection *Kolchan*, which translates as "the quiver." "The War to End All Wars," as World War I became known, slaughtered so many young men, some of whom produced some of the most haunting war poetry ever written.

Poetry Continues to Fight the Good Fight

Sadly, World War II would engulf the world by the late 1930's. Not as many notable English-language war poets came out of this war; many of the most important poems about the war were composed by French poets, including Louis Aragon, René Char, Pierre Seghers, Paul Éluard, and Robert Desnos. The American poet Karl Shapiro wrote about his experiences serving in the Pacific in such collection as *Person, Place, and Thing* (1942), *The Place of Love* (1942), and the Pulitzer Prize-winning *V-Letter and Other Poems* (1944). Several American poets who served in the Vietnam War during the 1960's, including W. D. Ehrhart and Walt McDonald, also immortalized their experiences in riveting poetry. John Balaban went to Vietnam through the International Volunteer Services as a conscientious objector. He taught in Vietnam but was wounded during the 1968 Tet Offensive, and his 1974 collection *After the War* is a harrowing portrait of how the experience changed him forever. The highly acclaimed Nigerian writer Chinua Achebe dealt with the tragedy of the Nigerian Civil War by responding with highly charged poetry. His 1971 collection *Beware: Soul Brother and Other Poems* includes poems that confront the failure of Biafra to become an independent nation.

Over the centuries, poets have felt obligated to take on all that makes up a war. Whether through firsthand experience or from a distance, these poets have had to come to terms with the very nature of man and his capacity to brutalize his fellow man on an ever-increasing scale.

Jeffry Jensen

BIBLIOGRAPHY

Chattarji, Subarno. *Memories of a Lost War: American Poetic Responses to the Vietnam War*. New York: Oxford University Press, 2001. A discussion of how poets responded to an unpopular war.

McLoughlin, Kate. *Authoring War: The Literary Representation of War from the "Iliad" to Iraq*. Cambridge, England: Cambridge University Press, 2011. A study of how writers have portrayed conflicts throughout the ages.

Rodman, Selden. "The Vision of Armies." Introduction to *War and the Poet: An Anthology of Poetry Expressing Man's Attitude to War from Ancient Times to the Present*, edited by Richard Eberhart and Selden Rodman. New York: Devin-Adair, 1945. An introduction to the purpose of war poetry.

Stallworthy, Jon. Introduction to *The Oxford Book of War Poetry*. New York: Oxford University Press, 1984. Discusses the special skill a poet must have in order to write honestly about something as terrifying as war.

Templeton, Alice. "What's the Use? Writing Poetry in Wartime." *College Literature* 34, no. 4 (Fall, 2007): 43-63. Considers whether poetry can retain its value while standing up to the reality of war.

Silkin, Jon. Introduction to *The Penguin Book of First World War Poetry*. London: Allen Lane, 1979. An introduction to the soldier-poets of World War I.

Winn, James Anderson. *The Poetry of War*. Cambridge, England: Cambridge University Press, 2008. Speaks to how the master war poets are able to confront the "terrible beauty" that is war.

CHINUA ACHEBE

Born: Ogidi, Nigeria; November 16, 1930

PRINCIPAL POETRY
Beware, Soul Brother, and Other Poems, 1971, 1972
Christmas in Biafra, and Other Poems, 1973
Collected Poems, 2004

OTHER LITERARY FORMS

Chinua Achebe (ah-CHAY-bay) is a writer who has made important contributions in every literary genre. He is known primarily for his first novel, *Things Fall Apart* (1959). His other novels include *No Longer at Ease* (1960), *Arrow of God* (1964), *A Man of the People* (1966), and *Anthills of the Savannah* (1987). Achebe's short stories are collected in *The Sacrificial Egg, and Other Stories* (1962) and *Girls at War, and Other Stories* (1972). He has also published collections of essays: *Morning Yet on Creation Day* (1975), *An Image of Africa* (1977), *The Trouble with Nigeria* (1983), *Hopes and Impediments* (1988), *Home and Exile* (2000), and *Education of a British-Protected Child* (2009). In addition to his contributions as a poet, novelist, short-story writer, and essayist, Ache has written books for children: *Chike and the River* (1966), *How the Leopard Got His Claws* (1972; with John Iroaganachi), *The Flute* (1977), and *The Drum* (1977). He has also edited numerous works, including *Don't Let Him Die: An Anthology of Memorial Poems for Christopher Okigbo, 1937-1967* (1978; with Dubem Okafor).

ACHIEVEMENTS

Chinua Achebe is known as the founder of modern African writing. His many awards include the Margaret Wrong Memorial Prize (1959) for *Things Fall Apart*, the Nigerian National Trophy for Literature (1961), the Jock Campbell-*New Statesman* Award for Literature for *Arrow of God* (1966), the Commonwealth Poetry Prize (1972, joint winner), the Afro-Asian Writers Association's Lotus Award (1975), the Nigerian National Merit Award (1979), the Triple Eminence Award from the Association of Nigerian Authors (1990), the Langston Hughes Award (1993), the Campion Medal and Order of Kilimanjaro Award (both 1996), the German Booksellers Peace Prize (2002), and the Man Booker International Prize (2007). He was named Officer of the Order of the Federal Republic (Nigeria) in 1979, a fellow of the Royal Society of Literature in 1981, an honorary foreign fellow of the American Academy and Institute of Arts and Letters in 1982, and an honorary fellow of the American Academy of Arts and Science in 2002. In 1998, he was the McMillan-Steward Lecturer at Harvard University and the Presidential Fellow Lecturer at the World Bank.

Biography

Albert Chinualumogu Achebe was born the fifth of six children of educated Igbo parents, Isaiah Okafor Achebe and Janet Anaenechi Achebe. He was born in Ogidi, a town in the eastern region of Nigeria. After converting to Christianity, Achebe's father served as a catechist for the Church Missionary Society. From 1944 to 1948, Achebe attended the Government College, Umuahia, a highly competitive school, then received a scholarship to the University College, Ibadan (University of Ibadan). Initially, Achebe's collegiate goal was to study medicine; however, his goals changed because of his interest in the academic areas of religion, history, and English literature. While at the University College, Achebe and several other students founded a literary journal, *The University Herald*. In addition to publishing works in the journal, Achebe served as the editor during his third year of matriculation at the institution.

After graduation in 1953, Achebe served as a teacher at the Merchant of Light School. He began working for the Nigerian Broadcasting Corporation in 1954, and two years later, he trained at the British Broadcasting Corporation. He published the inaugural text for the Heinemann African Writers series, *Things Fall Apart*, in 1959. The publication of this novel significantly changed the trajectory of Achebe's writing career and his life. The novel has been published in many languages and has sold more than eight million copies. Moreover, *Things Fall Apart* ushered Achebe into the center of the critical conversation on African literature and social-political thought, giving him a central place in the canon of world literature.

In addition to a prolific writing career, Achebe has had an outstanding academic portfolio. His visiting professorships include posts at the University of Massachusetts at Amherst (1972-1975), the University of Connecticut (1975-1976), and City College of the City University of New York (1989). In 1986, Achebe was appointed pro-vice-chancellor of the State University of Anambra in Enugu. Achebe was the Charles P. Stevenson Professor of Languages and Literature at Bard College in 1990-2009. In September, 2009, he became the David and Marianna Fisher University Professor and professor of Africana studies at Brown University.

In addition to being one of Africa's most influential writers, Achebe is a family man. On September 10, 1961, he married Christie Chinwe Okoli, a professor of psychology. The couple had four children, Chinelo, Ikechukwu, Chidi, and Nwando.

Analysis

The thematic concern of Chinua Achebe's life and writing is to articulate the meaning of what it is to be African from the perspective of one who is authentically African. Critic Nahem Yousaf has said that Achebe's intent as a writer is to "challenge the insidious stories in which the colonized and dispossessed are rendered inhuman and inept in order to make heroes of the 'hunter' colonialists, and to shore up the memoirs of colonial apologists." Achebe expresses his love for and critique of Africa, specifically Nigeria, in all of his writing. Achebe's political and social critique of his country comes out of his love for the people and the place that he identifies as home.

CHRISTMAS IN BIAFRA

Christmas in Biafra is a poetic response to the Biafran War (1967-1970; also known as the Nigerian Civil War). In this collection, Achebe relates the stories of the people who suffered during the war. The images created, as in "Benin Road," are portraits of a country tortured by the reality that on a highway sometimes, "Speed is violence/ Power is violence/ Weight violence."

The book is divided into five sections: "Prologue," "Poems About War," "Poems Not About War," "Gods, Men, and Others," and "Epilogue." Although the main theme of the book is war, the book has a religious tone. Poems such as "Lazarus" suggest that this collection is a spiritual polemic grounded in the complex depictions of war and its aftermath. Achebe helps the reader realize that when a war is over, a country—and all that is associated with it—must regroup, writing that "life catches desperately at passing hints of normalcy."

COLLECTED POEMS

Collected Poems is a broad representation of Achebe's poetry, with its themes of the cultural effects of imperialism and colonialism. In its introductory "parable," Achebe details the need for this collection, which was published because the author received an "urgent call from a lady who identified herself as Curator of *Another Africa*," an exhibition that included his work. In the postmodern sense, Achebe's *Collected Poems* was called into being because of the synergistic relationship between an author and his prospective audience.

OTHER MAJOR WORKS

LONG FICTION: *Things Fall Apart*, 1959; *No Longer at Ease*, 1960; *Arrow of God*, 1964; *A Man of the People*, 1966; *Anthills of the Savannah*, 1987.

SHORT FICTION: "Dead Men's Path," 1953; *The Sacrificial Egg, and Other Stories*, 1962; *Girls at War, and Other Stories*, 1972.

NONFICTION: *Morning Yet on Creation Day*, 1975; *An Image of Africa*, 1977; *The Trouble with Nigeria*, 1983; *Hopes and Impediments*, 1988; *Conversations with Chinua Achebe*, 1997 (Bernth Lindfors, editor); *Home and Exile*, 2000; *Education of a British-Protected Child*, 2009.

CHILDREN'S LITERATURE: *Chike and the River*, 1966; *How the Leopard Got His Claws*, 1972 (with John Iroaganachi); *The Drum*, 1977; *The Flute*, 1977.

EDITED TEXTS: *Don't Let Him Die: An Anthology of Memorial Poems for Christopher Okigbo, 1937-1967*, 1978 (with Dubem Okafor); *Aka wega: Egwu aguluagu egwu edeluede*, 1982 (with Obiora Udechukwu); *African Short Stories*, 1985 (with C. L.

Innes); *Beyond Hunger in Africa*, 1990 (with others); *The Heinemann Book of Contemporary African Short Stories*, 1992 (with Innes).

MISCELLANEOUS: *Another Africa*, 1998 (poems and essay; photographs by Robert Lyons).

BIBLIOGRAPHY

Booker, M. Keith, ed. *The Chinua Achebe Encyclopedia*. Westport, Conn.: Greenwood Press, 2003. This comprehensive guide to Achebe's life and works provides substantive discussions of his fiction, nonfiction, and poetry. Contains several hundred entries, a bibliography, and a chronology.

Egejuru, Phanuel Akubueze. *Chinua Achebe: Pure and Simple—An Oral Biography*. Ikeja, Nigeria: Malthouse Press, 2002. A biography of Achebe written from the Nigerian point of view.

Emenyonu, Ernest N., and Iniobong I. Uko, eds. *Emerging Perspectives on Chinua Achebe*. Trenton, N.J.: Africa World Press, 2004. Contains two essays on Achebe as a poet, one focusing on *Beware, Soul Brother, and Other Poems*, and the other discussing Achebe as a war poet.

Lindfors, Bernth. *Early Achebe*. Trenton, N.J.: Africa World Press, 2009. Although this work deals primarily with the novels, essays, and stories published between 1951 and 1966, it helps the reader understand what formed Achebe's main themes.

Morrison, Jago. *The Fiction of Chinua Achebe*. New York: Palgrave Macmillan, 2007. Although the focus of this work is Achebe's fiction, it examines the key areas of criticism surrounding his work.

Nwodo, Christopher S. *Philosophical Perspective on Chinua Achebe*. Port Harcourt, Nigeria: University of Port Harcourt Press, 2004. Looks at the philosophical aspects of Achebe's writings, focusing on the Igbo people and questions of racism.

Opata, Damian U., ed. *The Eagle in Ascendance: More Papers from the Chinua Achebe International Symposium, 1990, with New Essays Added*. Ibadan, Nigeria: Heinemann Educational Books, 2005. This collection, which adds new critical essays to those originally from a 1990 symposium, covers most aspects of Achebe's writing.

Sallah, Tijan M., and Ngozi Okonjo-Iweala. *Chinua Achebe, Teacher of Light: A Biography*. Trenton, N.J.: Africa World Press, 2003. A biography of Achebe that looks at his life and work, discussing the intellectual life of Nigeria in the twentieth century.

Ramona L. Hyman

ENDRE ADY

Born: Érdmindszent, Austro-Hungarian Empire (now Ady Endre, Romania);
November 22, 1877
Died: Budapest, Hungary; January 27, 1919

PRINCIPAL POETRY
Versek, 1899
Még egyszer, 1903
Új versek, 1906 (*New Verses*, 1969)
Vér és arany, 1908 (*Blood and Gold*, 1969)
Az Illés szekerén, 1909 (*On Elijah's Chariot*, 1969)
A minden titkok verseiből, 1910 (*Of All Mysteries*, 1969)
Szeretném, ha szeretnének, 1910 (*Longing for Love*, 1969)
A menekülő élet, 1912 (*This Fugitive Life*, 1969)
A magunk szerelme, 1913 (*Love of Ourselves*, 1969)
Ki látott engem?, 1914 (*Who Sees Me?*, 1969)
A halottak élén, 1918 (*Leading the Dead*, 1969)
Margita élni akar, 1921
Az utolsó hajók, 1923 (*The Last Ships*, 1969)
Rövid dalok egyről és másról, 1923
Poems of Endre Ady, 1969 (includes *New Verses, Blood and Gold, On Elijah's Chariot, Longing for Love, Of All Mysteries, This Fugitive Life, Love of Ourselves, Who Sees Me?, Leading the Dead,* and *The Last Ships*)

OTHER LITERARY FORMS

Endre Ady (O-dee) was a journalist who wrote numerous articles, reports, reviews, criticisms, essays, and short stories for the press. These were collected after his death under the titles *Az új Hellász* (1920; new Hellas), *Levelek Párizsból* (1924; letters from Paris), *Párizsi noteszkönyve* (1924; Paris notebook), and *Ha hív az aczélhegyű ördög* (1927; if the steel-tipped devil calls). In his lifetime, Ady published *Vallomások és tanúlmányok* (1911; confessions and studies), containing his important prose writings, both political and literary. Some of these writings are available in English translation in *The Explosive Country: A Selection of Articles and Studies, 1898-1916* (1977). His collections of short stories combine subjective, personal confession with a depiction of early twentieth century Hungary. They are *Sápadt emberek és történetek* (1907; pale men and stories), *Így is történhetik* (1910; it can happen thus also), *A tízmilliós Kleopátra és egyébb történetek* (1910; Cleopatra of the ten millions and other stories), *Új csapáson* (1913; on a new track), and *Muskétás tanár úr* (1913; Professor Muskétás).

His letters have been published in *Ady Endre válogatott levelei* (1956; selected letters of Endre Ady), with an introduction by Béla György.

Achievements

Endre Ady is one of Hungary's greatest lyric poets. Inspired by Western European models, primarily French, he created a new lyrical style that both shocked and inspired his contemporaries. At the same time, he revitalized indigenous Hungarian literary traditions, looking back to the seventeenth and eighteenth centuries rather than to the example of his immediate predecessors. His topics, too, were considered revolutionary: physical passion and erotic love, political and social reform. He remained, however, within the tradition of the great nineteenth century Hungarian poets who expressed the spirit of the nation in their works.

Biography

Endre Ady's heritage and birthplace had a profound influence on his poetry. His ancestry was the relatively poor nobility, or gentry, which on his mother's side also boasted a tradition of Calvinist ministers. In the small village of Érdmindszent, he came to know the peasantry intimately, for his own family's life differed little from theirs. His father wished him to enter the civil service, so he was educated with a view to obtaining a legal degree. The area in which Ady grew up (today Salaj, Romania) is situated in the Partium, a region of eastern Hungary that had stormy ties to Transylvania during the sixteenth and seventeenth centuries, when that principality had been a bulwark of Hungarian autonomy and traditions while the rest of the country was under Turkish or Habsburg rule. The Partium was thus doubly a frontier area in whose Calvinist and *kuruc* (anti-Habsburg) traditions Ady saw justification for his own rebellious, individualistic nature. He was always proud of his ancestry and considered himself much more Magyar than many of his contemporaries with more mixed ethnic backgrounds.

After completing five elementary grades in his village, Ady was sent first to the Piarist school in Nagykároly, then to the Calvinist gymnasium at Zilah, which he regarded as his alma mater; he always fondly remembered his teachers there. Several of his classmates were later to become prominent among the more radical thinkers and politicians of the early years of the twentieth century. He also read voraciously, both earlier Hungarian literature and European naturalistic writers, and became acquainted with the works of Arthur Schopenhauer. After a brief period in law school in Debrecen and time spent as a legal clerk in Temesvár (Timisoara, Romania) and Zilah (Zalau), he realized that his true vocation was in journalism. He followed this career until his death.

Ady first worked in Debrecen, and in this period not only did his horizons widen, but his critical theses began to crystallize as well. "Life" and "truth" became important bywords for him, and he continued his readings: Auguste Comte, Herbert Spencer, Friedrich Nietzsche, Henrik Ibsen, Fyodor Dostoevski, and especially the late eighteenth century poet Mihály Csokonai Vitéz, a native of Debrecen. It was in Nagyvárad (today Oradea, Romania) that Ady became familiar with the life of a large city and the more cosmopolitan society it represented. He wrote for liberal papers, and for a while his political views agreed with the pro-government stance of such journals. In time, however, he became disillusioned with their reluctance to press for universal suffrage and other reforms affecting the poor and the national minorities. It was at this time that he became acquainted with *Huszadik század*, a progressive journal begun in 1900.

The years in Nagyvárad were also important in Ady's personal life and poetic development, for it was during this period that he met Adél Brüll, whom he was to immortalize as the Leda of his poems. This older, married woman (her married name was Diósi)—more experienced, more worldly, more cultured than he—was an important influence on his life. Their passionate and at times tempestuous love affair, which finally ended in 1912, is recorded in poems that were to revolutionize Hungarian love poetry. When Ady went to Paris as the foreign correspondent of his paper, Brüll was there, and his impressions of the French city were acquired under her tutelage. When he returned from the 1904 trip, he burst on the world with a new poetic style.

By 1905, Ady was working in Budapest for the liberal *Budapesti napló*. In numerous articles, he wrote of the need for radical reforms; independence from Austria was also debated. At this time, Ady turned his attention to the social problems that were destroying the country; in both his poetry and his prose writings, he championed the disenfranchised. The important journal *Nyugat* was started in 1908, and Ady soon became associated with it—all the more so as his increasingly radical views did not agree with the middle-of-the-road liberalism of the *Budapesti napló*.

When war broke out in 1914, Ady opposed Hungarian participation in the conflict, increasing his isolation from official political life. His antiwar poems were inspired by humanism and patriotism. The poor and the politically powerless suffered most heavily, Ady argued, and he believed that the war was being fought against Hungarian interests, purely for Austrian goals. During this time, Ady lived mostly in Érdmindszent and at Csucsa, the estate of Berta Boncza, whom he had met in 1914 and married the following year. Berta, the daughter of a well-to-do nobleman and prominent politician, was considerably younger than Ady; she had been attracted to him some time earlier, when she read his *Blood and Gold* while still in school in Switzerland. The poems written to her reflect a different mood from that of the Leda poems: The love is deeper and less intensely erotic. They project the hope that Csinszka (as Berta is called in the poems addressed to her) will preserve the thoughts and ideals of the poet. By this time, Ady was gravely ill with the syphilis that had been progressively destroying him since his Nagyvárad days.

The revolution that Ady had awaited came to Hungary in October of 1918. Ady went to Budapest, where the revolutionary government celebrated him, even though he had reservations about the Socialist system. He also doubted whether the Karolyi government's courting of the Entente powers would bring any positive results. As it turned out, his instincts were right, and the Entente did little for Hungary. Ady died in January of 1919, spared the knowledge that Hungary's territory would be drastically reduced and that his own birthplace and home region would be awarded to Romania.

Analysis

Endre Ady came from the deep center of the nation, and he sought to raise the nation to a new consciousness, just as János Arany and others had done before him. Ady was an innovator because the literary and political establishment had failed to grasp the need for change. Ady's "Hungarianness" is a central part of his work; he was intensely aware of his struggle "with Europe for Europe."

Ady never abandoned his native traditions. He built instead on folklore, the *kuruc* poetry of the eighteenth century , the folk-song-inspired lyrics of Mihály Csokonai Vitéz, and the revolutionary verse of the great national poet of nineteenth century Hungary, Sándor Petőfi. Ady also drew heavily on Hungarian Calvinism and the rich vernacular tradition of Protestant writings to create a highly personal modern style, animated by the tension between Hungarian and Western European influences. His great love poems to Leda and Csinszka, his poems on materialism and on national traditions—all incorporated European philosophies, preoccupations, and styles, reflecting the influence of Friedrich Nietzsche and Henri Bergson as well as of Charles Baudelaire and Paul Verlaine. Today, Ady is recognized as one of the most important of the generation of writers and thinkers who transformed the intellectual life of Hungary in the first decades of the twentieth century.

New Verses

Ady's first two volumes of verse, *Versek* (poems) and *Még egyszer* (once more), did not attract great interest; they were relatively insignificant collections in the traditional vein. In 1906, however, Ady's own style emerged in *New Verses*. Here, he presented new subjects and new themes, new images and a fresh, new style. The emphasis in *New Verses*—an emphasis continued in Ady's next three collections—was on brevity and impact: short, concise lines; short poems packed with meaning; condensed language with multiple levels of reference. Many of the early poems develop a single metaphor. A very conscious innovator, Ady prefaced *New Verses* with a manifesto that identifies the tension that persists throughout his oeuvre: Hungary is a nation caught at the crossroads between East and West. While proudly claiming his descent from the conquering Hungarians of the ninth century, who came through the Eastern gate, he asks if *he* can break in from the *West* with "new songs of new times." Answering in a defiant affirmative, he states that, in spite of opposition by conservatives, these poems are "still victorious, still new and Hungarian."

Transformations

After the burst of energy that characterized his style in the period from 1906 to 1909, Ady paused in mid-career to adopt a quieter style and grayer moods. His themes and concerns remained much the same, but there was a deepening of thought, and a more pessimistic note entered his poems. His concern for the fate of the country, particularly its ordinary citizens, grew as he saw policies that could only bring ruin being blindly followed by the political elite. His relationship with Brüll also cooled.

After 1914, during the war years, Ady's style underwent another transformation. His sentences became more complex as his verse became increasingly reflective, and he turned from softer, French-inspired tones to the somber and sublime style of the Bible and of sixteenth century Calvinist poetry. In this late poetry, Ady retained two themes from his earlier collection: patriotism, which broadened into humanitarianism, and love—no longer the unfulfilled and unsatisfying erotic encounters of earlier years but the deeper, more fulfilling passion of the Csinszka poems.

Leda poems

Ady's poems can be organized thematically into four large groups (love, death, religion, patriotism), though there is considerable overlapping; also, some important minor themes are eventually subsumed into one or another of the major ones reflecting Ady's intellectual development. One of Ady's most enduring themes was romantic love. The Leda cycles, with their portrayal of destructive yet irresistible passion, reveal the influence of Baudelaire. These poems represented a break with Hungarian tradition in their emphasis on the physical aspects of love. Ady's poems to his wife, on the other hand, are more in the tradition of Petőfi, in which the emotional-spiritual content is on a par with the physical. It would be misleading, however, to dismiss the Leda poems as purely physical: Brüll offered Ady much more than physical excitement, and these poems reflect a world of shared ideas. They are more significant and generally more successful than the poems on fleeting alliances with insignificant partners.

"Félig csókolt csók" ("Half-Kissed Kiss"), from *New Verses*, and "Léda a kertben" ("Leda in the Garden"), from *Blood and Gold*, emphasize the intense desire that cannot be satisfied even in physical union. The "half-kissed kiss" is a metaphor for an erotic relationship that leaves the lovers still restless for fulfillment: "tomorrow, then perhaps tomorrow." Nature sympathizes with them in their eternal hunger, as an image from "Leda in the Garden" suggests: "even the poppy/ pities us, [itself] satisfied." Consummation, Ady suggests in "Héja nász az avaron" ("Kite-Wedding on the Loamy Earth"), can come only in death. In "A mi násznagyunk" ("Our Best Man"), Ady returns to this theme. There are also love poems of great tenderness in the Leda cycles, as "Add nekem a szemeidet" ("Give Me Your Eyes") illustrates. The beloved's eyes "always see him grand . . . always build, have mercy . . . see him in a better light," yet "they kill, burn, and desire." The poem, comprising four stanzas of three lines each, repeats the title line as the first line of each stanza and follows it with two rhymed lines. This *abb* tercet in anapestic meter echoes the lyrical mood and the melody of the words as well as the expansive ideas.

OF ALL MYSTERIES

The 1910 volume *Of All Mysteries* chronicles the waning of Ady's love for Brüll. This collection offers a virtual outline of Ady's characteristic themes, as is indeed suggested in the poem's motto: "youthful All vanquished, with the spear of Secrecy, Death in my heart: but my heart lives, and God lives." Here, Ady seems determined to hope in spite of disappointments. The Decadent pose of earlier poems is shed as the poet develops a real faith in humankind that culminates in the humanism of the war poems. Each of the six cycles in *Of All Mysteries* is devoted to a "secret": of God, of love, of sorrow, of glory, of life, and of death. In the "Love" cycle, dedicated to Leda, the poem "A türelem bilincse" ("The Fetters of Patience") significantly refers to the "fetters" of their love in the past tense. Their whole life was fetters, yet the "kisses, exhaustions, flames, oaths" were all good fetters. The farewell becomes explicit in "Elbocsátó, szép üzenet" ("Dismissing, Beautiful Message"), where pity wins over the regretful remembrance of love.

LOVE POEMS

The poems of 1912 to 1914 show a man in search of love. In the final volumes, this love is found. "A Kalota partján" ("On the Banks of the Kalota") records the "security, summer, beauty and peace" brought to his life by Berta Boncza. The poem's two long free-verse stanzas depict a summer Sunday in which the peace and joy of the service and of the feast (Pentecost) mingle to overwhelm the poet, and the eyes of his beloved draw him into a magic circle.

DEATH

Ady saw life and death not as opposing forces but as two components of the same force. "Párizsban járt az ősz" ("Autumn Passed Through Paris") is a beautiful evocation, through the breath of autumn on a summer day, of the presence of death. Although death comes for all people, it need not be accepted passively, as Ady suggests in the melodic "A halál lovai" ("Death's Horsemen"). The riderless horse with the unclaimed saddle is always in the troop of death's horses, but "He before whom they stop/ Turns pale and sits into the saddle." The act is presented as voluntary. In "Hulla a búza-földön" ("Corpse on the Wheat-Field"), a corpse, forgotten on the snowy plain, will not have carnations, artemisia, and basil blooming on its grave, but "the victorious wheat-kernel" will win through; life will triumph.

RELIGIOUS POEMS

To some extent, Ady's God-fearing poems continue the life-death theme. They chronicle the same doubts and seek answers to the same questions. In time, Ady found the answers and the refuge, but as with John Donne, the struggle was a fierce one; indeed, Ady's love poems, much as in Donne's case, have a close and direct relationship to his religious verse. Although many of Ady's religious poems describe his struggle to achieve union with God, others reflect the peace of childlike faith. Ady seeks rest and forgiveness and creates powerful symbols to concretize these feelings.

In "A Sion-hegy alatt" ("Under Mount Sion"), he creates an image of God as a man in a huge bell coat inscribed with red letters, ringing for the dawn Mass. The figure is kindly yet sad; he cannot answer the poet's plea for simple, unquestioning faith. The poem is a poignant expression of the dilemma of modern humankind. In "Hiszek hitetlenül Istenben" ("I Believe, Unbelieving, in God"), Ady longs for belief in the great mystery of God, convinced that such faith will bring peace to his tormented soul.

The poems from the cycle "Esaias könyvének margójára" ("To the Margins of the Book of Isaiah"), often prefaced by biblical quotations that emphasize their prophetic intentions, transcend the personal religious quest and become pleas for the nation and for humanity. "Volt egy Jézus" ("There Was a Jesus") not only testifies to a personal acceptance of Jesus Christ but also proclaims the need for all humankind to heed his teachings on peace and brotherhood. "A szétszóródás elött" ("Before the Diaspora"), another poem with a biblical inspiration, scourges the nation for its sins, concluding with the powerful line: "And we were lost, for we lost ourselves."

PATRIOTIC POEMS

Many of Ady's poems can be classified as patriotic. This group, however, unites several different themes that were significant at different points in his career. Two important early threads are the "I" poems and the "money" poems. The I poems are more than personal lyrics; they present the speaker (the poet) as a representative of the nation. As such, they evolve into the patriotic poems in a fairly direct line. The money poems startled readers with their "nonpoetic" theme: Ady went beyond complaints against poverty to question the role of money in society at large.

THE KURUC THEME

An important thread in Ady's patriotic-revolutionary poetry is the use of the *kuruc* theme. *Kuruc* was the name applied to the supporters of Ferenc Rákóczi II, who had led a popular uprising against the Habsburgs in the eighteenth century. In Ady's vocabulary, the *kuruc* is the true but disenfranchised Hungarian, a fighter for national goals betrayed by his self-serving masters to Austrian interests. In the war years, Ady identified the *kuruc* with the common person everywhere, oppressed by political power plays.

"MAN IN INHUMANITY"

Ady's last poem, "Ember az embertelenségben" ("Man in Inhumanity"), was an appeal to humanity addressed to the victors of the war. He appealed, fruitlessly, to the Allies "not to tread too harshly" on Hungarian hearts. The nation sought reform, but suffered instead "War, the Horror." Defeated in a war fought against Hungarian sentiments and interests, Hungary paid for its all-too-recent union with Austria with the loss of much of its territory and millions of its citizens. Foreseeing this tragedy even before the war, Ady offered a poignant comment on its aftermath.

Although Ady was a very subjective poet, one of the first purely personal lyric voices in Hungarian poetry, he did not break with the national tradition of committed literature. Deeply influenced by Western European models, he transformed what he took by the force of his genius, exploiting the rich resources of the Hungarian tradition in the service of a powerfully modern vision. Thus, it is not surprising that Ady continues to inspire poets in Hungary today.

OTHER MAJOR WORKS
SHORT FICTION: *Sápadt emberek és történetek*, 1907; *Így is történhetik*, 1910; *A tízmilliós Kleopátra és egyébb történetek*, 1910; *Muskétás tanár úr*, 1913; *Új csapáson*, 1913.

NONFICTION: *Vallomások és tanúlmányok*, 1911; *Az új Hellász*, 1920; *Levelek Párizsból*, 1924; *Párizsi noteszkönyve*, 1924; *Ha hív az aczélhegyű ördög*, 1927; *Ady Endre válogatott levelei*, 1956; *The Explosive Country: A Selection of Articles and Studies, 1898-1916*, 1977.

BIBLIOGRAPHY
Bóka, Lazlo. "Endre Ady the Poet." *New Hungarian Quarterly* 3, no. 5 (January-March, 1962): 83-108. A biographical and critical study of Ady's life and work.
Cushing, G. F. Introduction to *The Explosive Country: A Selection of Articles and Studies, 1898-1916*, by Endre Ady. Budapest: Corvina Press, 1977. Cushing offers some biographical insight into Ady's life.
Frigyesi, Judit. *Béla Bartók and Turn-of-the-Century Budapest*. Berkeley: University of California Press, 1998. A broad perspective on Bartók's art grounded in the social and cultural life of turn-of-the-century Hungary. Includes a discussion of Ady and his influence on Bartók.
Hanák, Péter. *The Garden and the Workshop: Essays on the Cultural History of Vienna and Budapest*. Princeton, N.J.: Princeton University Press, 1998. Ady is one of the central figures in his collection of essays. Deals with Ady's transition from journalism to poetry.
_____. *The Start of Endre Ady's Literary Career (1903-1905)*. Budapest: Akadémiai Kiadó, 1980. A brief study of Ady's early work, with bibliography.
Land, Thomas. "Endre Ady: Six Poems." *Contemporary Review* 279, no. 1627 (August, 2001): 100-105. Land briefly describes Ady's life, particularly his political activism, and translates six personal poems.

Nyerges, Anton N. Introduction to *Poems of Endre Ady*. Buffalo, N.Y.: Hungarian Cultural Foundation, 1969. Nyerges gives some biographic details of Ady's life.

Reményi, Joseph. *Hungarian Writers and Literature*. New Brunswick, N.J.: Rutgers University Press, 1964. A history and critical analysis of Hungarian literature including the works of Ady.

Enikő Molnár Basa

RAFAEL ALBERTI

Born: Puerto de Santa María, Spain; December 16, 1902
Died: Puerto de Santa María, Spain; October 28, 1999

PRINCIPAL POETRY
Marinero en tierra, 1925
La amante, 1926
El alba del alhelí, 1927
Cal y canto, 1929
Sobre los ángeles, 1929 (*Concerning the Angels*, 1967)
Consignas, 1933
Verte y no verte, 1935 (*To See You and Not to See You*, 1946)
Poesía, 1924-1938, 1940
Entre el clavel y la espada, 1941
Pleamar, 1944
A la pintura, 1945 (*To Painting*, 1997)
Retornos de lo vivo lejano, 1952
Baladas y canciones del Paraná, 1954 (*Ballads and Songs of the Parana*, 1988)
Poesías completas, 1961
Rafael Alberti: Selected Poems, 1966 (Ben Belitt, translator)
The Owl's Insomnia, 1973
Alberti tal cual, 1978

OTHER LITERARY FORMS

Although Rafael Alberti (ol-BEHR-tee) established his reputation almost entirely on the basis of his poetry, he became involved in drama after emigrating to Argentina, writing plays of his own and adapting Miguel de Cervantes' *El cerco de Numancia* (wr. 1585, pb. 1784; *Numantia: A Tragedy*, 1870) for the modern stage in 1944.

Alberti's most notable achievement in prose, a work of considerable interest for the student of his poetry, was his autobiography, *La arboleda perdida* (1942; *The Lost Grove*, 1976). In addition, he was a talented painter and supplied illustrations for some of his later volumes.

ACHIEVEMENTS

Rafael Alberti had at once the ill luck and the singular good fortune to flourish during Spain's second great literary boom. Despite his acknowledged worth, he was overshadowed by several of his contemporaries—in particular, by Federico García Lorca. Although Alberti's name is likely to come up in any discussion of the famous *generación del 27*, or Generation of '27, he generally languishes near the end of the list. On the other hand, the extraordinary atmosphere of the times did much to foster his talents; even among the giants, he earned acceptance and respect. He may occasionally have been lost in the crowd, but it was a worthy crowd.

His *Marinero en tierra* (sailor on dry land) won Spain's National Prize for Literature in 1925, and throughout his long career, his virtuosity never faltered. Always a difficult poet, he never gave the impression that his obscurity stemmed from incompetence. His political ideology—Alberti was the first of his circle to embrace communism openly—led him to covet the role of "poet of the streets," but Alberti will be remembered more for his poems of exile, which capture better than any others the poignant aftermath of the Spanish Civil War.

Ultimately, Alberti stands out as a survivor. Many of his great contemporaries died in the civil war or simply lapsed into a prolonged silence. Despite his wholehearted involvement in the conflict, Alberti managed to persevere after his side lost and to renew his career. He continued to publish at an imposing rate, took up new activities, and became a force in the burgeoning literary life of Latin America, as evidenced by his winning of the Cervantes Prize, the Spanish-speaking world's highest literary honor, in 1983. Consistent in his adherence to communism, he received the Lenin Prize for his political verse in 1965. Oddly enough, then, Alberti emerges as a constant—an enduring figure in a world of flux, a practicing poet of consistent excellence during six decades.

Biography

Rafael Alberti was born near Cádiz in Andalusia, and his nostalgia for that region pervades much of his work. His genteel family had fallen on hard times, and Alberti's schoolmates made him painfully aware of his inferior status. In 1917, the family moved to Madrid, where Alberti devoted himself to painting in the cubist manner, attaining some recognition. Illness forced him to retire to a sanatorium in the mountains—a stroke of luck, as it happened, for there he subsequently met such luminaries as García Lorca, Salvador Dalí, and Luis Buñuel and began seriously to write poetry. He won the National Prize for *Marinero en tierra* and thereby gained acceptance into the elite artistic circles of the day. Personal difficulties and an increasing awareness of the plight of his country moved Alberti to embrace communism. In 1930, he married María Teresa León, also a writer, and together they founded the revolutionary journal *Octubre* in 1934.

Alberti's new political credo enabled him to travel extensively and to encounter writers and artists from all parts of Europe and the Americas. After participating actively in the civil war, he emigrated to Argentina in 1940. There, he began to write for the theater, gave numerous readings, and resumed painting. Hard work and fatherhood—his daughter Aitana was born in 1941—preserved Alberti from embittered paralysis, and his production of poetry never slackened. Indeed, many of his readers believe that he reached his peak in the late 1940's.

In 1964, Alberti moved to Rome, where he lived until 1977, when he was finally able to return to Spain, after almost thirty-eight years in exile. He was welcomed by more than three hundred communists carrying red flags as he stepped off the airliner. "I'm not coming with a clenched fist," he said, "but with an open hand." He enjoyed a resurgence of popularity after his return and proceeded to run for the Cortes, giving poetry readings instead of speeches, and won. Alberti resigned his seat after three months to devote himself to his art. He became a well-respected literary figure in his last two decades in Spain; the lost Andalusian had returned home. He died there on October 28, 1999, from a lung ailment; he was ninety-six years old.

Analysis

Throughout his long career, Rafael Alberti proved to be a remarkably versatile poet. His facility of composition enabled him to shift smoothly from fixed forms to free verse, even within the confines of a single poem. Whether composing neomedieval lyrics, Baroque sonnets, or Surreal free verse, he always managed to be authentic. His deep emotions, sometimes obscured by his sheer virtuosity, found expression in all modes. His technical skill did not allow him to stagnate: Commentators on Alberti agree in their praise of his astonishing technical mastery. He might continue in the same vein for three volumes, but he would invariably break new ground in the fourth. His massive corpus of poetry comprises a remarkable array of styles, themes, and moods.

Although he was a natural poet with little formal training, Alberti always kept abreast of current developments in his art—indeed, he kept himself in the vanguard. He associated with the best and brightest of his time and participated in their movements. When the luminaries of Spain reevaluated Luis de Góngora y Argote, Alberti wrote accomplished neo-Baroque poetry; when Dalí and Buñuel were introducing Surrealism in Spanish art and film, Alberti adapted its principles to Spanish poetry; when most of the intellectuals of Spain were resisting General Franciso Franco and embracing communism, Alberti was the "poet of the streets." He remained withal a genuine and unique lyric voice. Even his political verses are not without poetic merit—an exception, to be sure. Alberti changed by adding and growing, never by discarding and replacing; thus, he became a richer talent with each new phase of his creative development.

Alberti's poetry is suffused with nostalgia. The circumstances of his life decreed that he should continually find himself longing for another time, a distant place, or a lost friend, and in his finest poems, he achieves an elegiac purity free of the obscurity and self-pity that mar his lesser works. From first to last, the sadness for things lost remains Alberti's great theme, one he explored more fully than any other poet of his generation.

Alberti was a poet who could grow without discarding his past. The youthful poet who composed marvelous lyrics persisted in the nostalgia of exile; the angry poet of the streets reasserted himself in diatribes against Yankee imperialism in Latin America. At ease in all forms and idioms, forever the Andalusian in exile, always growing in his art and his thought, Alberti wrote a staggering number of excellent poems. In the vast treasure trove of twentieth century Spanish poetry, he left a hoard of pearls and sapphires—hidden at times by the rubies and the emeralds, but worthy nevertheless.

MARINERO EN TIERRA

The doyens of Spanish letters received *Marinero en tierra* with immediate enthusiasm, and the young Alberti found himself a de facto member of the Generation of '27, eligible to rub elbows with all the significant writers of the day. Although Alberti seems to have been happy in the mid-1920's, his early volumes glow with poignant nostalgia for the sea and the coasts of his native Andalusia. He expresses his longing in exquisite lyrics in the medieval tradition. Ben Belitt, introducing his translations collected in *Selected Poems*, confesses that he could find no way to render these lyrics in English. They depend entirely on a native tradition, the vast trove of popular verses from Spain's turbulent Middle Ages. Alberti's genius is such that the poems have no savor of pedantry or preciosity. Luis Monguió, in his introduction to Belitt's translations, suggests that "it is far from unlikely that they are being sung in the provinces today by many in complete ignorance of their debt to Rafael Alberti." The notion is a tribute both to the poet and to the tradition he understood so well.

The verses themselves may seem enigmatic, but only because the modern reader is accustomed to probe so far beneath the surface. One of the best of them, "Gimiendo" ("Groaning"), presents the plaint of a sailor who remembers that his shirt used to puff up in the wind whenever he saw the shore. The entire poem consists of only six brief lines; there is only one image, and only one point. That single image conveys a feeling close to the hearts of those born within smell of the sea—a need unfulfilled for Alberti. He speaks for all seafarers who are marooned inland, the sailors on land.

"Pradoluengo," an aubade in the same style, is only seven lines long and conveys an equally simple message. The beloved to whom the poem is addressed is told that the cocks are crowing, that "we need cross only river waters, not the sea," and is urged to get up and come along. With all the richness of the genre, Alberti hints at a wealth of erotic possibilities and natural splendors. Only William Butler Yeats, in modern English poetry, matches this exquisite simplicity and feeling for tradition.

CAL Y CANTO

As noted above, Alberti took a leading role in the Góngora tricentennial of 1927, and many of the poems in *Cal y canto* owe much to the Baroque model. Here, Alberti reveals a new facet of his technical mastery, particularly in his handling of the sonnet, perhaps the most difficult of forms. "Amaranta," a sonnet that frequently appears in anthologies, shows how completely Alberti was able to assimilate the poetics of Góngora and to adapt them to the twentieth century. The octave describes, in ornate and lavish terms, the beauty of Amaranta; as with Góngora, the very exuberance of the description disquiets the reader. Her breasts, for example, are polished "as with the tongue of a greyhound." The sestet conceals the scorpion sting so often found in Góngora's conclusions: Solitude, personified, settles like a glowing coal between Amaranta and her lover. In this poem, Alberti displays his affinity with Góngora in two respects: an absolute control of his idiom and an obscurity that has deprived both poets of numerous readers. As Alberti himself remarked in his autobiography, "this was painterly poetry—plastic, linear, profiled, confined."

CONCERNING THE ANGELS

Concerning the Angels differs sharply from Alberti's previous work. Bouts of depression and a loss of faith in his former ideals drove him to abandon nostalgia and to confront despair. Suddenly, all the joy and tender sorrow of his early work is gone, replaced by anguish and self-pity. The revolution in content corresponds to a rebellion in form: Free verse prevails as more appropriate to the poet's state of mind than any traditional order. Alberti does not despair utterly, as Monguió indicates, but the overall tone of the collection is negative.

"Tres recuerdos del cielo" ("Three Memories of Heaven"), a tribute to the great Romantic poet Gustavo Adolfo Bécquer, constitutes a noteworthy exception to the depressing tone of the volume. Here, Alberti displays the subtlety and tenderness that characterize his work at its most appealing. Evoking a condition of being before time existed, Alberti recaptures the tenuous delicacy of Bécquer, the sense of the ineffable. The meeting between the lovers, for example, takes place in a world of clouds and moonlight: "When you, seeing me in nothingness/ Invented the first word." Alberti imitates Bécquer masterfully, at the same time finding a new way to express his own nostalgia.

"Three Memories of Heaven," however, is atypical of the collection. Virtually all the other poems treat of "angels" and ultimately of a world turned to wormwood and gall. "El ángel desengañado" ("The Angel Undeceived") debunks the ideals of the younger Alberti, particularly in its desolate conclusion: "I'm going to sleep./ No one is waiting for me." "El ángel de carbón" ("Angel of Coals") ends no less grimly: "And that octopus, love, in the shadow:/ evil, so evil." Several of the poems offer a kind of hope, but it is a wan hope, scarcely better than despair. Like the T. S. Eliot of "The Hollow Men," however, Alberti maintains his poetic control, even with the world withering away around him.

TO SEE YOU AND NOT TO SEE YOU

Two pivotal events in Alberti's life helped him out of this quagmire: meeting his future wife and becoming a communist. The political commitment, while it did little to benefit his poetry, provided him with a set of beliefs to fill the void within. Of his proletarian verse, one can say only that it is no worse than most political poetry. Like his friend and contemporary Pablo Neruda, Alberti mistook a sincere political commitment for an artistic imperative; like Neruda, he eventually returned to more personal themes, although he never wholly abandoned doctrinaire verse.

Even at the height of his political activism, however, Alberti was capable of devoting his gifts to the elegy; the death of Ignacio Sánchez Mejías in the bullring moved him to write the sonnet series that makes up *To See You and Not to See You* in 1935. The same tragedy also inspired Federico García Lorca to compose one of the most famous poems in the Spanish language, "Llanto por Ignacio Sánchez Mejías" ("Lament for Ignacio Sánchez Mejías"). A comparison of the two poems reveals the radical differences between these two superficially similar poets. García Lorca chants compellingly, "At five in the afternoon," evoking the drama of the moment and the awful immediacy of the bull. Alberti reflects on the bull's calfhood, its callow charges as it grew into the engine of destruction that destroyed Sánchez Mejías. García Lorca goes on to convey, in muted tones, his sense of loss. Alberti expresses that sense of loss in terms of distance: As his friend dies in the bullring, Alberti is sailing toward Romania on the Black Sea. The memory of the journey becomes permanently associated with the loss of the friend and thus a redoubled source of nostalgia.

In García Lorca's Shadow

As usual, García Lorca enjoys the fame, and Alberti is lost in his shadow. No doubt García Lorca's elegy speaks more clearly and more movingly; it probably *is* better than its counterpart. Alberti himself admired the "Lament for Ignacio Sánchez Mejías" without reservation. The pattern, however, is only too familiar: Alberti, so like García Lorca in some ways, found himself outmatched at every turn while his friend and rival was still alive. Alberti wrote exquisite medieval lyrics, but García Lorca outdid him with the *Romancero gitano* (1928; *The Gypsy Ballads*, 1953). Alberti captured the essence of Andalusia, but the public identified Andalusia with García Lorca. Alberti wrote a noble and moving elegy for Ignacio Sánchez Mejías, but his rival composed such a marvelous lament that Alberti's has been neglected.

All this is not to imply conscious enmity between the two poets. Alberti had cause to envy his contemporary's fame, and his bitterness at playing a secondary role may have been reflected in *Concerning the Angels*. Indeed, although Alberti gave many indications, in verse and prose, of his profound regard for García Lorca, his relationship with the poet of Granada represents an analogue to the dilemma of his literary life. The competition must have stimulated him, but, because his poetry was less accessible and less dramatic in its impact, he tended to be eclipsed. After the Spanish Civil War, Alberti emigrated to Argentina, mourning his slain and dispersed comrades, including García Lorca, who was senselessly gunned down at the outset of the hostilities. The war poems in the Alberti canon compare favorably with any on that subject, not least because his lively imagination enabled him to look beyond the slaughter.

ENTRE EL CLAVEL Y LA ESPADA

For all his faith, the poet soon found himself across the Atlantic, listening to reports of World War II, picking up the pieces. Somehow he managed to recover and to emerge greater than ever. A poem from his first collection published outside Spain, *Entre el clavel y la espada* (between sword and carnation), sounds the keynote of his renewed art:

> After this willful derangement, this harassed
> and necessitous grammar by whose haste I must live,
> let the virginal word come back to me whole and
>   meticulous,
> and the virginal verb, justly placed with its rigorous
>   adjective.

The poem, written in Spain, anticipates the purity of Alberti's poetry in exile. The poet forgot neither the horrors he had seen nor his love for his homeland.

Another elegy deserves mention in this context. Written after news of the death of the great poet Antonio Machado, "De los álamos y los sauces" (from poplar and willow) captures the plight of Alberti and his fellow exiles in but a few lines. The man in the poem is caught up "in the life of his distant dead and hears them in the air." Thus, Alberti returns grimly to his leitmotif, nostalgia.

RETORNOS DE LO VIVO LEJANO

With his return to his nostalgic leitmotif, Alberti reached his full potential as a poet during the 1940's and 1950's. He poured forth volume after volume of consistently high quality. *Retornos de lo vivo lejano* (returns of the far and the living), a book wholly devoted to his most serviceable theme, may well be the finest volume of his career. The poems are at once accessible and mysterious, full of meaning on the surface and suggestive of unfathomed depths.

"Retornos del amor en una noche de verano" ("Returns: A Summer Night's Love") recalls in wondrous imagery the breathlessness of a time long past. For example, two pairs of lips, as they press together, become a silent carnation. "Retornos de Chopin a través de unas manos ya idas" ("Returns: Chopin by Way of Hands Now Gone") evokes some of the poet's earliest memories of his family. After many years, the poet is reunited with his brothers by an act of imagination, supported by the memory of Frédéric Chopin's music as played by the poet's mother. This is the quintessential Alberti, the master craftsman and the longing man in one.

To Painting

Amid the melancholy splendor of his poems of exile, Alberti distilled a curious volume entitled *To Painting*. In contrast to all that Alberti lost in exile, painting stands as a rediscovered treasure, and the Alberti of the early 1920's comes face to face with the middle-aged émigré. The collection includes sonnets on the tools of painting, both human and inanimate; free-verse meditations on the primary colors; and poems on various painters, each in a style reminiscent of the artist's own. Beyond its intrinsic value, the volume reveals much about the mutual attraction of the two arts.

"Ballad of the Lost Andalusian"

A poem from *Ballads and Songs of the Parana*, deserves special mention. "Balada del Andaluz perdido" ("Ballad of the Lost Andalusian"), as much as any single poem, reflects Alberti's self-image as a poet in exile. Written in terse, unrhymed couplets, it tells of a wandering Andalusian who watches the olives grow "by the banks of a different river." Sitting alone, he provokes curious questions from the Argentine onlookers on the opposite bank of the river, but he remains a mystery to them. Not so to the reader, who understands the pathos of the riderless horses, the memory of hatred, the loneliness. The final question admits of no answer and in fact needs none: "What will he do there, what is left to be done/ on the opposite side of the river, alone?"

Other major works

PLAYS: *El hombre deshabitado*, pb. 1930; *El trébol floride*, pb. 1940; *El adefesio*, pb. 1944; *El cerco de Numancia*, pr. 1944 (adaptation of Miguel de Cervantes' play).

NONFICTION: *La arboleda perdida*, 1942 (*The Lost Grove*, 1976).

Bibliography

Gagen, Derek. "Marinero en tierra: Alberti's first 'Libro organico de poemas'?" *Modern Language Review* 88, no. 1 (January, 1993): 91. Alberti's *Marinero en tierra* is examined in detail.

Havard, Robert. *The Crucified Mind: Rafael Alberti and the Surrealist Ethos in Spain*. London: Tamesis Books, 2001. A biographical and historical study.

Herrmann, Gina. *Written in Red: The Communist Memoir in Spain*. Urbana: University of Illinois Press, 2009. This work examining memoirs of Communists in Spain contains a chapter on Maria Teresa León and Alberti.

Jiménez-Fajardo, Salvador. *Multiple Spaces: The Poetry of Rafael Alberti*. London: Tamesis Books, 1985. A critical analysis of Alberti's poetic works. Includes bibliographic references.

Manteiga, Robert C. *Poetry of Rafael Alberti: A Visual Approach*. London: Tamesis Books, 1978. A study of Alberti's literary style. Text is in English with poems in original Spanish. Includes bibliographic references.

Nantell, Judith. *Rafael Alberti's Poetry of the Thirties*. Athens: University of Georgia Press, 1986. This study puts Alberti's work in historical and social context by analyzing the influences from a turbulent decade in which civil war erupts, ignites a European conflagration, and ends in societal crises. The author discusses political poems that are not as memorable as his earlier works but deserve recognition for their artistic as well as social value.

Soufas, C. Christopher. *The Subject in Question: Early Contemporary Spanish Literature and Modernism*. Washington, D.C.: Catholic University of America Press, 2007. This overview of Spanish literature and modernism contains a chapter examining the poetry of Alberti and Luis Cernuda.

Ugarte, Michael. *Shifting Ground: Spanish Civil War Exile Literature*. Durham, N.C.: Duke University Press, 1989. Examination of the importance of Spanish exile literature during and after the civil war. The second section of the book explores the intellectual diaspora of the civil war, and an analysis of Alberti's *The Lost Grove* is featured prominently.

Philip Krummrich
Updated by Carole A. Champagne and Sarah Hilbert

GUILLAUME APOLLINAIRE

Born: Rome, Italy; August 26, 1880
Died: Paris, France; November 9, 1918
Also known as: Wilhelm Apollinaris; Guillelmus Apollinaris de Kostrowitzki

PRINCIPAL POETRY
Le Bestiaire, 1911 (*Bestiary*, 1978)
Alcools: Poèmes, 1898-1913, 1913 (*Alcools: Poems, 1898-1913*, 1964)
Calligrammes, 1918 (English translation, 1980)
Il y a, 1925
Le Guetteur mélancolique, 1952
Tendre comme le souvenir, 1952
Poèmes à Lou, 1955
Œuvres poétiques, 1956

OTHER LITERARY FORMS

Besides poetry, Guillaume Apollinaire (ah-pawl-ee-NEHR) wrote a number of prose works. Among the most significant of his short stories and novellas are *L'Enchanteur pourrissant* (1909; "the putrescent enchanter"), published by Henry Kahnweiler and illustrated with woodcuts by André Derain; *L'Hérésiarque et Cie.* (1910; *The Heresiarch and Co.*, 1965), a contender for the Prix Goncourt; and *Le Poète assassiné* (1916; *The Poet Assassinated*, 1923). They are contained in the Pléiade edition, *Œuvres en prose* (1977), edited by Michel Décaudin.

Apollinaire collaborated on numerous plays and cinema scripts. His best-known individual works in these genres are two proto-Surrealist plays in verse: *Les Mamelles de Tirésias* (pr. 1917; *The Breasts of Tiresias*, 1961), first published in the magazine *SIC* in 1918, and *Couleur du temps* (the color of time; pr. 1918), which first appeared in the *Nouvelle Revue française* in 1920. They are available in the Pléiade edition of *Œuvres poétiques*. Apollinaire also published a great deal of art criticism and literary criticism in journals, newspapers, and other periodicals. In 1913, the articles published before that year were collected in *Peintres cubistes: Méditations esthétiques* (*The Cubist Painters: Aesthetic Meditations*, 1944). In 1918, *Mercure de France* published his famous manifesto "L'Esprit nouveau et les poètes" ("The New Spirit and the Poets"), which later appeared, along with many other articles, in *Chroniques d'art, 1902-1918* (1960), edited by L. C. Breunig. This collection has been translated into English as *Apollinaire on Art: Essays and Reviews, 1902-1918* (1972).

Achievements

After Guillaume Apollinaire, French poetry was never the same again. Writing at the end of the long Symbolist tradition, a tradition very apparent in his early works, Apollinaire moved into a new perception of the world and of poetry. In the world of his mature verse, spatial and temporal relations are radically altered. Apollinaire's was one of the first voices in French poetry to attempt to articulate the profound discontinuity and disorientation in modern society. At the same time, however, his works reflect hope, frequently ecstatic, in the promise of the future.

Apollinaire's sense of radical discontinuity was reflected in his formal innovations, analyzed in considerable depth by Jean-Claude Chevalier in *Alcools d'Apollinaire* (1970). Immediately before the publication of *Alcools*, Apollinaire went through the volume and removed all punctuation, a device that he continued to use in most of his later works. His most notable poems, such as "Zone," "Liens" ("Chains"), and "Les Fenêtres" ("Windows"), use free verse with irregular rhyme and rhythm; his most startling works are the picture poems of *Calligrammes*, a form that he falsely claimed to have invented. They consist of verses arranged to give both a visual and an auditory effect in an effort to create simultaneity.

Like the cubists and other modern painters who sought to go beyond the traditional boundaries of space and time, Apollinaire desired to create the effect of simultaneity. This ambition is evident in "Zone," with its biographical, geographical, and historical discontinuity. In this single poem, the poet leaps from his pious childhood at the Collège Saint-Charles in Monaco to the wonders of modern aviation and back to the "herds" of buses "mooing" on the streets of Paris. Perhaps his most obvious achievement in simultaneity, though less profound, is in "Lundi rue Christine" ("Monday in Christine Street"), which records overheard bits of conversation in a "sinistre brasserie," a low-class café-restaurant that Apollinaire had frequented as early as 1903.

The friend and collaborator of many important painters during the exciting years in Paris just before World War I, Apollinaire began associating with artists when he met Pablo Picasso in 1904, after which he frequented the famous Bateau-Lavoir on the rue Ravignan with Max Jacob, André Derain, Maurice Vlaminck, Georges Braque, and others. After 1912, he moved into the world of art criticism, not always appreciated by the artists themselves, as critic Francis Steegmuller has noted. Not unrelated to this interest was Apollinaire's tumultuous liaison with Marie Laurencin from 1907 to 1912. He frequently inspired works and portraits by artists, including Laurencin, Henri Rousseau, and Picasso. Apollinaire's own works further testify to his links with painters: *Bestiary* was illustrated by Raoul Dufy, and "Windows" was the introductory poem to the catalog of the Robert Delaunay exhibit in 1912. His poems often parallel the work of the painters in their spirit of simultaneity; in their subjects, such as the *saltimbanques* of Picasso; and in their moods, such as those of Marc Chagall's dreamworld and inverted figures.

After 1916, Apollinaire became the *chef d'école*, the leader of a new generation of poets and painters. Among them were Pierre Reverdy, Philippe Soupault, Jean Cocteau, André Breton, and Tristan Tzara. His own works appeared in the most avant-garde journals: Reverdy's *Nord-Sud*, Picabia's *391*, and Albert Birot's *SIC*. His lecture "The New Spirit and the Poets" called poets to a new prophetic vision, imploring them to create prodigies with their imagination like modern Merlins. Like Paul Claudel, Apollinaire regarded the poet as a creator. The modern poet, he believed, must use everything for his (or her) creation: new discoveries in science, in the subconscious and the dreamworld, and in the cinema and visual arts.

The Surrealists, in their desire to revolutionize art and literature, saw in Apollinaire their precursor. It was he who coined the word *surréaliste*, in the preface to his drama in verse *The Breasts of Tiresias*. In it, he explains that an equivalent is not always an imitation, even as the wheel, though intended to facilitate transportation, is not a reproduction of the leg. Apollinaire conveys his message with a lighthearted tone, employing incongruous rhythms, parody, and sexual imagery. This is essentially the technique he employs in his most avant-garde poetry, and *The Breasts of Tiresias* echoes poems from "Ondes" ("Waves," the first part of *Calligrammes*) such as "Zone," "Le Brasier" ("The Brazier"), "Les Fiançailles" ("The Betrothal"), and "Le Larron" ("The Thief"). Thus, Apollinaire indicated the path to follow in revolutionizing poetry, although much of his work was in some respects traditional. Like Victor Hugo, he served subsequent poets chiefly as a guide rather than as a model, but it was his "esprit nouveau" that gave considerable impetus to a new form of modern poetry.

Biography

Born in Rome on August 26, 1880, Guillaume Albert Wladimir Alexandre Apollinaire de Kostrowitzky was an illegitimate child; in "The Thief," he says that his "father was a sphinx and his mother a night." In reality, his mother was a Polish adventurer of noble ancestry, Angelique Kostrowicka, known in Paris mostly as "Olga." His father's identity has never been definitively ascertained. The most plausible supposition points to Francesco Flugi d'Aspermont, who was from a noble Italian family that included many prelates. This theory is based on the careful investigation of biographer Marcel Adéma. Apollinaire's mysterious and involved parentage haunted the poet throughout his life, leaving unmistakable marks on his character and works.

Apollinaire received his only formal education at the Collège of Saint-Charles in Monaco and the Collège Stanislas at Cannes, from 1890 to 1897, where he acquired a solid grounding in religious and secular knowledge. Although his Catholic training was to remain firmly implanted in his memory and is evident in his poetry, he moved away from any outward adherence to religious beliefs after 1897. In 1899, he arrived in Paris, his home for most of the next nineteen years of his life and the center and inspiration of his literary activity. First, however, he made a significant trip to Germany's Rhineland in 1901, as tutor to Gabrielle, the daughter of the viscountess of Milhau. There, he met and fell in love with Annie Playden, Gabrielle's English governess. This ill-fated romance and the beauty of the Rhineland inspired many of Apollinaire's early poems, which were later published in *Alcools*.

Apollinaire's return to Paris coincided with the beginning of friendships with artists and writers such as André Salmon, Alfred Jarry, Max Jacob, and especially Picasso. In 1903, he began his collaboration on many periodicals, which he continued throughout his lifetime. Most of his prose and poetry was first published in such journals, many of which—such as *Le Festin d'Esope* and *La Revue immoraliste*—were of very short duration. His works appeared under several pseudonyms, of which "Apollinaire" was the most significant. Others included "Louise Lalame," "Lul," "Montade," and "Tyl." In 1907, he met Marie Laurencin, an artist, whose talent Apollinaire tended to exaggerate. Their liaison continued until 1912 and was an inspiration and a torment to both of them. During this period, Apollinaire was deeply marked by the false accusation that he was responsible for the theft of the *Mona Lisa* from the Louvre. A series of six poems in *Alcools*, "À la Santé" ("At the Santé") describes his brief stay in the prison of La Santé in Verlainian imagery.

The year 1912 marked Apollinaire's break with Laurencin and his definite espousal of modern art, of which he became a staunch proponent. During the two years preceding World War I, he gave lectures and wrote articles on modern art and prepared *Alcools* for publication. The beginning of the war, in 1914, was to Apollinaire a call to a mission. Although not a French citizen until the year 1916, he embraced with great enthusiasm his *métier de soldat* as an artilleryman and then as an infantryman, according an almost mystical dimension to his military service. His poetry of these first two years reveals the exaltation of war and the idealization of two women, "Lou" (Louise de Coligny-Châtillon) and Madeleine Pagès, to whom he was briefly engaged.

Wounded in the head in 1916, Apollinaire required surgery and was then discharged from the service. He returned to the world of literature and art with numerous articles, lectures, two plays, and a volume of poetry, *Calligrammes*. In May of 1918, he married Jacqueline Kolb ("Ruby"), the "jolie rousse" ("pretty redhead") of the last poem in *Calligrammes*. The marriage was of short duration, however, as Apollinaire died of Spanish influenza on November 9 of the same year.

Analysis

In his poetic style, Guillaume Apollinaire might be characterized as the last of the Symbolists and the first of the moderns. He is considered a revolutionary and a destroyer, yet the bulk of his work shows a deep influence of traditional symbolism, especially biblical, legendary, and mythical. Very knowledgeable in Roman Catholic doctrine from his years with the Marianists at Monaco and Cannes, he uses extensive biblical imagery: Christ, the Virgin Mary, and the Holy Spirit in the form of a dove.

Robert Couffignal has analyzed Apollinaire's religious imagery in detail and considers his comprehension of the Bible to be "a cascade of superficial weavings." Scott Bates sees the Last Judgment, with its apocalyptic implications, as central to Apollinaire's works. The concept of messianism and the advent of a new millennium is evident in both the early works and the war poems, which predict a new universe. In the Symbolist tradition, the poet is the seer of the new kingdom.

Many of Apollinaire's symbols are from the realm of legend and myth. Rosemonde, the idealized woman of the Middle Ages, is present in several poems, though she appears also as a prostitute. In "Merlin et la vieille femme" ("Merlin and the Old Woman"), the medieval seer foreshadows Apollinaire's vision of the future. Ancient mythology is the source for Orpheus, under whose sign *Bestiary* is written. Orpheus is also the symbol of Christ and the poet, as is Hermès Trismègiste. Ancient Egypt appears in frequent references to the Nile, the Israelites in bondage, and Pharaoh, the image of the poet himself. The fantastic abounds in Apollinaire's works: ghosts, diabolic characters, and phantoms, as found, for example, in "La Maison des Morts" ("The House of the Dead") and especially in the short stories.

Much of Apollinaire's early symbolism is directed toward the quest for self-knowledge; his choice of the name Apollinaire is a clue to his search. Though it was the name of his maternal grandfather and one of the names given to him at baptism, he seems to have chosen it for its reference to Apollo, the god of the sun. Indeed, solar imagery is central to his poetry, and the introductory poem of *Alcools*, "Zone," ends with the words "Soleil cou coupé" ("Sun cut throat"). Bates argues that the violent love-death relationship between the sun and night, with its corresponding symbolism, is as crucial to the interpretation of Apollinaire as it is to a reading of Gérard de Nerval or Stéphane Mallarmé. Along with love and death is death and resurrection. Apollinaire chooses the phoenix as a sign of rebirth and describes his own psychological and poetic resurrection in "The Brazier" and "The Betrothal," poems that he regarded as among his best. Fire seems to be his basic image, with its multiple meanings of passion, destruction, and purification.

Passion as a flame dominated Apollinaire's life and poetry. Of the many women whom he loved, five in particular incarnated his violent passion and appear in his work: Playden and Laurencin in *Alcools*; Lou, Madeleine, and Jacqueline in *Calligrammes* and in several series of poems published after his death. Apollinaire is capable of expressing tender, idealistic love, as in the "Aubade chantée à Lætare un an passé" ("Aubade Sung to Lætare a Year Ago") section of the "La Chanson du mal-aimé" ("The Song of the Poorly Loved") and in "La Jolie Rousse" ("The Pretty Redhead"), which closes *Calligrammes*. In most cases, Apollinaire is the *mal-aimé*, and as he himself says, he is much less the poorly beloved than the one who loves poorly. His first three loves ended violently; his last was concluded by his death. Thus, the death of love is as important as its first manifestation, which for him resembles the shells bursting in the war.

Autumn is the season of the death of love, wistfully expressed in such nostalgic works as "L'Adieu" ("The Farewell") and "Automne" ("Autumn"). Because the end of love usually involved deep suffering for him, the image of mutilation is not uncommon. The beloved in "The Song of the Poorly Loved" has a scar on her neck, and the mannequins in "L'Émigrant de Landor Road" ("The Emigrant from Landor Road") are decapitated, much like the sun in "Zone." Apollinaire perceives love in its erotic sense, and in many cases he resorts to arcane symbolism, as in the seven swords in "The Song of the Poorly Loved." "Lul de Faltenin" ("Lul of Faltenin") is also typical, with its subtle erotic allusions. Such themes are more overt in Apollinaire's prose; indeed, Bates has compiled a glossary of erotic symbolism in the works of Apollinaire.

Apollinaire was both a lyric poet and a storyteller. In the lyric tradition, he writes of his emotions in images drawn from nature. His work is particularly rich in flora and fauna. *Bestiary* shows his familiarity with and affection for animals and his ability, like the fabulists, to see them as caricatures of people. *Alcools*, as the title indicates, often evokes grapes and wine; it also speaks of fir trees (in "Les Sapins") and falling leaves. "Zone" contains a catalog of birds, real and legendary. The Seine comes alive in Apollinaire's ever-popular "Le Pont Mirabeau" ("Mirabeau Bridge"). In *Calligrammes*, the poet often compares the explosion of shells to bursting buds.

Apollinaire was the author of many short stories, and he maintains a narrative flavor in his poetry. "The House of the Dead" was originally a short story, "L'Obituaire," and it reads like one. Many of the picture poems in *Calligrammes* tell a story; "Paysage" ("Landscape"), for example, portrays by means of typography a house, a tree, and two lovers, one of whom smokes a cigar that the reader can almost smell. Apollinaire's technique often involves improvisation, as in "Le Musicien de Saint-Merry" ("The Musician of Saint-Merry"). Although he claims almost total spontaneity, there are revised versions of many of his poems, and he frequently borrowed from himself, rearranging both lines and poems. In particular, Apollinaire tells stories of the modern city, imitating its new structures as Arthur Rimbaud did in his innovative patterns, and like Charles Baudelaire, Apollinaire peoples his verse with the forgotten and the poor, the prostitutes and the clowns.

Apollinaire had a remarkable sense of humor, displayed in frequent word-plays, burlesques, and parodies. The briefest example of his use of puns is the one-line poem "Chantre" ("Singer"): "Et l'unique cordeau des trompettes marines" ("and the single string of marine trumpets"). *Cordeau*, when read aloud, might be *cor d'eau*, or "horn of water," another version of a marine trumpet, as well as *corps d'eau* ("body of water") or even *cœur d'eau* ("heart of water"). The burlesque found in his short stories appears in poetry as dissonance, erotic puns, and irreverent parodies, such as in "Les Sept Epées" ("The Seven Swords") as well as in "The Thief," a poem that Bates interprets as parodying Christ. Apollinaire's lighthearted rhythm and obscure symbolism tend to prevent his verse from becoming offensive and convey a sense of freedom, discovery, and surprise.

BESTIARY

Bestiary is one of the most charming and accessible of Apollinaire's works. The idea for the poem probably came from Picasso in 1906, who was then doing woodcuts of animals. In 1908, Apollinaire published in a journal eighteen poems under the title "La Marchande des quatre saisons ou le bestiaire moderne" (the costermonger or the modern bestiary). When he prepared the final edition in 1911, with woodcuts by Raoul Dufy, he added twelve poems and replaced the merchant with Orpheus. According to mythology, Orpheus attracted wild beasts by playing on the lyre he had received from Mercury. He is the symbol of Gnosis and Neoplatonic Humanism and is also identified with Christ and poetry, in a mixture of mystical and sensual imagery.

Apollinaire himself wrote the notes to the volume and uses as its sign a δ (the Greek letter delta) pierced by a unicorn. He interprets it to mean the delta of the Nile and all the legendary and biblical symbols of ancient Egypt, also suggesting a *D* for Deplanche, the publisher, in addition to the obvious sexual symbolism. He added the motto "J'émerveille" ("I marvel"), thus giving a fantastic aura to the work. Roger Little sees in the volume a "delicious and malicious" wit, with metamorphoses, syncretism, pride in poetry, carnal love, and mysticism. Like all Apollinaire's early works, it is full of self-analysis. In "La Souris" ("The Mouse"), the poet speaks of his twenty-eight years as "mal-vécus" ("poorly spent").

The animals represent human foibles; the peacock, for example, displays both his best and, unbeknownst to him, his worst. They also speak of love: the serpent, the Sirens, the dove, and Orpheus himself. They point to God and things divine: the dove, the bull, or, again, Orpheus. They speak of poetry: the horse, the tortoise, the elephant, and the caterpillar. For Apollinaire, poetry is a divine gift. He concludes his notes by observing that poets seek nothing but perfection, which is God himself. Poets, he says, have the right to expect after death the full knowledge of God, which is sublime beauty.

ALCOOLS

The most analyzed and the best known of Apollinaire's works is *Alcools*, a slender volume published in 1913 with the subtitle *Poèmes, 1898-1913*. A portrait of Apollinaire, an etching by Picasso, serves as the frontispiece. Apollinaire chose fifty-five of the many poems he had written from his eighteenth to his thirty-third year and assembled them in an order that has continued to fascinate and baffle critics. Michel Décaudin says that the order in *Alcools* is based entirely on the aesthetic and sentimental affinities felt by the author, or their discrete dissonances. Very few poems have dates, other than "Rhénanes" (September, 1901, to May, 1902) and "At the Santé" (September, 1911); nevertheless, critics have succeeded in dating many, though not all, of the poems.

The poems have several centers, though not all of those from one group appear together. More than twenty were inspired by Apollinaire's trip to the Rhineland in 1901, including the nine in the cycle "Rhénanes." Several of these poems and some others, such as "The Song of the Poorly Loved," "Annie," and "The Emigrant from Landor Road," refer to his unhappy love affair with Playden. These poems and an interview with her as Mrs. Postings in 1951 by Robert Goffin and LeRoy Breunig are the only sources of information about this significant period in Apollinaire's life. Three poems, "Mirabeau Bridge," "Marie," and "Cors de chasse" ("Hunting Horns"), scattered throughout the volume, refer to Laurencin.

The poems exhibit great variety in form, tone, and subject matter. They range from the one-line "Chantre" to the seven-part "The Song of the Poorly Loved," the longest in the collection. Most of them have regular rhyme and rhythm, but "Zone" and "Vendémiaire," the first and the last, give evidence of technical experimentation. The poems range from witty ("The Synagogue") to nostalgic ("Autumn," "Hunting Horns") and from enigmatic ("The Brazier") to irreverent ("The Thief"). Critics have arranged them in various ways. Bates, for example, sees the volume as a "Dionysian-Apollonian dance of life in three major symbols: fire, shadow, alcools."

Apollinaire chose the beginning and concluding poems of the collection, "Zone" and "Vendémiaire," with great care. "Zone" is overtly autobiographical in a Romantic-Symbolist ambience, yet its instant leaps in space and time make it very modern. Also modern is the image of the city, where Apollinaire can see beauty in a poster, a traffic jam, and a group of frightened Jewish immigrants. The city is also the central focus in the concluding poem, "Vendémiaire" (the name given the month of vintage, September 22-October 21, in the revolutionary calendar), a hymn to the glory of Paris. The poet exuberantly proclaims his immortality and omnipresence: "I am drunk from having swallowed all the universe." Bates sees the end of the poem as a hymn to joy reminiscent of Walt Whitman and Friedrich Nietzsche.

The bizarre juxtapositions, the inner borrowings of lines from one poem to the next, and the absence of punctuation provoked various responses from critics. Cubists hailed Apollinaire as a great poet. Georges Duhamel, writing in the June 15, 1913, issue of *Mercure de France*, called the volume a junk shop. Critics such as Adéma, Décaudin, and Marie-Jeanne Durry analyze *Alcools* with depth and scholarship. They discover many platitudes and much mediocrity but find it redeemed by what Steegmuller identifies as a spirit of freedom.

CALLIGRAMMES

Intended as a sequel to *Alcools*, *Calligrammes* is much more unified than *Alcools*, yet its importance was seen only much later. It consists of six parts. The first part, "Waves," is the most innovative and was written before World War I in the frenzied stimulation of artistic activity in Paris. The other five contain poems inspired by the war and by the poet's love for Lou, Madeleine, and—in the final poem—his future wife, Jacqueline.

Philippe Renaud sees the difference between *Alcools* and "Waves" as one of nature rather than degree. Even the most enigmatic poems of *Alcools* follow a familiar plan, he maintains, whereas in "Waves" the reader is in unfamiliar territory, disoriented in space and time. In "Waves" one feels both the insecurity and the indefiniteness that can only be called modern art. The introductory poem, "Chains," uses the elements recommended by Apollinaire in "The New Spirit and the Poets" yet remains anchored in the past. It leaps from the Tower of Babel to telegraph wires in disconcerting juxtapositions, speaking of humankind's eternal, frustrating quest for unity. In "The Windows," the window opens like an orange on Paris or in the tropics and flies on a rainbow across space and time.

Beginning with "Waves" and throughout *Calligrammes*, Apollinaire uses what he calls ideograms, or picture poems. They are the most attractive pieces in the book, though not necessarily the most original. They became excellent vehicles for the war poems, where brevity and wit are essential. The theme of war dominates the majority of poems in *Calligrammes*. The war excited Apollinaire, promising a new universe. He experienced exhilaration as he saw shells exploding, comparing them in the poem "Merveilles de la guerre" ("Wonders of War") to constellations, women's hair, dancers, and women in childbirth. He saw himself as the poet-hero, the omnipresent seer, the animator of the universe. In "La Tête étoilée" ("The Starry Head"), his wound was a crown of stars on his head.

Apollinaire was as dependent on love as he was on air, and he suffered greatly in the solitary trenches of France. His brief romance with Lou was intense and violent, as his pun on her name in "C'est Lou qu'on la nommait" ("They Called Her Lou") indicates; instead of "Lou," the word *loup* (which sounds the same in French but means "wolf") is used throughout the poem. In his poems to Madeleine, he devours images like a starving man. The anthology ends serenely as he addresses Jacqueline, "la jolie rousse," the woman destined to be his wife, as poetry was destined to be his life. This final poem is also his poetic testament, in which he bequeaths "vast and unknown kingdoms, new fires and the mystery of flowers to anyone willing to pick them."

OTHER MAJOR WORKS

LONG FICTION: *L'Enchanteur pourrissant*, 1909; *Le Poète assassiné*, 1916 (*The Poet Assassinated*, 1923).

SHORT FICTION: *L'Hérésiarque et Cie.*, 1910 (*The Heresiarch and Co.*, 1965).

PLAYS: *Les Mamelles de Tirésias*, pr. 1917 (*The Breasts of Tiresias*, 1961); *Couleur du temps*, pr. 1918; *Casanova*, pb. 1952.

NONFICTION: *Peintres cubistes: Méditations esthétiques*, 1913 (*The Cubist Painters: Aesthetic Meditations*, 1944); *Chroniques d'art, 1902-1918*, 1960 (*Apollinaire on Art: Essays and Reviews, 1902-1918*, 1972).

MISCELLANEOUS: *Œuvres complètes*, 1966 (8 volumes); *Œuvres en prose*, 1977 (Michel Décaudin, editor).

BIBLIOGRAPHY

Adéma, Marcel. *Apollinaire*. Translated by Denise Folliot. New York: Grove Press, 1955. This is the prime source of biographical material, the bible of scholars researching the poet and his epoch.

Bates, Scott. *Guillaume Apollinaire*. Rev. ed. Boston: Twayne, 1989. This book offers detailed erudite analyses of Apollinaire's major works and informed judgments on his place in French literature and in the development of art criticism. It emphasizes the importance to the entire world of Apollinaire's vision of a cultural millennium propelled by science and democracy and implemented by poetry. Included are a chronology, a twenty-six-page glossary of references, notes, and selected bibliographies of both primary and secondary sources.

Bohn, Willard. *The Aesthetics of Visual Poetry: 1914-1928*. New York: Cambridge University Press, 1986. Chapter 3, "Apollinaire's Plastic Imagination," reveals the lyric innovations that Apollinaire brought to visual poetry with *Calligrammes*: new forms, new content, multiple figures in a unified composition, a dual sign system used to express a simultaneity, and a difficulty of reading that mirrors the act of creation. Chapter 4, "Toward a Calligrammar," offers a sophisticated structural and statistical analysis of the calligrammes to demonstrate metonymy as the principal force binding the visual tropes, whereas metaphor and metonymy occur evenly in the verbal arena.

_____. *Apollinaire and the Faceless Man: The Creation and Evolution of a Modern Motif*. Rutherford, N.J.: Fairleigh Dickinson University Press, 1991. Traces the history of Apollinaire's faceless man motif as a symbol of the human condition, from its roots in the poem "Le Musicien de Saint-Mercy" to its dissemination to the arts community through the unproduced pantomime "A quelle heure un train partira-t-il pour Paris?"

_____. *Apollinaire and the International Avant-Garde*. Albany: State University of New York Press, 1997. Chronicles the early artistic and critical reception of Apollinaire in Europe, North America, and Latin America. Especially interesting is the discussion of Argentina, exported through the Ultraism of Jorge Luis Borges, and Apollinaire's place in the revolutionary circles of Mexico.

Cornelius, Nathalie Goodisman. *A Semiotic Analysis of Guillaume Apollinaire's Mythology in "Alcools."* New York: Peter Lang, 1995. Examines Apollinaire's use of linguistic and mythological fragmentation and reordering to mold his material into an entirely new system of signs that both encompasses and surpasses the old. Chapters give close semiotic readings of four poems: "Claire de lune," "Le Brasier," "Nuit rhëane," and "Vendémaine."

Couffignal, Robert. *Apollinaire*. Translated by Eda Mezer Levitine. Tuscaloosa: University of Alabama Press, 1975. This is a searching analysis of some of Apollinaire's best-known works, including "Zone," strictly from the Roman Catholic point of view. It traces his attitude toward religion from his childhood to his death. The book contains a chronology; translations of ten texts, both poems and prose, with the author's comments; a bibliographical note; and an index.

Matthews, Timothy. *Reading Apollinaire: Theories of Poetic Language*. New York: Manchester University Press, 1987. Uses a variety of historical, biographical, and stylistic approaches to offer an accessible point of entry into often difficult texts. Matthews's detailed discussion of *Alcools* focuses heavily on "L'Adieu" and "Automne malade," which allows for a reading that may be transferred to the rest of the book. His chapter "Poetry, Painting, and Theory" offers a solid historical background that leads directly into his examination of *Calligrammes*.

Shattuck, Roger. *The Banquet Years*. Rev. ed. New York: Vintage Books, 1968. In the two long chapters devoted to Apollinaire, "The Impresario of the Avant-garde" and "Painter-Poet," the author gives a year-by-year and at times even a month-by-month account of his life, loves, friends, employment, writings, and speeches. The tone is judicial, the critical judgments fair and balanced. Includes a bibliography and an index.

Steegmuller, Francis. *Apollinaire: Poet Among the Painters*. New York: Farrar, Straus, 1963. This is an exhaustive, extremely well-documented, unbiased, and highly readable biography. Contains a preface, translations, numerous photographs and illustrations, two appendixes, notes, and an index.

Irma M. Kashuba
Updated by David Harrison Horton

LOUIS ARAGON

Born: Paris, France; October 3, 1897
Died: Paris, France; December 24, 1982

PRINCIPAL POETRY
Feu de joie, 1920
Le Mouvement perpétuel, 1925
La Grande Gaîté, 1929
Persécuté persécuteur, 1931
Hourra l'Oural, 1934
Le Crève-coeur, 1941
Brocéliande, 1942
Les Yeux d'Elsa, 1942
En Français dans le texte, 1943
Le Musée grévin, 1943
La Diane française, 1945
Le Nouveau Crève-coeur, 1948
Les Yeux et la mémoire, 1954
Le Roman inachevé, 1956
Elsa, 1959
Les Poètes, 1960
Le Fou d'Elsa, 1963
Les Chambres, 1969
Aux abords de Rome, 1981
Les Adieux, et autres poèmes, 1982

OTHER LITERARY FORMS

Louis Aragon (ah-rah-GAWN) was one of the most prolific French authors of the twentieth century, and although lyric poetry was his first medium, to which he always returned as to a first love, he also produced many novels and volumes of essays. As a young man, he participated in the Surrealist movement, and his works of this period defy classification. In addition to the exercises known as automatic writing, which had a considerable impact on his mature style in both prose and poetry, he wrote a number of Surrealist narratives combining elements of the novel (such as description and dialogue) and the essay. The most important of these, *Le Paysan de Paris* (1926; *Nightwalker*, 1970), is a long meditation on the author's ramblings in his native city and on the "modern sense of the mythic" inspired by its streets, shops, and parks.

In the 1930's, after his espousal of the Communist cause, Aragon began a series of

Louis Aragon
(Library of Congress)

novels under the general title of *Le Monde réel* (1934-1944), which follow the tenets of Socialist Realism. These are historical novels dealing with the corruption of bourgeois society and the rise of Communism. His later novels, however, beginning with *La Semaine sainte* (1958; *Holy Week*, 1961), show greater freedom of form and lack the explicit "message" characteristic of Socialist Realism; these later works incorporate an ongoing meditation on the novel as a literary form and on its relation to history and biography.

An important characteristic of Aragon's style that cuts across all his works of fiction and poetry is the use of spoken language as a model: His sentences reproduce the rhythms of speech, full of parentheses, syntactic breaks, and interjections, and his diction, especially in prose, is heavily interlarded with slang. This trait is true to some extent even of his essays, although the latter tend to be more formal to both diction and rhetorical strategy. His nonfiction works are voluminous, for he was an active journalist for much of his life, producing reviews and essays on politics, literature, and the visual arts for a variety of Surrealist and then Communist publications.

Achievements

Like most writers who have taken strong political stands, Louis Aragon was, during the course of his lifetime, the object of much praise and blame that had little to do with the literary value of his work. This was especially true of his series of novels, *Le Monde réel*, which was hailed by his fellow Communists as a masterpiece and criticized by most non-Communist reviewers as contrived and doctrinaire. He was, with André Breton, one of the leaders of the Surrealist movement; his poetry after the mid-1940's combined elements of Romanticism and modernism, but his style evolved in a direction of its own and cannot be identified with that of any one school.

After his Surrealist period, during which he wrote for an intellectual elite, Aragon sought to make his work accessible to a wider public and often succeeded. The height of his popularity was achieved in the 1940's, when his poems played an important role in the French Resistance: written in traditional meters and using rhyme, so that they might more easily be sung, they became rallying cries for French patriots abroad and in occupied France. (Many of Aragon's poems have, in fact, been set to music by writers of popular songs, including Léo Ferré and George Brassens.) Beginning in the late 1950's, Aragon's work became much less overtly political, which contributed to its acceptance by non-Communist critics. At the time of his death in 1982, Aragon was considered even by his political opponents as a leading man of letters. Writers of lesser stature have been elected to the French Academy, but Aragon never applied for membership, and it is hard to imagine such an ardent advocate of commoners, who used slang liberally in his own work, sitting in judgment on the purity of the French language.

For Aragon, who wrote his first "novel" at age six (and dictated a play to his aunt before he could write), writing was like breathing, a vital activity coextensive with living. He was a novelist whose eye (and ear) for telling detail never dulled, a poet whose lyric gifts did not diminish with age.

BIOGRAPHY

Until late in life, Louis Aragon was reticent about his childhood, and many biographical notices describe it as idyllic; in fact, his family (which consisted of his grandmother, mother, and two aunts) was obsessed with a concern for appearances that caused the boy considerable pain. The illegitimate son of a prominent political figure, Louis Andrieux, who chose the name Aragon for his son and acted as his legal guardian, Aragon was reared as his mother's younger brother, and although as a boy he guessed much of the truth, it was not until his twentieth year that he heard it from his mother (at the insistence of his father, who had previously insisted on her silence). Since his maternal grandfather had also deserted the family, his mother, Marguérite Toucas-Masillon, supported them all as best she could by painting china and running a boardinghouse. According to his biographer, Pierre Daix, the circumstances of Aragon's childhood left him with an instinctive sympathy for outsiders, especially women, and a great longing to be accepted as a full member of a group. This longing was first satisfied by his friendship with André Breton and later by Aragon's adherence to the Communist Party. (Indeed, his deep need to "belong" may help to account for his unswerving loyalty to the party throughout the Stalinist era.)

Breton, whom he met in 1917, introduced Aragon to the circle of poets and artists that was to form the nucleus of the Dadaist and Surrealist movements. Horrified by the carnage of World War I (which Aragon had observed firsthand as a medic), these young people at first embraced the negative impulse of Dada, an absurdist movement founded in Zurich by Tristan Tzara. Their aim was to unmask the moral bankruptcy of the society that had tolerated such a war. Realizing that a philosophy of simple negation was ultimately sterile, Breton and Aragon broke away from the Dadaists and began to pursue the interest in the subconscious, which led them to Surrealism. Through the technique of automatic writing, they tried to suppress the rational faculty, or "censor," which inhibited free expression of subconscious impulses.

Politically, the Surrealists were anarchists, but as they became increasingly convinced that profound social changes were necessary to free the imagination, a number of them, including Aragon, joined the French Communist Party. At about the same time (1928), Aragon met the Russian poet Vladimir Mayakovsky and his sister-in-law, the novelist Elsa Triolet, at the Coupole, a Paris café. As Aragon put it, describing his meeting with Elsa many years later, "We have been together ever since" (literally, "We have not left each other's side"). In Elsa, Aragon found the "woman of the future," who could be her husband's intellectual and social equal while sharing with him a love in which all the couple's aspirations were anchored. Aragon celebrated this love in countless poems spanning forty years; some of the most ecstatic were written when the two were in their sixties. Elsa introduced Aragon to Soviet Russia, which they visited together in the early 1930's; she also took part with him in the French Resistance during World War II, publishing clandestine newspapers and maintaining a network of antifascist intellectuals. Although he followed the "party line" and tried to rationalize the Soviet pact with the Nazis, Aragon was an ardent French patriot; he was decorated for bravery in both world wars and wrote hymns of praise to the French "man (and woman) in the street," who became the heroes of the Resistance.

After the war, Aragon redoubled his activities on behalf of the Communist Party, serving as editor of the Communist newspaper *Ce Soir* and completing his six-volume novel *Les Communistes* (1949-1951). In 1954, he became a permanent member of the Central Committee of the French Communist Party, and in 1957, the Soviet Union awarded him its highest decoration, the Lenin Peace Prize. He was vilified by many of his fellow intellectuals in France for failing to criticize Stalin; not until 1966, during the much-publicized trial of two Soviet writers, Andrei Sinyavsky and Yuli Daniel, did he venture to speak out against the notion that there could be a "criminality of opinion." In 1968, he joined with the French Communist Party as a whole in condemning the Russian invasion of Czechoslovakia. Throughout his life, Aragon continued to produce a steady stream of poetry, fiction, and essays. His wife's death in 1970 was a terrible blow, but he survived it and went on to write several more books in the twelve years that were left to him.

ANALYSIS

Despite the length of Louis Aragon's poetic career and the perceptible evolution of his style in the course of six decades, there is a remarkable unity in the corpus of his poetry. This unity results from stylistic as well as thematic continuities, for even when he turned from free verse to more traditional metric forms, he managed to preserve the fluency of spoken language. In fact, his most highly structured verse has some of the qualities of stream-of-consciousness narrative. There are a variety of reasons for this. Aragon began to write as a very young boy and continued writing, steadily and copiously, throughout his life. As critic Hubert Juin has observed, Aragon never needed to keep a journal or diary because "his work itself was his journal," into which he poured his eager questions and reflections on what most closely concerned him.

This confessional impulse was reinforced and given direction in Aragon's Surrealist period by experiments with automatic writing, a technique adapted for literary use primarily by Breton and Philippe Soupault. By writing quickly without revising and by resisting the impulse to edit or censor the flow of words, the Surrealistis hoped to tap their subconscious minds and so to "save literature from rhetoric" (as Juin puts it). Literature was not all they hoped to save, moreover, for "rhetoric" had poisoned the social and political spheres as well; in liberating the subconscious, Aragon and his friends sought to break old and unjust patterns of thought and life. They also expected this powerful and hitherto untapped source to fuel the human imagination for the work of social renewal. Although Aragon repudiated the Surrealist attitude (which was basically anarchistic) when he embraced Communism as the pattern of the future, he never lost the stylistic freedom that automatic writing had fostered, nor did he become complacent about the "solution" he had found. Like his relationship with his wife, in which his hopes for the future were anchored, Aragon's Communism was a source of pain as well as of fulfillment: the deeper his love and commitment, the greater his vulnerability. Thus, poetry remained for him, as it had been in his youth, a form of questioning in which he explored the world and his relation to it.

There were, nevertheless, perceptible changes in Aragon's style during the course of his career. After the Dadaist and Surrealist periods, when he wrote mainly free verse (although there are metrically regular poems even in his early collections), Aragon turned to more traditional prosody—including rhyme—in the desire to make his verses singable. At the same time, he sought to renew and broaden the range of available rhymes by adopting new definitions of masculine and feminine rhyme based on pronunciation rather than on spelling. He also applied the notion of enjambment to rhyme, allowing not only the last syllable of a line but also the first letter or letters of the following line to count as constituent elements of a rhyme. Partly as a result of the conditions under which they were composed, Aragon's Resistance poems are for the most part short and self-contained, although *Le Musée grévin* (the wax museum) is a single long poem, and the pieces in *Brocéliande* are linked by allusions to the knights of the Arthurian cycle, whom Aragon saw as the symbolic counterparts of the Resistance fighters.

Aragon's postwar collections are more unified, and beginning with *Les Yeux et la mémoire* (eyes and memory), they might almost be described as book-length poems broken into short "chapters" of varying meters. Many of these "chapters," however, can stand alone as finished pieces; good examples are the love lyrics in *Le Fou d'Elsa* (Elsa's madman), some of which have been set to music, like the war poems, and the vignette from *Le Roman inachevé* (the unfinished romance) beginning "Marguerite, Madeleine, et Marie," which describes Aragon's mother and aunts—whom he thought of as his sisters—dressing for a dance. Within his longer sequences, Aragon skillfully uses shifts of meter to signal changes of mood and does not hesitate to lapse into prose when occasion warrants—for example, when, in *Le Roman inachevé*, he is suddenly overwhelmed by the weariness and pain of old age: "The verse breaks in my hands, my old hands, swollen and knotted with veins." Such disclaimers to the contrary, Aragon was never in greater control of his medium than in these poems of his old age, culminating in *Elsa, Le Fou d'Elsa*, and *Les Chambres* (the rooms). *Le Fou d'Elsa* is perhaps his greatest tour de force, a kind of epic (depicting the end of Muslim rule in Spain, with the fall of Granada in 1492) made up of hundreds of lyric pieces, along with some dialogue and prose commentary. As Juin has remarked, Aragon tends to alternate between two tones, the epic and the elegiac, and *Le Fou d'Elsa* is a perfect vehicle for both. The grand scale of the book gives full sweep to Aragon's epic vision of past and future regimes, while the inserted lyrics preserve the reduced scale proper to elegy.

To appreciate the texture of Aragon's poetry—his characteristic interweaving of image and theme, diction and syntax—it is necessary to examine a few of his poems in detail. Choosing one poem from each of the three distinct phases of his career (the Surrealist, Resistance, and postwar periods), all dealing with his central theme, the love of a woman, makes it possible to demonstrate both the continuities and the changes in his poetry during the greater part of his career. All three poems are in his elegiac vein, the mode easiest to examine at close range and the most fertile for Aragon. The occasional false notes in his verse tend to be struck when he assumes the triumphalist pose of the committed Marxist. When he speaks of his wife, his very excesses suggest a shattering sincerity, especially when the subject is separation, age, or death.

"Poem to Shout in the Ruins"

"Poème à crier dans les ruines" ("Poem to Shout in the Ruins"), although addressed to a woman, is not addressed to Elsa, whom Aragon had yet to meet when it was written. The poem records the bitterness of an affair that has recently ended and from which the poet seems to have expected more than his lover did. Like most of Aragon's work, the poem is heavily autobiographical; the woman involved was American heir Nancy Cunard, with whom Aragon had lived for about a year, and the allusions to travel throughout the poem recall trips the couple had taken together. Although the poem opens with a passage that might be described as expository, and although it moves from particular details to a general observation and closes with a sort of reprise, it strikes the reader as more loosely organized than it actually is. This impression results from its rhythm being that of association—the train of thought created when a person dwells on a single topic for a sustained period of time. Because the topic is unhappy love and the bitterness of rejection, the process of association takes on an obsessive quality, and although the resulting monologue is ostensibly addressed to the lover, the title suggests that neither she nor anyone else is expected to respond. The overall effect, then, is that of an interior monologue, and its power stems not from any cogency of argument (the "rhetoric" rejected by the Surrealists) but from the cumulative effects of obsessive repetition. Thus, the speaker's memories are evoked in a kind of litany ("I remember your shoulder/ I remember your elbow/ I remember your linen."); later, struck by the realization that memory implies the past tense, he piles up verbs in the *passé simple* (as in "Loved Was Came Caressed"), the tense used for completed action.

The lack of a rhetorical framework in the poem is paralleled by the absence of any central image or images. Although many arresting images appear, they are not linked in any design but remain isolated, reinforcing the sense of meaninglessness that has overwhelmed the speaker. The "little rented cars" and mirrors left unclaimed in a baggage room evoke the traveling the couple did together, which the speaker now sees as aimless. Some of the details given remain opaque because they have a private meaning that is not revealed ("Certain names are charged with a distant thunder"); others seem to be literary allusions, such as Mazeppa's ride (described in a poem by George Gordon, Lord Byron) and the bleeding trees, which to a reader who knows the works of Dante suggest that poet's "wood of the suicides." (Not until many years later did Aragon reveal that he had attempted suicide after the breakup with Cunard.)

The use of such arcane personal and literary allusions was a legacy of the Symbolist movement; as a young man, Aragon admired both Arthur Rimbaud and Stéphane Mallarmé, two of the most gifted Symbolists. The Surrealist approach to imagery evolved directly out of Symbolism in its more extreme forms, such as "Le Bateau ivre" ("The Drunken Boat") of Rimbaud and the *Chants de Maldoror* (1869) of Comte de Lautréamont. Despite its hopelessness, "Poem to Shout in the Ruins" conveys the almost hallucinatory power the Surrealists saw in imagery: its ability to charge ordinary things with mystery by appealing to the buried layers of the subconscious. "Familiar objects one by one were taking on . . . the ghostly look of escaped prisoners. . . ." The poem also suggests, however, that Aragon is not content merely to explore his subconscious; he hungers for a real connection to a real woman. In his desperate desire to prolong the liaison, he tries fitfully to make a "waltz" of the poem and asks the woman to join him, "since *something* must still connect us," in spitting on "what we have loved together." Despite its prevailing tone of negation and despair, the poem anticipates two central themes of Aragon's mature works: the belief that love between man and woman should be infinitely more than a source of casual gratification and the awareness of mortality (which the finality of parting suggests). This awareness is not morbid but tragic—the painful apprehension of death in a man whose loves and hopes were lavished on mortal existence.

"Elsa's Eyes"

"Les Yeux d'Elsa" ("Elsa's Eyes"), the opening poem in the collection of that name, is a good example of the metrically regular pieces Aragon produced in the 1940's (and continued to produce, together with free verse, until the end of his life). It is particularly characteristic in that, while each stanza has internal unity, the stanzas do not follow one another in a strictly necessary order; like those of a folk song or lyrical ballad, they offer a series of related insights or observations without logical or narrative progression. Many of Aragon's mature poems *do* exhibit such a progression (notably "Toi qui es la rose"—"You Who Are the Rose"), but in most cases it is subordinated to the kind of associative rhythm observed in "Poem to Shout in the Ruins."

The imagery of "Elsa's Eyes" is more unified than that of the earlier poem. Taking his wife's eyes as the point of departure, the poet offers a whole array of metaphors for their blueness (sky, ocean, wildflowers), brilliance (lightning, shooting stars), and depth (a well, far countries, and constellations). The last four stanzas are more closely linked than the preceding ones and culminate in an apocalyptic vision of Elsa's eyes surviving the end of the world. The poem as a whole, however, cannot be said to build to this climax; its power stems from the accumulation of images rather than from their arrangement. It should be noted that Aragon's Surrealist formation is still very much in evidence here, not only in the hallucinatory quality of his images but also in their obvious connection with subconscious desires and fears. The occasional obscurities are no longer the result of a deliberate use of private or literary allusions; Aragon was already writing with a wider public in mind. Nevertheless, he continued to evoke his own deepest desires and fears in language whose occasional ambiguity reflects the ambiguity of subconscious impulses.

A relatively new departure for Aragon in this period, the serious use of religious imagery, is reflected in the references to the Three Kings and the Mother of the Seven Sorrows in "Elsa's Eyes." Although reared a Catholic, Aragon became an atheist in his early youth and never professed any religious faith thereafter. During World War II, however, he was impressed by the courage of Christian resisters and acquired a certain respect for the faith that sustained them in the struggle against fascism. For his own part, Aragon began to use the vocabulary of traditional religion to extol his wife. Thus, for example, in "Elsa's Eyes," Elsa is described as the Mother of the Seven Sorrows, an epithet of the Virgin Mary; at the same time, Elsa is assimilated by natural forces and survives the cataclysm of the last stanza like a mysterious deity. This is partly attributable to Aragon's rediscovery, at about this time, of the courtly love tradition in French poetry, in which the lady becomes the immediate object of the knight's worship, whether as a mediatrix (who shows the way to God) or as a substitute for God himself. Repeatedly in Aragon's postwar poetry, Elsa is endowed with godlike qualities, until, in *Le Fou d'Elsa*, a virtual apotheosis takes place: The "holy fool" for whom the book is named (a Muslim, not a Christian) is convicted of heresy for worshiping a woman—Elsa—who will not be born for four centuries.

Whenever he was questioned on the subject, Aragon insisted that his aim was not a deification of Elsa but the replacement of the transcendent God of traditional religions with a "real" object, a woman of flesh and blood who could serve as his partner in building the future. Thus, Elsa's madman tells his judge, "I can say of her what I cannot say of God: She exists, because she *will be*." At the same time, the imagery of "Elsa's Eyes" clearly indicates that on some level there is an impulse of genuine worship, compounded of love, fear, and awe, in the poet's relation to his wife; he turned to the courtly tradition because it struck a deep chord in him. From the very first stanza, Elsa is identified with forces of nature, not all of which are benevolent: "Your eyes are so deep that in stooping to drink/ I saw all suns reflected there/ All desperate men throw themselves there to die." In most of the early stanzas, emphasis is laid on her grief (presumably over the effects of war), which only enhances her beauty, but the insistence on her eyes also suggests that, like God, she is all-seeing. Aragon himself often referred to his wife as his conscience, and Bernard Lecherbonnier has suggested in *Le Cycle d'Elsa* (1974) that the circumstances of Aragon's upbringing created in him, first in regard to his mother and later in regard to his wife, "an obsession with self-justification that permitted the myth of god-as-love to crystallize around the person, and in particular the eyes, of Elsa." Such an attitude is especially suggested by the final images of the poem, that of "Paradise regained and relost a hundred times" and that of Elsa's eyes shining over the sea after the final "shipwreck" of the universe.

"YOU WHO ARE THE ROSE"

An attitude of worship can also be seen in "You Who Are the Rose," from the collection *Elsa*, but it is tempered considerably by the vulnerability of the rose, the central image around which the poem is built. Its tight construction makes this a somewhat uncharacteristic poem for Aragon, yet his technique is still that of association and accumulation rather than logical or rhetorical development. As in "Poem to Shout in the Ruins," short syntactic units give the impression of spoken (indeed, in this poem, almost breathless) language. With an obsessiveness reminiscent of the earlier poem, the speaker worries over the flowering of the rose, which he fears will not bloom "this year" because of frost, drought, or "some subterranean sickness." The poem has a clear dramatic structure: The tension of waiting builds steadily, with periodic breaks or breathing spaces marked by the one-line refrain "*(de) la rose*," until the miraculous flowering takes place and is welcomed with a sort of prayer. The images that accumulate along the way, evoked by the poet in a kind of incantation designed to call forth the rose, are all subordinated to this central image of flowering, yet by their startling juxtaposition and suggestiveness, they clearly reflect Aragon's Surrealist background. Thus, the dormant plant is compared to "a cross contradicting the tomb," while two lines later its roots are "like an insinuating hand beneath the sheets caressing the sleeping thighs of winter." The use of alliteration is excessive—as when six words beginning with *gr-* appear in the space of three lines—and although this serves to emphasize the incantatory quality of the verse, to hostile critics it may look like simple bad taste. Hubert Juin, a friendly critic, freely acknowledges that a certain kind of bad taste is evident in Aragon; he ascribes it to the poet's "epic" orientation, his desire to include as much of the world as possible in his design, which precludes attention to every detail. It seems more to the point to recall that for the Surrealists, editing was a kind of dishonesty; by writing rapidly and not revising, they sought to lay bare what was most deeply buried in their psyches. What often saves Aragon from *préciosité*, or literary affectation, is the realism of this stream-of-consciousness technique. Caught up in the speaker's own anxiety or fantasy, the reader does not stop to criticize the occasional banalities and lapses of taste; he follows in the poet's wake, eager to see where the train of thought will lead.

The poignancy of "You Who Are the Rose," as of so many of Aragon's late poems, stems from the contrast between his exaggerated hopes—still virtually those of a young man—and the fact of old age, which threatens to deprive him of his wife and of his poetic voice. There is also, in some of his later work, a hint of sadness (although never of disillusionment) at the failure of Communism to fulfill its promise within his own lifetime. It is worth noting that in France the rose has long been associated with Socialist ideals; the poet's fear for his wife in "You Who Are the Rose" may be doubled by a tacit fear that the promise of Marxism will not be fulfilled. The two fears are related, moreover, because Aragon saw the harmony between husband and wife as the hope of the future, the cornerstone of a just and happy (Communist) society. His anguish is that of the idealist who rejects the possibility of transcendence: His "divinity" is mortal, like him. This helps to account for the fact that he continued to write with undiminished passion until the very end of his life, for poetry held out the only prospect of immortality in which he believed. The rose is mortal, but she has a name, and the poet can conjure with it (as his conclusion emphasizes: "O rose who are your being and your name"). What is more, Elsa Triolet was herself a writer, and in the preface to an edition combining her own and her husband's fiction, she described their mutually inspired work as the best possible memorial to their love. Aragon will probably be remembered primarily as the poet of Elsa—"Elsa's Madman," perhaps, in his anguished self-disclosure—but above all as Elsa's troubadour, an ecstatic love poet who insists on the possibility of earthly happiness because he has tasted it himself.

OTHER MAJOR WORKS
LONG FICTION: *Anicet: Ou, le panorama*, 1921; *Les Aventures de Télémaque*, 1922 (*The Adventures of Telemachus*, 1988); *Le Paysan de Paris*, 1926 (*Nightwalker*, 1970); *Les Cloches de Bâle*, 1934 (*The Bells of Basel*, 1936); *Le Monde réel*, 1934-1944 (includes *Les Cloches de Bâle*, 1934; *Les Beaux Quartiers*, 1936; *Les Voyageurs de l'impériale*, 1942; and *Aurélien*, 1944); *Les Beaux Quartiers*, 1936 (*Residential Quarter*, 1938); *Les Voyageurs de l'impériale*, 1942 (*The Century Was Young*, 1941); *Aurélien*, 1944 (English translation, 1947); *Les Communistes*, 1949-1951; *La Semaine sainte*, 1958 (*Holy Week*, 1961); *La Mise à mort*, 1965; *Blanche: Ou, L'oubli*, 1967; *Théâtre/roman*, 1974.

SHORT FICTION: *Servitude et grandeur de français*, 1945; *Le Mentir-vrai*, 1981.

NONFICTION: *Le Traité du style*, 1928; *Pour une réalisme socialiste*, 1935; *L'Homme communiste*, 1946, 1953; *Introduction aux littératures soviétiques*, 1956; *J'abats mon jeu*, 1959; *Les Deux Géants: Histoire parallèle des États-Unis et de l'U.R.S.S.*, 1962 (with André Maurois; 5 volumes; partial translation *A History of the U.S.S.R. from Lenin to Khrushchev*, 1964); *Entretiens avec Francis Crémieux*, 1964; *Écrits sur l'art moderne*, 1982.

BIBLIOGRAPHY

Adereth, M. *Aragon: The Resistance Poems*. London: Grant & Cutler, 1985. A brief critical guide to Aragon's poetry.

_____. *Elsa Triolet and Louis Aragon: An Introduction to Their Interwoven Lives and Works*. Lewiston, N.Y.: Edwin Mellen Press, 1994. An introductory biography of Triolet and Aragon and their lives together including critical analysis of their work and a bibliography.

Becker, Lucille Frackman. *Louis Aragon*. New York: Twayne, 1971. An introductory biography of Aragon and critical analysis of selected works. Includes bibliographic references.

Benfey, Christopher, and Karen Remmler, eds. *Artists, Intellectuals, and World War II: The Pontigny Encounters at Mount Holyoke College, 1942-1944*. Amherst: University of Massachusetts Press, 2006. Contains a chapter on Aragon, Gustave Cohen, and the poetry of the Resistance. Provides a general perspective on World War II literature.

Josephson, Hannah, and Malcolm Cowley, eds. *Aragon, Poet of the French Resistance*. New York: Duell, Sloan and Pearce, 1945. A study of Aragon's poetic works produced between 1939 and 1945.

Lillian Doherty

JOHN BALABAN

Born: Philadelphia, Pennsylvania; December 2, 1943

PRINCIPAL POETRY
After Our War, 1974
Scrisori de peste mare/Letters from Across the Sea, 1979
Blue Mountain, 1982
Words for My Daughter, 1991
Locusts at the Edge of Summer: New and Selected Poems, 1997
Path, Crooked Path, 2006

OTHER LITERARY FORMS

Apart from his volumes of poetry, John Balaban (BAHL-uh-bahn) published a novel, *Coming Down Again* (1985, 1989); a juvenile fable, *The Hawk's Tale*(1988); and several nonfiction books about his Vietnam experience, which include *Vietnam: The Land We Never Knew* (1989) and a memoir, *Remembering Heaven's Face: A Moral Witness in Vietnam* (1991). With coeditor Nguyen Qui Duc, Balaban edited a collection of seventeen short stories, *Vietnam: A Traveler's Literary Companion* (1996). He wrote a screenplay titled *Children of an Evil Hour*, produced in 1969. Balaban has translated Vietnamese poetry into English; some of these translations are in his *Ca Dao Vietnam: A Bilingual Anthology of Vietnamese Folk Poetry* (1974).

ACHIEVEMENTS

John Balaban's deep concern for humanity on the brink of annihilation, which he witnessed during the Vietnam War, is the hallmark of his poetry. Although he explored other areas of human experience, both geographically and historically, as well as his own inner world, the Vietnam factor stayed with him as a sounding board for whatever else came under his scrutiny. In three decades of steady publication, his work accumulated the needful critical mass to secure him an enduring place among the very best poets writing in the United States at the dawn of the twenty-first century.

Among his numerous awards and honors, his first book of poetry published in the United States, *After Our War*, was named the Lamont Poetry Selection by the Academy of American Poets in 1974 and was nominated for the National Book Award in Poetry. His third book, *Words for My Daughter*, was a National Poetry Series selection in 1990; his fourth book of poetry, *Locusts at the Edge of Summer*, was nominated for the National Book Award and won the Poetry Society of America's William Carlos Williams Award.

Balaban was the recipient of literary distinctions or prizes in Romania, the Steaua Prize of the Romanian Writers' Union (1978), and the Prize for Poetry at the Lucian

Blaga International Poetry Festival (1999). In Bulgaria, he won the Vaptsarov Medal given by the Union of Bulgarian Writers (1980). In Romania, he held a Fulbright-Hayes Lectureship for 1976-1977 and a Fulbright Distinguished Visiting Lectureship in 1979. After he completed his alternative military service in 1969, he visited Vietnam in 1971 to work on his translation of folk poetry, in 1985 to study the institutions of the unified country, and in 1989 to lecture for a few days at the University of Hanoi.

Between 1994 and 1997, he was president of the American Literary Translators Association. He earned two Pushcart Prizes: for his *Hudson Review* essay "Doing Good" (1978-1979) and for his poem "For the Missing in Action" (1990), originally published in *Ploughshares* and collected in *Words for My Daughter*. Balaban won the National Artist Award of the Phi Kappa Phi Honor Society for 2001-2004 and a John Simon Guggenheim Fellowship in 2003. Balaban has contributed poems, translations, essays and reviews to such periodicals as *American Scholar*, *Asian Art and Culture*, *Hudson Review*, *Modern Poetry in Translation*, *Sewanee Review*, *Southern Review*, *Steaua* (Cluj- Napoca, Romania), *The New Yorker*, and *TriQuarterly*.

BIOGRAPHY

John Balaban was born to Romanian immigrant parents, Phillip Balaban and Alice (Georgies) Balaban, both of peasant stock. The family name Balaban comes from a Polish count who led a force against the Turks in about 1510. Balaban's father, Filip Balaban, was born in Lovrin, a village in the Banat; his mother, Alexandra Georgies, came from a nearby village in southwestern Transylvania. The population was predominantly Romanian in the countryside; however, the people did not enjoy any civic rights and freedoms. After their respective families immigrated to the United States before World War I, Balaban's parents met in 1930 in the United States. They married and had two children, John and his sister, and their assimilation was quick and thorough.

Balaban showed an early bent toward the humanities, became a student at Pennsylvania State University, and majored in English. In 1966, he earned his bachelor's degree with the highest honors. He secured a much-coveted place at Harvard University, where the next year, he received his master's degree. Balaban accepted a position with the International Voluntary Services, a predecessor of the Peace Corps; he fulfilled his alternative service as a conscientious objector during the Vietnam War. As a graduate of Harvard, he received appointment as instructor in literature and descriptive linguistics at the University of Can Tho in South Vietnam (1967-1968).

The next year, Balaban served as field representative for the Committee of Responsibility to Save War-Burned and War-Injured Children, a Boston-based group that offered hospital care to children. It was at this time that he met his future wife, Lana "Lonnie" Flanagan, a teacher. Between 1970 and 1992, he taught English and creative writing at his alma mater, Pennsylvania State University, and taught twice as a Fulbright lecturer in Romanian universities.

In the early 1980's, John's and Lana's only child—a daughter, Tally—was born. A westward trip across the United States, during which he hitchhiked through the desert to escape the "technological sublime," helped him cope with his memories of Vietnam. He recorded what happened during that trip in *Blue Mountain. Words for My Daughter* continues his attempt to contain the past, make sense of what happened, and offer wisdom and guidance to his daughter.

From 1992 to 2000, Balaban served as professor of English at the University of Miami. In 2000, he earned appointment as professor of English and poet-in-residence at North Carolina State University in Raleigh.

Analysis

John Balaban's unique experiences as a conscientious objector and eyewitness to the destruction of Vietnam's rural population often figure into his poetry. The uncompromising picture Balban so powerfully paints details the plight of the indiscriminate war casualties among children, women, and elderly peasants. Caught in the crossfire between the belligerent armies, these groups were often victims of "collateral damage."

Balaban's was not a straightforward journalistic account but instead a young humanist's response. To develop a rapport with the centuries-long tradition of Vietnamese folk and written poetry, he went back to Vietnam in 1971 and became fluent in the language of this tradition. The development of his craft came from a sense of urgency and outrage; many of his later experiences yielded poetry from early traumatic events.

"After Our War"

"After Our War," the concluding piece of Balaban's first volume of poetry, is a meditation in the wake of the peace agreement signed between the United States and North Vietnam on January 27, 1973, in Paris. According to that agreement, the United States military would withdraw from the conflict. The poem opens with an apocalyptic vision:

> After our war, the dismembered bits
> —all those pierced eyes, ear slivers, jaw splinters,
> gouged lips, odd tibias, skin flaps, and toes—
> came squinting, wobbling, jabbering back.
> The genitals, of course, were the most bizarre,
> inching along roads like glowworms and slugs.

The tone is bemused, detached, and slightly ironic. The concreteness and specificity of the depiction mark the intensity of the experience. After more details of a like nature, the shocked reader realizes that:

> Since all things naturally return to their source,
> these snags and tatters arrived, with immigrant uncertainty,
> in the United States.

The poem concludes with a sequence of questions:

> After the war, with such Cheshire cats grinning in our trees,
> will the ancient tales still tell us new truths?
> Will the myriad world surrender new metaphor?
> After our war, how will love speak?

In "Gerontion," T. S. Eliot had asked a somewhat similar question: "After such knowledge, what forgiveness?" However, there is a significant difference here: Balaban's knowledge reflects the nightmare of history. Under such circumstances, the poet asks, is it worthwhile to seek after new truths, mediated by new metaphors? Art seems helpless and impotent in the face of twentieth century genocide.

"SITTING ON BLUE MOUNTAIN..."

"Sitting on Blue Mountain, Watching the Birds Fly South and Thinking of St. Julien Ravenel Childs," a poem from Balaban's *Blue Mountain*, develops the topic of war and violence in the United States. Sitting, watching, thinking aloud, and addressing the person mentioned in the title is a common stance for Balaban. The poem bears an ominous motto from Harriott Horry Rutledge Ravenel's book on the city of Charleston, South Carolina:

> *If the new is, or shall be, better,*
> *purer, braver or higher, it will be well.*
> *This is the tale of the old and it is done.*

While there may be some hope for the future, the past is beyond mending. Forgetful of human history for the moment, the first stanza is about migratory birds heading south toward the Carolinas. After a Whitmanesque catalog, the poet stops and asks himself: "Are these birds worth a whole stanza? Sure,/ they point our noses south; our hearts, to memory."

The entire second stanza is a splendid account of the burgeoning American Civil War, the secession of South Carolina, and the battering of Fort Sumter. The title character of the poem, St. Julien Ravenel Childs, is a southerner steeped in the colonial mentality of the slave-owning class and the grandson of Ravenel, whose book was the source of the motto. Balaban addresses Childs:

> In 1922, you soldiered in Santo Domingo.
> With Marines led by a latter General Lee
> you chased bandits through riverine jungles
> and saved the cane crop for a New York bank.

The next stanza casts the same doubt as to the scope and potency of poetry: "We live in a world with a simple sense of use/ that doesn't include poetry and musings." In spite of that declaration, the poet confesses he is a prisoner of his vocation and craft and cannot abandon himself to other pursuits; likewise, his addressee cannot escape his delusions. The poem ends on a resigned note, with an implicit comparison between the Blue Mountain of the poet's sublime idealism and the Atlantis of his interlocutor's incurable "dynastic mind."

"Words for My Daughter"

Balaban attempts a solution to the poet's dilemmas in "Words for My Daughter," a frequently anthologized poem. The title recalls William Butler Yeats's "A Prayer for My Daughter"; a comparison of the two poems yields some insight. Balaban seems aware that there is no point in sheltering one's offspring from the harsh reality of living. Yeats, in contrast, directs his prayer toward God and entreats God to protect, insulate, and endow his infant daughter with the graceful arts of gentility. For his daughter, the middle-class Balaban provides an account of his own rough childhood environment to educate her in the difficult art of survival; in this moment, Balaban becomes aware of the healing power he feels as he holds his daughter and of a renewal of hope in his alienated self.

Path, Crooked Path

Path, Crooked Path opens with "Highway 61 Revisited," set in June following the September 11, 2001, terrorist attacks on the United States. The poem reminds readers of the countryside along the legendary road and of Bob Dylan's album *Highway 61 Revisited* (1965). The narrator hopes to find both relief from the summer heat of the city and normality in the farmlands and the songs of crickets and songbirds; the speaker hopes to forget scenes of "the couples holding hands in their slow-motion leaps/ from the skyscraper windows billowing smoke." Reality presents itself, however, when he encounters a soldier who has been mugged and a man who cannot lift his prosthetic legs into a car.

Balaban includes some translations in *Path, Crooked Path*: "Ovid, Tristia V.x: 15-22" (from Ovid), "A Vision" (translated with Elena Christova from the Bulgarian of Kolyo Sevov), "Let Him Be" (translated with Alexandra Veleva from the Bulgarian of Georgi Borrisov), and "Van Gogh" (translated from the Bulgarian with the author, Lyubomir Nikolov). Their inclusion suggests the variety of topics in this collection.

Through his poetry, Balaban chronicles an array of individuals, some famous, some not, and some living, some dead. Balaban offers tribute to his teachers in "The Great Fugue" and to his dog Apples, to Dr. Alice Magheru, and to Vincent van Gogh in the poems named after their subjects. Balaban mentions more than twenty poets, including Georgi Borrisov and Hayden Carruth in the poems bearing their names and Denise Levertov, Theodore Roethke, Sylvia Plath, Cicero, Victor Hugo, and James Wright in "The Lives of the Poets."

Balaban's tolerance of others is apparent throughout the volume but particularly in

"Let Him Be," "If Only," and "Leaving." Balaban exhibits respect for other people: a paraplegic in "Eddie," a member of the Sex Change Band in "Poor Boy Slim," and even a feral cat tamed by his daughter in "Big Boy." Balaban's pacifist leanings are evident in "The Lives of the Poets" when he wonders if poetry can "calm the guns" and in "Varna Snow" when he concludes: "Only poetry lasts."

As might be expected for a collection titled *Path, Crooked Path*, Balaban mentions various locales, including Venice Beach (California), Hanoi, and Romania in "Some Dogs of the World"; the Volga River in "Ibn Fadhlan"; Camp Lejeune in "Soldier Home"; the Rio Grande in "Sotol"; the Miami area in "Remembering Miami" and "Dinner in Miami"; and Spain in "Butter People." Not all his scenes are pleasant: an accident victim in "Eddie," Chernobyl and America's cardboard huts in "Acropolis," losing others in "Goodbyes," and soldiers "smeared on the bushes and grass" in "Soldier Home."

Just as the first poem "Highway 61 Revisited," sets *Path, Crooked Path* on a journey, "Driving Back East with My Dad"—one of the last poems in the collection—ends the trip, mentioning various sites such as Kitty Hawk, North Carolina; the Danube; Philadelphia and Scranton, Pennsylvania; and Kansas. The poet and his father had a difficult trip; at one point, Balaban's father even turns off his hearing aid. Still, Balaban describes their trip—like life itself—as good; they had been ". . . alive together, taking in the road,/ mindful of where we had come, and moving on." Balaban, throughout the entire collection, reminds the reader to value the past, to appreciate the present, and to look forward to the future.

OTHER MAJOR WORKS

LONG FICTION: *Coming Down Again*, 1985, 1989.
SCREENPLAY: *Children of an Evil Hour*, 1969.
NONFICTION: *Vietnam: The Land We Never Knew*, 1989; *Remembering Heaven's Face: A Moral Witness in Vietnam*, 1991.
TRANSLATIONS: *Ca Dao Vietnam: A Bilingual Anthology of Vietnamese Folk Poetry*, 1974; *Vietnam: A Traveler's Literary Companion*, 1996; *Spring Essence: The Poetry of Ho Xuan Huong*, 2000.
CHILDREN'S LITERATURE: *The Hawk's Tale*, 1988.

BIBLIOGRAPHY

Balaban, John. "John Balaban." http://www.john balaban.com. The official Web site of Balaban contains information on his books and poetry as well as links to interviews with him and articles about him.

Beidler, Philip D. *Late Thoughts on an Old War: The Legacy of Vietnam*. Athens: University of Georgia Press, 2004. In his memoir on the Vietnam War, Beidler, an Army calvary platoon leader during the war, describes how his life paralleled that of Balaban in the chapter "Wanting to Be John Balaban."

_____. *Re-writing America: Vietnam Authors in Their Generation.* Athens: University of Georgia Press, 1991. Beidler discusses *After Our War*, which he says shows Balaban's sense of the crucial role of the Vietnam poet in remaking Americans' collective cultural experience of this conflict.

Erhart, W. D. "Soldier-Poets of the Vietnam War." In *America Rediscovered: Critical Essays on Literature and Film of the Vietnam War*, edited by Owen W. Gilman, Jr., and Lorrie Smith. New York: Garland, 1990. The work describes the great effort to absorb the Vietnamese culture made by Balaban, who learned the language and even suffered wounds.

Hillstrom, Laurie Collier. *The Vietnam Experience: A Concise Encyclopedia of American Literature, Songs, and Films.* Westport, Conn.: Greenwood Press, 1998. Contains a chapter on *After Our War*, which discusses the work and Balaban.

Kriesel, Michael. Review of *Path, Crooked Path. Library Journal* 131, no. 3 (February 15, 2006): 119-121. Kriesel notes how Balaban takes readers on a road trip, peopling his poetry with poets and figures ordinary and historical in various locales.

Rignalda, Don. *Fighting and Writing the Vietnam War.* Jackson: University Press of Mississippi, 1994. In the chapter on Vietnam War poetry, Rignalda calls Balaban the "most insistent" of the war poets on "translating the war—on both a figuratively literal and literally figurative level."

Seaman, Donna. Review of *Path, Crooked Path. Booklist*, 102, no. 17 (May 1, 2006): 65. Seaman calls Balaban a "roaming bard" who considers all of humanity and its storms. She notes Balaban's communication of his love of others in his writings although he recognizes their frequent reliance on violence.

Smith, Lorrie. "Resistance and Revision by Vietnam War Veterans." In *Fourteen Landing Zones: Approaches to Vietnam War Literature*, edited by Philip K. Jason. Iowa City: University of Iowa Press, 1991. Smith argues that Balaban implicates the reader in the decision to fight in Vietnam by calling it "our" war in the title of *After Our War*.

Stefan Stoenescu
Updated by Anita Price Davis

EDMUND BLUNDEN

Born: London, England; November 1, 1896
Died: Long Melford, Suffolk, England; January 20, 1974

PRINCIPAL POETRY
Poems, 1914
The Harbingers, 1916
Pastorals, 1916
The Waggoner, and Other Poems, 1920
The Shepherd, and Other Poems of Peace and War, 1922
To Nature: New Poems, 1923
English Poems, 1925
Masks of Time: A New Collection of Poems, Principally Meditative, 1925
Retreat, 1928
Undertones of War, 1928 (poetry and prose)
Near and Far: New Poems, 1930
The Poems of Edmund Blunden, 1914-1930, 1930
To Themis: Poems on Famous Trials, with Other Pieces, 1931
Halfway House: A Miscellany of New Poems, 1932
Choice or Chance: New Poems, 1934
An Elegy, and Other Poems, 1937
Poems, 1930-1940, 1940
Shells by a Stream: New Poems, 1944
After the Bombing, and Other Short Poems, 1949
Poems of Many Years, 1957
A Hong Kong House, 1962
Eleven Poems, 1965
Selected Poems, 1982
Overtones of War, 1996

OTHER LITERARY FORMS

The reputation of Edmund Blunden as a major British poet is founded primarily, and perhaps unfairly, on the poems he wrote about his service in World War I. Similarly, his popular prose works were connected to his wartime experiences. His most famous prose work, *Undertones of War* (1928), which includes a section of poems at the end, is one of the least vituperative of postwar British memoirs. Blunden's wartime experiences also featured prominently in the novel *We'll Shift Our Ground: Or, Two on a Tour* (1933), written in collaboration with Sylva Norman, in which two central characters visit the former battlefields of Flanders.

In contrast to his poetry and popular prose, Blunden's scholarly writing consisted primarily of biographies of important British literary figures—including Percy Bysshe Shelley, Lord Byron, and Charles Lamb—and rather impressionistic literary criticism. His scholarly approach was to focus on an author's life to understand his or her writings. Toward this end, Blunden wrote studies of a wide variety of major English poets, including the seventeenth century poet Henry Vaughan (1927), the Romantic poets Leigh Hunt (1930) and Shelley (1946), the Romantic essayist Lamb (1933), the early modern poet and novelist Thomas Hardy (1942), and fellow World War I poet Wilfred Owen (1931).

Achievements

Edmund Blunden's formal honors had little to do with his war poetry. In 1950, for example, Blunden was elected an honorary member of the Japan Academy, mainly for his educational work with the United Kingdom Liaison Mission in Tokyo after World War II. In 1963, the Japanese government awarded Blunden the Order of the Rising Sun, Third Class. Blunden's greatest honor had to do with his work in education and criticism: In 1966, he was elected Professor of Poetry at Oxford.

Biography

Although he was born in London, Edmund Charles Blunden's early years were spent in Yalding, a small English village, where his father was employed as a schoolmaster. For the next thirteen years, Blunden's experience of life was formed in Yalding, where the age-old rhythms of agriculture held sway. In 1909, Blunden entered Christ College, a public school in London. Already endowed with both scholarly interests and a desire to write, Blunden won the Senior Classics scholarship to Queen's College, Oxford, in 1914. As it did for many in his generation, World War I interrupted Blunden's further studies.

In 1915, Blunden earned a commission in the Royal Sussex Regiment and was in active service until 1917. Although two books of his poetry were accepted for publication before enlisting—*The Harbingers* and *Pastorals*—Blunden developed his poetic voice during active service. After the war and a brief stint at Oxford, he soon joined the staff of the *Athenaeum*, a literary journal. For most of the next four decades, Blunden's work life oscillated between literary journalism and teaching. For instance, a teaching post at Merton College, Oxford, lasted from 1931 to 1941 and was immediately followed by a job with the *Times Literary Supplement*, from 1941 to 1947.

From 1947 until his retirement in 1964, Blunden lived in Asia, first working in Japan and later taking a professorship of English literature at the University of Hong Kong. In 1966, after returning to England, Blunden was elected Professor of Poetry at Oxford

University, a post he almost rejected because of ill health. By the early 1970's, the long-term effects of his war wounds forced him to retire from active life. He died in Long Melford, Suffolk, England, on January 20, 1974.

Analysis

In *Heroes' Twilight* (1965, 1996), a study of World War I literature, the critic Bernard Bergonzi emphasizes the literariness of the average British officer, who "had received a classical education and [was] very well read in English poetry, so that [William] Shakespeare and [John] Milton, [William] Wordsworth and [John] Keats would be constantly quoted or alluded to when they wrote about the war." However true this observation may be of others, it is perfectly suited to Edmund Blunden. Blunden was the epitome of the well-educated, humane, and literary-minded British officer of World War I. Support for this argument comes in Blunden's *Undertones of War* when Blunden's commanding officer summons him to headquarters to express his admiration on learning that a published author serves under him. The respect accorded poetry is almost unbelievable until one considers Bergonzi's further point about the value of poetry during the war. Poetry provided "a sense of identity and continuity, a means of accommodating to life in a bizarre world as well as a source of consolation." As a form of shared experience and as a form of therapy, poetry helped many British soldiers endure the barbaric conditions they faced.

In the 1960's, Bergonzi pointed out that Blunden could be distinguished from his contemporaries by "the intensity of his absorption in the countryside." Blunden was almost always considered a nature poet; that is, his interest lay in representing the interconnection between humans and the natural world. The critical status of nature poetry varies greatly over time; correspondingly, Blunden's critical reputation also varied. During the late 1920's and early 1930's, he was compared unfavorably to more experimental poets like T. S. Eliot and Ezra Pound; in the mid-1960's, his poetry seemed hopelessly old-fashioned to many Oxford University undergraduates, who vocally opposed his candidacy for Professor of Poetry. It is questionable whether either set of critics truly understood the value of nature for Blunden. Nature was to Blunden a complex and compelling subject for poetry.

Nature as the art of God

The strongest of Blunden's reasons for writing nature poetry was to convey his deep love for the English countryside. As Bergonzi points out, "He knows the country with a deep knowledge and a deep love and it pervades the whole structure of his mind and feelings." This sense of deep intermingling of nature and the human mind is central to Blunden's poetry. In another critical study of Blunden's work, Thomas Mallon makes the same point, writing, "Poetry's chief task in describing nature [is] to capture its spirit, to communicate those feelings it gave to man." In a public address, Blunden endorsed the belief that "Nature hath made one World, and Art another. In brief, all things are artificial; for Nature is the Art of God." Thus, through his poetry Blunden could posit himself within this process of creation and understand more deeply the proper relationship of human beings, nature, and God. Seen in this way, Blunden's poetry is classifiable in terms of a series of interpenetrations of human beings and nature: the effect of nature on the human being, the effects of war on nature, the effect of war on humanity, and, finally, the effect of humans on nature.

Poems, 1914-1930

This collection of previously published works contains some of Blunden's earliest and most accessible poems. Blunden often offered a straightforward view of nature as therapy for suffering humanity, particularly those who are facing death during war. In "The Pagoda," the speaker dwells on the crumbled building and the animals that inhabit it:

> The small robin reconnoitres,
> Unabashed the woodmouse loiters:
> Brown owls hoot at shadow-fall
> And deathwatch ticks and beetles drone.

Apart from a few suggestive words such as "reconnoiters," there is little to suggest that the speaker is in active service during wartime. Blunden pointed out, however, that the poem was provoked by a visit to "some château in ruins" near the front. It is characteristic of much of his earlier poetry that war should be almost entirely absent; for nature to provide therapy, it must first allow the sufferer to distance himself or herself from the war.

As Blunden puts it in "Bleue Maison," the speaker longs to

> attune [his] dull soul, . . .
> To the contentment of this countryside
> Where man is not for ever killing man
> But quiet days like these calm waters glide.

This poetic landscape is described in blissful terms that become even more clear as the speaker continues:

> And I will praise the blue flax in the rye,
> And pathway bindweed's trumpet-like attire,
> Pink rest-harrow and curlock's glistening eye,
> And poppies flaring like St. Elmo's fire.

There is little sense in this poem that nature here has suffered from the war; in fact, the landscape of "Bleue Maison" is almost unaffected by the war.

A similar sense of nature as a place of spiritual healing is presented in "Mont de Cassel," although the frightful fact of the war does intrude on this speaker's consciousness:

> Here on the sunnier scarp of the hill let us rest,
> And hoard the hastening hour
> Find a mercy unexpressed
> In the chance wild flower.

The mercy that the speaker seeks is unexpressed, unvoiced, but still present. In fact, as the speaker later puts it, the merciful therapy provided by the flower and "other things so small and unregarded" reduces the war to "a leering ghost now shriven."

Blunden frequently returned to the concept of nature as a place of healing in his poetry, yet many of his later poems present a different sense of the interpenetration of the natural and the human worlds. In some of his later poems, particularly those written after World War I, Blunden describes nature as scarred and suffering. In this second sense of the overall theme, Blunden shows the effect of war on nature. By "nature," Blunden does not mean untamed wilderness, but rather landscape and the plants and creatures that cling to existence in the face of human destructiveness.

THE SHEPHERD, AND OTHER POEMS OF PEACE AND WAR

In *The Shepherd, and Other Poems of Peace and War*, published in 1922, Blunden's emphasis on the effect of war on nature is stated both clearly and emphatically. For instance, in the short work "A Farm Near Zillebeke," a rural home becomes a casualty of the war:

> The Line is all hushed—on a sudden anon
> The fool bullets clack and guns mouth again.
> I stood in the yard of a house that must die,
> And still the black hame was stacked by the door,
> And harness still hung there, and the dray waited by.

The depersonalization of the soldiers, "The Line," contrasts with the humanized "house that must die." In a poetic gesture reaching back to the Romantic period, Blunden uses the landscape to underscore the emotional significance of the moment.

This technique, called the pathetic fallacy by Samuel Taylor Coleridge and others, appears in another poem from the same collection, "1916 Seen from 1921." This poem turns on a central irony: The speaker, who has survived the war, is hardly alive spiritually. It is strongly implied that the speaker suffers from a form of guilt that is common in people who have survived harrowing and deadly experiences. Those who survived the war often felt guilty for living and would fruitlessly wonder why they lived on while so many others died. In this poem, the speaker clearly manifests this guilt:

> Dead as the men I loved, [I] wait while life drags
>
> Its wounded length from those sad streets of war
> Into green places here . . .

The speaker implies that he was most alive during active service. The intensity of life during wartime cannot be replicated in peacetime, and the speaker cannot find solace in nature. The green places once "were my own;/ But now what once was mine is mine no more." The sense of guilt shouts down the voice of nature: "the charred stub outspeaks the living tree."

Undertones of War

At the end of his prose memoir of the war, *Undertones of War*, Blunden included a series of poems, most of which were published between 1918 and 1928. In them, Blunden clearly demonstrates the effect that war has had on human beings. As in "1916 Seen from 1921," survivor's guilt figures prominently in some poems, but not all. In poems like "II Peter ii 22," Blunden offers a thoroughly negative representation of the postwar world to the returning veteran. In this poem, the speaker castigates a society in which "slinking Slyness rules the roost/ And brags and pimps" and in which

> Quarrel with her hissing tongue
> And hen's eye gobbles gross along
>   To snap that prey
>   That marched away
> To save her carcass, better hung.

To this observer, the postwar society is corrupt and little understands or appreciates the sacrifices that World War I demanded of the British soldier.

"At the Great Wall of China"

If society ignores the sacrifice of the soldier, Blunden certainly did not. In the later poem "At the Great Wall of China," published in *Poems of Many Years* in 1927, the poet describes the wall clearly and concisely, pointing out its structure and fortifications, yet finds himself thinking more about the lonely sentry who stood guard long ago:

> But I half know at this bleak turret here,
> In snow-dimmed moonlight where sure answers quail,
> This new-set sentry of a long-dead year,
> This boy almost, trembling lest he may fail
> To espy the ruseful raiders, and his mind
> Torn with sharp love of the home left far behind.

Understanding Blunden's life, it is tempting to interpret this poem as a disguised representation of his own feelings while standing guard in the trenches of the western front. However, the import of this poem is more universal: Its overall sense is to convey the tragedy of war in compelling human terms and to offer nature as solace, victim, and alternative.

OTHER MAJOR WORKS

LONG FICTION: *We'll Shift Our Ground: Or, Two on a Tour*, 1933 (with Sylvia Norman).

NONFICTION: *The Bonadventure: A Random Journal of an Atlantic Holiday*, 1922; *On the Poems of Henry Vaughan: Characteristics and Imitations*, 1927; *Undertones of War*, 1928 (poetry and prose); *Leigh Hunt and His Circle*, 1930; *Charles Lamb and His Contemporaries*, 1932; *Votive Tablets*, 1932; *The Mind's Eye*, 1934; *Edward Gibbon and His Age*, 1935; *English Villages*, 1941; *Shelley: A Life Story*, 1947.

EDITED TEXT: *The Poems of Wilfred Owen*, 1931.

BIBLIOGRAPHY

Barlow, Adrian. *The Great War in British Literature*. New York: Cambridge University Press, 2000. Although intended more for the student reader, this short book does an effective job of covering the major issues faced by British writers like Vera Brittain, Robert Graves, Richard Aldington, and Blunden.

Bergonzi, Bernard. *Heroes' Twilight: A Study of the Literature of the Great War*. 1965. Reprint. Manchester, England: Carcanet Press, 1996. Bergonzi's book was one of the first critical studies of its subject written for the nonacademic. This work postulates that British writers represented the war in terms of a "complex fusion of tradition and unprecedented reality."

Cross, Tim, ed. *Lost Voices of World War I*. Iowa City: University of Iowa Press, 1990. A moving anthology of poetry and other short works by writers who were killed in the conflict. It includes a fine introduction by Robert Wohl, a leading scholar of modernism, who offers valuable insight into how Blunden's British contemporaries felt about literature and the role it plays in society.

Hibbard, Dominic. *The First World War*. London: Macmillan, 1990. This work offers a chronological study of the war seen through the eyes of the writers who represented it at the time and much later. Generally, Hibbard does not focus much attention on Blunden, although he does point out that writers were far from univocal in their treatment of the war; responses ranged from the kind produced by Blunden to the gossipy cynicism and outrage of Robert Graves and Siegfried Sassoon.

McPhail, Helen, and Philip Guest. *Edmund Blunden*. Barnsley, South Yorkshire, England: Cooper, 1999. A biography of Blunden that examines his life and works, focusing on his war writings.

Mallon, Thomas. *Edmund Blunden*. Boston: Twayne, 1983. Like other works in the Twayne series, this study of Blunden is a fine starting point for general readers who are unfamiliar with the poet or his poetry.

Scupham, Peter. "Edmund Blunden." In *British Writers: Supplement XI*, edited by Jay Parini. New York: Charles Scribner's Sons, 2006. A basic biography and analysis of Blunden's works.

Webb, Barry. *Edmund Blunden: A Biography*. New Haven, Conn.: Yale University Press, 1990. This biography goes into great detail about the difficulties he faced in finding suitable work and domestic happiness. The general picture that emerges is of a thoroughly decent, kindly man who made the best of the worst possible experiences.

Michael R. Meyers

BERTOLT BRECHT

Born: Augsburg, Germany; February 10, 1898
Died: East Berlin, East Germany (now Berlin, Germany); August 14, 1956

PRINCIPAL POETRY
Hauspostille, 1927, 1951 (*Manual of Piety*, 1966)
Lieder, Gedichte, Chöre, 1934 (*Songs, Poems, Choruses*, 1976)
Svendborger Gedichte, 1939 (*Svendborg Poems*, 1976)
Selected Poems, 1947
Hundert Gedichte, 1951 (*A Hundred Poems*, 1976)
Gedichte und Lieder, 1956 (*Poems and Songs*, 1976)
Gedichte, 1960-1965 (9 volumes)
Bertolt Brecht: Poems, 1913-1956, 1976 (includes *Buckower Elegies*)
Bad Time for Poetry: 152 Poems and Songs, 1995

OTHER LITERARY FORMS

A prolific writer, Bertolt Brecht (brehkt) experimented with several literary forms and subjected nearly everything he wrote to painstaking revision. He first became known as a dramatist when he won the distinguished Kleist Prize in 1922 for his plays *Baal* (pb. 1922; English translation, 1963), *Trommeln in der Nacht* (pr., pb. 1922; *Drums in the Night*, 1961), and *Im Dickicht der Städte* (pr. 1923; *In the Jungle of Cities*, 1961), and he remains perhaps best known for plays such as *Mutter Courage und ihre Kinder* (pr. 1941; *Mother Courage and Her Children*, 1941) and his groundbreaking operas *Die Dreigroschenoper* (pr. 1928; *The Threepenny Opera*, 1949) and *Aufstieg und Fall der Stadt Mahagonny* (pb. 1929; *Rise and Fall of the City of Mahagonny*, 1957). His longer prose works include the novels *Der Dreigroschenroman* (1934; *The Threepenny Novel*, 1937, 1956) and *Die Geschäfte des Herrn Julius Caesar* (1956; the affairs of Mr. Julius Caesar). Brecht also wrote about eighty short stories, as well as essays in his *Arbeitsjournal* (1938-1955, 1973; *Bertolt Brecht Journals*, 1993).

ACHIEVEMENTS

Just as he would have it, Bertolt Brecht remains a controversial figure. His literary works, his politics, and his biography spark disagreement, but one thing is clear: Brecht belongs among the great writers of the twentieth century and certainly among the great modern poets. When Brecht died, Lion Feuchtwanger praised him as the only originator of the German language in the twentieth century.

Brecht was a bit of a showman (he was immediately recognizable in Berlin with his leather jacket, his proletarian cap, and his nickel-rimmed glasses), but he was always more interested in what people thought of his work than in what they thought of him. Eric Bentley, for example, has called Brecht's *Manual of Piety* "one of the best of all books of modern poems." Brecht's initial success on the stage in 1922, the year in which he won the Kleist Prize, was echoed in 1928 with the sensational premiere of *The Threepenny Opera* in Berlin. He received a National Institute of Arts and Letters Award in 1948. Toward the end of his life, Brecht was awarded the East German National Prize (1951), the highest distinction conferred by the German Democratic Republic on one of its citizens. In 1954, he became vice president of the East German Academy of Arts. One year before his death, he traveled to Moscow to accept the Stalin Peace Prize.

Without a doubt, Brecht is best known for his concept of the epic theater and his staging and acting technique of *Verfremdung* (alienation). He sought the intellectual rather than the emotional engagement of the audience, and his propensity for didactic structure rather than sentimental discourse is evident in his poetry as well. Brecht embraced Karl Marx's thesis that "it is not a matter of interpreting the world, but of changing it." His anti-Aristotelian theater concentrated on the factual and sober depiction of human and social conflicts, but with humorous alienation and alienating humor. To do serious theater today without acknowledging Brecht in some way is nearly impossible.

An assessment of Brecht's achievements cannot overlook his relation to literary tradition. Brecht "borrowed" freely from his predecessors, and he frequently chose the forms of parody or satire to make his readers aware of historical change and social contradictions. His candid speech did not always win favor: Because of his antiwar poem "Legende vom toten Soldaten" ("Legend of the Dead Soldier"), which was appended to his play *Drums in the Night*, Brecht was high on the Nazis' list of undesirables. It must be ranked among Brecht's accomplishments that, with his pen, he fought doggedly against the forces of evil and injustice that he saw embodied in the figure of Adolf Hitler and in the Nazi regime. The intensity and range of Brecht's voice as an essayist and dramatist have long been recognized; in contrast, because of the publication history of his poetry, it is only since Brecht's death that the power and scope of his lyric voice have begun to be appreciated.

Biography

Eugen Bertolt Friedrich Brecht was born into a comfortable middle-class home. His father, the manager of a paper factory, was Catholic; his mother, Protestant. Brecht was reared in the Lutheran faith. Before long, he turned strongly against religion, but the language of Martin Luther's translation of the Bible continued to influence Brecht throughout his life. A local Augsburg newspaper carried his first poems and essays in 1914, under the pen name "Berthold Eugen." Brecht dropped the mask in 1916 with the publication of his poem "Das Lied der Eisenbahntruppe von Fort Donald" ("Song of the Fort Donald Railroad Gang"), in the same local paper.

A restless and arrogant student ("I did not succeed in being of any appreciable help to my teachers"), Brecht enrolled in the University of Munich in 1917. There, he claimed to study medicine (as his father wished) and learned to play the guitar (less to his father's liking, no doubt). He completed a brief term of military service in 1918 as a medical orderly in a hospital for patients suffering from venereal disease. (It was in this year that Brecht wrote the "Legend of the Dead Soldier.") In Munich, Brecht soon became more interested in the local cabarets than in the study of medicine. He especially enjoyed the comedian Karl Valentin, who, along with Frank Wedekind, became an important influence on Brecht's literary development. He turned increasingly to literature and began taking seminars at the university with Professor Arthur Kutscher in 1918; he wrote the first version of *Baal* between March and June of the same year. Brecht traveled to Berlin in 1920; the city impressed him, but he returned to Munich after failing to make substantial literary contacts.

Brecht was to make one more trip to Berlin before finally moving there in 1924. From then until 1933, he spent his time in the capital and cultural center of Germany. In 1926, he first became acquainted with the writings of Marx; in its profound impact on his work, Brecht's discovery of Marx could be compared to Friedrich Schiller's reading of Immanuel Kant. At the time, Brecht was working on the play "Wheat" (to be staged by Erwin Piscator), and he wanted to understand how the exchange market worked. In the short run, his effort proved futile: "From every point of view," he wrote, "the grain market remained one impenetrable jungle." The consequences of his study, however, were far-reaching. His planned drama was never completed. Instead, he began to read Marx intensely: "It was only then that my own jumbled practical experiences and impressions came clearly into focus." Brecht's conversion to the principles of communism had begun. What followed in its literary wake were the operas and several strongly didactic plays in the early 1930's. Brecht, the eminent political poet, wisely left Germany on February 28, 1933, the day after the burning of the Reichstag. Several years of exile ensued.

"Changing countries more often than shoes," as Brecht reflected once, he eventually found his way to a place near Svendborg in Denmark, after traveling through Prague, Zurich, Lugano, and Paris. In Denmark, Brecht was—for the time being, anyway—relatively settled. Still, he remained acutely sensitive toward "escape routes" (images of doors are frequent in the poetry of his exile). He traveled to Moscow and New York in 1935, to London in 1936, and to Paris in the next year. With the threat of Nazi invasion looming large, Brecht left Denmark for Sweden in 1939 and settled near Stockholm. Before long, this sanctuary, too, appeared endangered by the Nazis. Brecht fled to the United States in 1941.

Brecht's life in exile, coupled with his fascination for the exotic, drew him in particular to the Chinese poet, Bai Juyi (Po Chü-i), whose work he had come to know through the translation of Arthur Waley. In the United States, Brecht was particularly conscious of his displacement; having settled in Santa Monica near Hollywood, he never felt comfortable in the "tinsel town." His productivity slackened somewhat during his American years, though he collaborated with artists of the stature of Fritz Lang and Charles Laughton. On October 30, 1947, the day after he appeared before the House Un-American Activities Committee, Brecht flew to Paris and shortly thereafter moved to Switzerland.

Brecht's second wife, the accomplished actress Helene Weigel, was an Austrian citizen, and it is most likely for this reason that Brecht acquired Austrian citizenship as well, even though he finally settled in East Berlin in 1949. There, until his death in 1956, Brecht worked with the Berlin Ensemble. Meanwhile, his Austrian citizenship allowed his work to remain accessible to all the German-speaking countries (Brecht was also shrewd about the business and politics of publication). As he wished, Brecht's death was noted with a quiet ceremony. He lies buried in an old cemetery not far from his apartment, near the graves of Georg Wilhelm Friedrich Hegel and Johann Gottlieb Fichte.

Analysis

It is important to note that Bertolt Brecht's creativity as a poet resulted less from any inclination toward introspection than from his desire to communicate with others. Against the prevailing tone of German poetry in the 1920's, at least as it was represented by Rainer Maria Rilke, Hugo von Hofmannsthal, and Stefan George, Brecht's poetic voice startled and shocked his readers. "These poems [of Rilke and others] tell ordinary people nothing, sometimes comprehensibly, sometimes incomprehensibly," he wrote in his youth. One of Brecht's main objections to this style of poetry was that its sense of artistic order hid rather than disclosed the chaos he saw in modern life. For this reason, Brecht eventually came to see rhyme and rhythm as obstructive and to prefer "Rhymeless Verse with Irregular Rhythms," as the title of an essay in 1939 reads. As basic to Brecht's poems as their consideration of the reader is his notion of functionality. He first articulated this concept in 1927 when asked to judge a poetry contest that had brought more than four hundred entries. Brecht read them all and awarded no prize. Instead, he acknowledged an unsubmitted poem from a little-known writer, appreciating its simplicity, its engaging choice of topics, its melodiousness, and its documentary value. The notion that "all great poems have the value of documents" was central to Brecht's thought. Writing poetry was, for Brecht, no "mere expression," but a "social function of a wholly contradictory and alterable kind, conditioned by history and in turn conditioning it."

Brecht wrote his poems in, as he called it, "a kind of Basic German." His sensitivity for the "gestic" power of language was nurtured by his fondness for Luther's Bible (the term Brecht uses, *Gestus*, is difficult to render adequately in English: John Willet identifies it with "gesture" and "gist," attitude and point). At the root of Brecht's poetry, indeed all his work, are the notions of clarity ("The truth is concrete" was Brecht's favorite maxim from Hegel) and functionality. Form, of which Brecht was a master and not a slave, was a means toward an end, that being enlightenment. In tracing Brecht's poetic development, one can see how the forms and motifs change against the backdrop of these guiding concepts.

One attribute of the term "gestic" is that of performance. Brecht was always concerned with delivery (it is central to his theory of the epic theater), and his early poetry is characterized by its close links with song. Indeed, most of Brecht's early poems were written to be accompanied by the guitar. Verse and melody often came about simultaneously, the rhythm of the words combining with the flow of the song. It is not surprising that Brecht's early poems acknowledge such traditional forms as legends, ballads, and chronicles. He was aware that no poet who considered himself important was composing ballads at that time, and this fact, too, may have intrigued the young iconoclast. What drew Brecht to these older poetic forms was their attention to adventure, to nature, and to the role of the heroic individual. Brecht rejuvenated a tired literary tradition by turning to the works of François Villon and Rudyard Kipling. Brecht's ballads mark a decisive turning point in the history of that genre.

"Song of the Fort Donald Railroad Gang"

"Song of the Fort Donald Railroad Gang," written in 1916, exhibits Brecht's youthful keenness for the frontier spirit. It relates the struggle and demise of a railroad crew laying track in the wilderness of Ohio. The portrayal of nature as rugged and indifferent marks a distinct switch for Brecht from the mediocre war poems he had been writing earlier. A common denominator, however, was the element of destructive force. This poem leads, step by inevitable step, through six strophes toward the culminating catastrophe. Initially, nature tolerates the intruders, who can be seen as pilgrims of modern progress pitted against the dense forests, "forever soulless." With the onset of torrential rains, the tolerance of nature becomes indifference, but the railroad gang forges on. Striking up a song within a song, they take to singing in the night to keep themselves awake and posted of the dangers posed by the downpour and the swelling waters. For them, escape is not an option. Death simply comes, and comes simply, leaving only the echo of their melody: "The trains scream rushing over them alongside Lake Erie/ And the wind at that spot sings a stupid melody." A stupid melody? What has happened to these modern "heroes"? There are no modern heroes, Brecht answers—and this in the poetic form that traditionally extols them. Brecht debunks their melody, uses the ballad to put an end to the balladesque hero. Death and nature prevail.

"Remembering Marie A."

Death and nature, along with murder and love, are the elemental themes distinguishing Brecht's early poems. He was wont to treat these perennial subjects, though, in nontraditional ways. He does this with great effect in what is ostensibly a love poem, "Erinnerung an die Maria A." ("Remembering Marie A."), written in 1920 and later included in *Manual of Piety*. It is more lyrical than the balladesque forms Brecht had already mastered, but it does not get lost in sentimentality. Instead, Brecht achieves a parody of the melancholy youth remembering an early love, and in its attitude it is quintessential Brecht. What the speaker in the poem actually recalls is less his "love so pale and silent/ As if she were a dream that must not fade," than it is "a cloud my eyes dwelt long upon/ It was quite white and very high above us/ Then I looked up, and found that it had gone." Not even the woman's face remains present for Brecht's persona, only her kiss, and "As for the kiss, I'd long ago forgot it/ But for the cloud that floated in the sky." The idyllic atmosphere of the first strophe turns out to be nothing but cliché.

What Brecht does with the element of time in this poem is essential to its overall effect. He establishes an internal relationship on three levels: first, the love affair, located in the past; second, the passage of time, the forgetting that wastes all memory; and third, the making present, by means of the cloud, that September day long ago. The tension Brecht succeeds in creating between these different levels has ironic consequences. For one, his use of verb tenses renders as present what is actually narrated in the past tense, while the grammatical past tense functions on the level of present time. The hierarchy of experiences is also switched: the backdrop of nature, the embodiment of everything transitory, can be remembered, while the primary experience (or what convention dictates should be the primary experience)—namely, the relationship between the lovers—falls prey to bad memory. Ultimately, it is a poem about the inconstancy of feeling and the mistrust between people that renders meaningful and lasting relationships problematic. It treats an old theme originally; where others write poems directed toward those lovers in the present, those passed away, those absent, or even those expected in the future, Brecht writes of the lover forgotten.

"OF POOR B. B."

"I, Bertolt Brecht, came out of the black forests." So begins Brecht's famous autobiographical poem, "Vom armen B. B." ("Of Poor B. B."), first written in 1922 and later revised when he was preparing *Manual of Piety* for publication. It was composed when Brecht's feet were mostly in Augsburg and Munich, but his mind was mostly in Berlin. The poem marks a turning point for Brecht. He leaves behind the ballad form and takes up the theme of the city. Nature in the raw yields to the irrepressible life of the big city, although neither locus is ever idealized. Written literally while under way (apparently on a train to Berlin), the poem is about where one feels at home, "one" in this instance being no one but Brecht himself. "In the asphalt city I'm at home," he admits, and he goes on to describe the daily routine of city dwellers, situating himself in their midst: "I put on/ A hard hat because that's what they do./ I say: they are animals with a quite peculiar smell/ And I say: does it matter? I am too." The poem is full of cynicism and despair. The poet admits that he is undependable and remains convinced that all that will remain of the cities is what passed through them—that is, the wind: "And after us there will come: nothing worth talking about." Thematically, the change of emphasis in "Of Poor B. B." prepares the way for later poems. Formally, the delivery of the poem depends less on melody (song) and relies instead on the premise of conversation between poet and reader.

"IN DARK TIMES"

Brecht's poems of the 1930's reveal a heightened awareness of the function of the poet with regard to his readership. He had made this point quite polemically already in 1927 as the judge of the poetry contest noted above. The poem, he claimed, had functional value. Looking for the functional lyric caused Brecht to seek a new style and idiom. The often-quoted poem "In finsteren Zeiten" ("In Dark Times"), written in 1937 during Brecht's exile in Denmark, attests his self-conscious task as responsible poet. Brecht imagines what people will later say about these "dark times." "They won't say: when the child skimmed a flat stone across the rapids/ But: when the great wars were being prepared for." History, in other words, will ride along on the backs of the little people—as Brecht makes clear in "Fragen eines lesenden Arbeiters" ("Questions from a Worker Who Reads")—but what remain visible are only the "great powers." In the face of this adversity, Brecht remarks with chagrin: "However, they won't say: the times were dark/ Rather: why were their poets silent?"

"BAD TIME FOR POETRY"

Brecht refused to be silent. His "Schlechte Zeit für Lyrik" ("Bad Time for Poetry"), written in 1939, is a personally revealing poem about his own internal struggle to reconcile aesthetic demands with demands of social responsibility: "In my poetry a rhyme/ Would seem to me almost insolent." Still, as Brecht wrote in his essay on poetry and logic, also from the 1930's, "we cannot get along without the concept of beauty." The poem "Bad Time for Poetry" thus concludes:

> Inside me contend
> Delight at the apple tree in blossom
> And horror at the house-painter's speeches.
> But only the second
> Drives me to my desk.

Brecht seldom mentioned Hitler by name, preferring to call him only "the house-painter," ridiculing Hitler's artistic pretentions.

"LEGEND OF THE ORIGIN OF THE BOOK TAO-TÊ-CHING ON LAO-TZÛ'S ROAD INTO EXILE"

To appreciate Brecht's aesthetic sensitivities, one must realize that he saw the felicitous poem as one in which "feeling and reason work together in total harmony." For Brecht, too, there was no distinction between learning and pleasure, and thus a didactic poem was also cause for aesthetic pleasure. The sensual pleasure derived from knowledge is an important aspect of the title figure of Brecht's play *Leben des Galilei* (pr. 1943; *The Life of Galileo*, 1960). What to do with knowledge and wisdom was another question that, for Brecht, followed inevitably. He answered it in his poem "Legende von der Entstehung des Buches Taoteking" ("Legend of the Origin of the Book Tao-Tê-Ching on Lao-tzû's Road into Exile") written in 1938 and included in the *Svendborg Poems*.

This poem is a highly successful combination of Brecht's earlier fascination with legends, the balladesque narrative, and the aesthetics of functional poetry. It relates the journey of Laozi (Lao Tzu), "seventy and getting brittle," from his country, where "goodness had been weakening a little/ And the wickedness was gaining ground anew" (a topic of immediate interest to the exile Brecht). Brecht does not puzzle over Laozi's decision to leave; it is not even an issue. He states simply, "So he buckled his shoe." (One recalls Brecht's line that he had "changed countries more often than shoes.") Laozi needs little for the journey: books, pipe, and bread (note here the relation between knowledge and sensual pleasure). After four days, he and the boy accompanying him come across a customs official at the border: "'What valuables have you to declare here?'/ And the boy leading the ox explained: 'The old man taught'/ Nothing at all, in short." The customs official, however, is intrigued by the boy's modest assertion that the old man "'learned how quite soft water, by attrition/ Over the years will grind strong rocks away./ In other words, that hardness must lose the day.'" The official shouts to them before they are able to move on and requires them to dictate what it was the old man had to say about the water: "'I'm not at all important/ Who wins or loses interests me, though./ If you've found out, say so.'" The old man obliges him ("'Those who ask questions deserve answers'"), and he and the boy settle down for a week, the customs man providing them with food. When the dictation is finally done, "the boy handed over what they'd written./ Eighty-one sayings." This is the wisdom of Laozi, for which posterity has been grateful, but Brecht is quick to point out that "the honor should not be restricted/ To the sage whose name is clearly writ./ For a wise man's wisdom needs to be extracted./ So the customs man deserves his bit./ It was he who called for it."

Brecht's return to rhyme in this poem is consistent with its ballad form. Where rhyme no longer sufficed for what was to be said, Brecht applied his theory of rhymeless verse with irregular rhythms. He had already used this style occasionally in the 1920's but mastered it fully in the poetry of the 1930's and 1940's; the form corresponded to Brecht's perception of a society at odds with itself, and it dominated his later lyrical writings.

BUCKOWER ELEGIES

Brecht's later poetry tends to be at once more intimate and more epigrammatic than his earlier work. This late style is best illustrated in his last group of poems, the *Buckower Elegien* (*Buckower Elegies*), written in 1953. The poems are concise evidence of Brecht's fascination with the fragmentary nature of the lyric, which he viewed as an appeal to the reader. Many of the poems mimic the open form of the riddle, with a strong central image, as in "Der Radwechsel" ("Changing the Wheel"). In six brief lines, Brecht observes how a driver changes a wheel. He voices his own dissatisfaction with his course in life ("I do not like the place I have come from./ I do not like the place I am going to"). Brecht characteristically leaves this poem open toward the future: "Why with impatience do I/ Watch him changing the wheel?"

The critic Joachim Müller has written that

> In all its phases and in all its forms, Brecht's poetry is neither exclusively subjective confession, nor simply an agitator's call to arms; every confession becomes an appeal to human activity, and every appeal, however it may alienate us by its satire or its polemics, springs from the deep emotion of a rational heart that sees all conditions in the world dialectically and that always sides with what is human against every inhumanity.

OTHER MAJOR WORKS

LONG FICTION: *Der Dreigroschenroman*, 1934 (*The Threepenny Novel*, 1937, 1956); *Die Geschäfte des Herrn Julius Caesar*, 1956.

SHORT FICTION: *Geschichten vom Herrn Keuner*, 1930, 1958 (*Stories of Mr. Keuner*, 2001); *Kalendergeschichten*, 1948 (*Tales from the Calendar*, 1961); *Me-ti: Buch der Wendungen*, 1965; *Prosa*, 1965 (5 volumes); *Bertolt Brecht Short Stories, 1921-1946*, 1983 (translation of *Geschichten*, volume 11 of *Gesammelte Werke*); *Collected Stories*, 1998.

PLAYS: *Baal*, pb. 1922 (English translation, 1963); *Trommeln in der Nacht*, pr., pb. 1922 (wr. 1919-1920; *Drums in the Night*, 1961); *Im Dickicht der Städte*, pr. 1923 (*In the Jungle of Cities*, 1960); *Leben Eduards des Zweiten von England*, pr., pb. 1924 (with Lion Feuchtwanger; based on Christopher Marlowe's play *Edward II*; *Edward II*, 1966); *Die Hochzeit*, pr. 1926 (wr. 1919; pb. 1953 as *Die Keinbürgerhochzeit*; *The Wedding*, 1970); *Mann ist Mann*, pr. 1926 (*A Man's a Man*, 1961); *Die Dreigroschenoper*, pr. 1928 (libretto; based on John Gay's play *The Beggar's Opera*; *The Threepenny Opera*, 1949); *Aufstieg und Fall der Stadt Mahagonny*, pb. 1929 (libretto; *Rise and Fall of the City of Mahagonny*, 1957); *Das Badener Lehrstück vom Einverständnis*, pr. 1929 (*The Didactic Play of Baden: On Consent*, 1960); *Happy End*, pr. 1929 (libretto; lyrics with Elisabeth Hauptmann; English translation, 1972); *Der Jasager*, pr. 1930 (based on the Japanese Nō play *Taniko*; *He Who Said Yes*, 1946); *Die Massnahme*, pr. 1930 (libretto; *The Measures Taken*, 1960); *Die heilige Johanna der Schlachthöfe*, pb. 1931 (radio play; pr. 1959, staged; *St. Joan of the Stockyards*, 1956); *Der Neinsager*, pb. 1931 (*He Who Said No*, 1946); *Die Mutter*, pr., pb. 1932 (based on Maxim Gorky's novel *Mat*; *The Mother*, 1965); *Die Sieben Todsünden der Kleinbürger*, pr. 1933 (cantata; *The Seven Deadly Sins*, 1961); *Die Rundköpfe und die Spitzköpfe*, pr. 1935 (based on William Shakespeare's play *Measure for Measure*; *The*

Roundheads and the Peakheads, 1937); *Die Ausnahme und die Regel*, pb. 1937 (wr. 1930; *The Exception and the Rule*, 1954); *Die Gewehre der Frau Carrar*, pr., pb. 1937 (*Señora Carrar's Rifles*, 1938); *Furcht und Elend des dritten Reiches*, pr. 1938 (in French; pr. 1945, in English; pb. 1945, in German; *The Private Life of the Master Race*, 1944); *Die Horatier und die Kuriatier*, pb. 1938 (wr. 1934; *The Horatians and the Curatians*, 1947); *Mutter Courage und ihre Kinder*, pr. 1941 (based on Hans Jakob Christoffel von Grimmelshausen's *Der abenteuerliche Simplicissimus*; *Mother Courage and Her Children*, 1941); *Der gute Mensch von Sezuan*, pr. 1943 (wr. 1938-1940; *The Good Woman of Setzuan*, 1948); *Leben des Galilei*, pr. 1943 (first version wr. 1938-1939; second version, in English, wr. 1945-1947, pr. 1947; third version, in German, pr., pb. 1955, revised pb. 1957; *The Life of Galileo*, 1947; better known as *Galileo*); *Die Antigone des Sophokles*, pr., pb. 1948 (*Sophocles' Antigone*, 1990); *Herr Puntila und sein Knecht, Matti*, pr. 1948 (wr. 1940; *Mr. Puntila and His Hired Man, Matti*, 1976); *Der kaukasische Kreidekreis*, pr. 1948 (wr. 1944-1945, in English; pb. 1949 in German; based on Li Hsing-dao's play *The Circle of Chalk*; *The Caucasian Chalk Circle*, 1948); *Der Hofmeister*, pr. 1950 (adaptation of Jacob Lenz's *Der Hofmeister*; *The Tutor*, 1972); *Der Prozess der Jeanne d'Arc zu Rouen, 1431*, pr. 1952 (based on Anna Seghers' radio play; *The Trial of Jeanne d'Arc at Rouen, 1431*, 1972); *Don Juan*, pr. 1953 (adaptation of Molière's play; English translation, 1972); *Die Gesichte der Simone Machard*, pb. 1956 (wr. 1941-1943; with Feuchtwanger; *The Visions of Simone Machard*, 1961); *Pauken und Trompeten*, pb. 1956 (adaptation of George Farquhar's *The Recruiting Officer*; *Trumpets and Drums*, 1972); *Die Tage der Commune*, pr. 1956 (wr. 1948-1949; based on Nordahl Grieg's *Nederlaget*; *The Days of the Commune*, 1971); *Der aufhaltsame Aufstieg des Arturo Ui*, pb. 1957 (wr. 1941; *The Resistible Rise of Arturo Ui*, 1972); *Schweyk im zweiten Weltkrieg*, pr. 1957 (wr. 1941-1943, in Polish; pb. 1957 in German; based on Jaroslav Hašek's novel *Osudy dobrého vojáka Švejka za svetove války*; *Schweyk in the Second World War*, 1975); *Coriolan*, pb. 1959 (wr. 1952-1953; adaptation of William Shakespeare's play *Coriolanus*; *Coriolanus*, 1972); *Turandot: Oder, Der Kongress der Weisswäscher*, pr. 1970 (wr. 1950-1954).

SCREENPLAYS: *Kuhle Wampe*, 1932 (English translation, 1933); *Hangmen Also Die*, 1943; *Das Lied der Ströme*, 1954; *Herr Puntila und sein Knecht, Matti*, 1955.

RADIO PLAYS: *Der Ozeanflug*, pr., pb. 1929 (radio play; *The Flight of the Lindberghs*, 1930); *Das Verhör des Lukullus*, pr. 1940 (radio play; *The Trial of Lucullus*, 1943).

NONFICTION: *Der Messingkauf*, 1937-1951 (*The Messingkauf Dialogues*, 1965); *Arbeitsjournal*, 1938-1955, 1973 (3 volumes; *Bertolt Brecht Journals*, 1993); *Kleines Organon für das Theater, 1948* (*A Little Organum for the Theater*, 1951); *Schriften zum Theater*, 1963-1964 (7 volumes); *Brecht on Theatre*, 1964; *Autobiographische Aufzeichnungen, 1920-1954*, 1975 (partial translation *Diaries, 1920-1922*, 1979); *Letters*, 1990; *Brecht on Film and Radio*, 2000.

MISCELLANEOUS: *Gesammelte Werke*, 1967 (20 volumes).

BIBLIOGRAPHY

Bartram, Graham, and Anthony Waine, eds. *Brecht in Perspective*. London: Longman, 1982. Thirteen excellent essays by highly qualified scholars. The topics range from German drama before Brecht through Brecht's manifold innovations to Brecht's legacy for German and English playwrights. Indispensable reading for understanding the broader context of his works.

Dickson, Keith A. *Towards Utopia: A Study of Brecht*. Oxford, England: Clarendon Press, 1978. Places Brecht's works in the context of literary, philosophical, social, and political history. German quotations are translated at the end of the book.

Giles, Steve, and Rodney Livingstone, eds. *Bertolt Brecht: Centenary Essays*. Atlanta: Rodopi, 1998. A collection of essays on Brecht written one hundred years after his birth. Bibliography.

Hayman, Ronald. *Brecht: A Biography*. London: Weidenfeld and Nicolson, 1983. A lengthy, dispassionately objective biography with many interesting details. Hayman skillfully integrates the facts of Brecht's private life with the discussion of his works. Opens with a chronology and a list of performances.

Martin, Carol, and Henry Bial. *Brecht Sourcebook*. New York: Routledge, 2000. Collection of protean essays in three sections: Brecht's key theories, his theories in practice, and, most successful, the adoption of his ideas internationally.

Mews, Siegfried, ed. *A Bertolt Brecht Reference Companion*. Westport, Conn.: Greenwood Press, 1997. An indispensable guide for the student of Brecht. Includes bibliographical references and an index.

Speirs, Ronald, ed. *Brecht's Poetry of Political Exile*. New York: Cambridge University Press, 2000. A collection of essays that examine the poetry Brecht wrote while in exile from Germany during World War II.

Thomson, Peter, and Glendyr Sacks, eds. *The Cambridge Companion to Brecht*. New York: Cambridge University Press, 1994. This extensive reference work contains a wealth of information on Brecht. Part of the Cambridge Companions to Literature series. Bibliography and index.

Willett, John. *Brecht in Context: Comparative Approaches*. Rev. ed. London: Methuen, 1998. A comparative analysis of the works of Brecht. Bibliography and index.

Richard Spuler

RUPERT BROOKE

Born: Rugby, England; August 3, 1887
Died: Aboard a hospital ship on the Aegean Sea; April 23, 1915

PRINCIPAL POETRY
Poems, 1911
Collected Poems, 1915
1914, and Other Poems, 1915
Complete Poems, 1932
The Poetical Works of Rupert Brooke, 1946 (Geoffrey Keynes, editor)

OTHER LITERARY FORMS

Rupert Brooke's lasting work is to be found exclusively in his poetry, but his work in several other literary forms at least deserves mention. Brooke was attracted to the theater, and two of his works, one as a critic and one as an artist, reflect this interest. *John Webster and the Elizabethan Drama* (1916) was written as his fellowship dissertation and later published; although much criticized for its lack of scholarly decorum, it reveals a lively style and an author fascinated with the remarkable developments in Elizabethan theater. His only play, a one-act tragedy titled *Lithuania* (pb. 1935), can be read with some satisfaction despite its bizarre plot and uncertain tone. As always with Brooke, his skill with language helps camouflage his errors and excesses. As a journalist, Brooke mixed with strong effect the lyricism of a poet with the enthusiastic observations of an excited traveler, most prominently in a series of articles that described his tour of the United States, Canada, and the South Seas, written for the *Westminster Gazette*. In these delightful pieces, he adeptly and wittily penetrates such subjects as the American personality, a baseball game at Harvard, and the grandeur of the Rocky Mountains. These display British wonder, sometimes dismay, at the "new world" but always stop short of tasteless condescension. Finally, Brooke was a masterful and enthusiastic correspondent; his letters contain enchanting representations of matters both personal and universal as he comments on a variety of subjects.

ACHIEVEMENTS

Any attempt to measure the achievement of Rupert Brooke as a poet must also account for the impact of Brooke as a dashing public figure in life, and as a hero and martyr in death. This is not to devalue the richness of his best verse, for his canon is mostly sound, and the tragedy of his early death is amplified by the tragedy of artistic potential cut short. Still, if ever a poet has been linked with an era, his physical presence and intellectual attributes defining the sentiments of a nation and its people, then that poet is

Rupert Brooke
(Library of Congress)

Brooke. Any evaluation of his work is at once confused and enriched by the clamor that surrounded his life, art, and death. His life as student, citizen, and soldier reflects values prized by the British as they entered the twentieth century and endured World War I. His art is complex, but not in a metaphysical way. Rather, its mystery can be ascribed to the tension produced when the convictions of a traditionalist in matters of form and structure are linked with the passionate voice of an exuberant Romantic. Brooke's preference for sonneteering is well known. His topics and themes are more often quaint and predictable than unique and shocking (an effect he often desired to achieve). The poetry is classically graceful and romantically intense, always ultimately sustained by a gift for language. Finally, however, Brooke's death during World War I, the sometimes crude publicity that surrounded it and his memory, and the subsequent legendary status accorded him ensured for all time that critics would find it difficult to separate his life from his art, in an attempt to assess his legacy.

BIOGRAPHY

Rupert Chawner Brooke was born in Rugby, England, on August 3, 1887. His father, William Parker Brooke, was a Rugby schoolmaster, an undistinguished but competent classical scholar, a person perhaps most noticeable for his very lack of noticeable traits. Rupert's mother, Mary Ruth Cotterill, dominated the family and is often described as an organizer—energetic, efficient, strict, even domineering. One of Rupert's brothers, Dick, died after a short illness in 1907; another, Alfred, was killed in World War I three months after Rupert's death. Several commentators have made much of the death of a child who would have been Rupert's older sister, implying that somehow Rupert was always affected by the notion of being a disappointing replacement for an adored and much-lamented daughter.

Rupert Brooke realized many benefits from, but at the same time was assuredly strained by, his family's association with the British educational system. Although not unhealthy, neither was he robust, and he was heartily encouraged to develop his intellectual skills first and foremost. As a youth he exhibited a tendency to role-play, most often typified by world-weariness and grandiloquent language. His more engaging qualities included an active mind, interest if not excellence in some sports, and (to understate) a pleasing appearance that later became a significant part of his legend.

Brooke's life at Rugby was notable for the variety of his academic, social, and even athletic interests, and for his ability to develop close friendships with interesting people, a trait that stayed with Brooke always. Many of his friends were remarkable and passionately loyal to him; even mere acquaintances could not deny intense curiosity about him. As a poet, his early works show a young man enchanted with words and full of the impulse to parody the masters. He was more enthusiastic than polished, becoming increasingly so with each English poet whose secrets he discovered, digested, and imitated. Brooke adored writing contests and seemed to delight in shocking the sensibilities of his friends and family.

As a student at King's College, Cambridge, Brooke continued these activities, but now for the first time found real independence from his family in a stimulating and glamorous setting. In addition to his reading and writing, he now discovered the delights of political debate, the mysteries of such disciplines as psychology, and the pleasures of acting. He excitedly joined political discussions, joined the Cambridge Fabian Society, and worked diligently on its behalf. As an actor he exhibited no real talent, in spite of his ability to deliver poetic lines with great enthusiasm and a physical presence that, according to many, was spectacular. His career at Cambridge, undistinguished academically, was nevertheless solid. He cultivated still more fascinating friends, showed a preference for "modern" works, and matured as a poet. At the same time, he confessed a weary tolerance for life, an attitude that his many activities would seem to contradict.

After his formal education and before World War I, Brooke found both peace and adventure. He spent some time reading and writing in a charming setting, Grantchester, and reveled in his surroundings and leisure, a welcome relief from his school years. For excitement, Brooke embarked in 1913 to explore the Americas and the South Seas, an excursion financed by the *Westminster Gazette*; the newspaper had commissioned him to send back impressions of his tour. He must have enjoyed himself; the pace was hectic, and he was greeted enthusiastically and with respect by his various hosts. His articles, often supremely "British" and critical of a general lack of culture in the Americas, are nevertheless important and enjoyable, suggesting increasing powers of observation and description.

Brooke's return to Britain was personally triumphant and satisfying. He had confessed homesickness during his travels but was little prepared for his outright joy at once again reaching British soil. His friends greeted him exuberantly, and a series of social and artistic activities kept him busy. His future, as artist, as critic, even perhaps as politician, seemed assured.

Brooke's dreams were to be stalled, shattered, and canceled by World War I. It is a curious measure of the impact of Brooke's work and personality that he, with limited exposure to battle, eventually dying of blood poisoning, should ultimately be accorded the lavish praise of his countrymen, who saw him as the spokesperson for a generation of heroes. With many of his friends, he had expressed early disgust for the very notion of war, but he changed attitudes quickly, voicing the desire to find high adventure while ridding the world of the Prussian menace. He joined the Artists' Rifles, sought a commission, and eventually landed a post as a sublieutenant in the Royal Naval Division. His only significant action was to march with a brigade in relief of Antwerp, where he witnessed the realities of war. The column, however, retreated quickly after a few days of occupying trenches.

Later, Brooke's division received its orders for the Aegean and Gallipoli. En route, Brooke contracted dysentery; his condition weakened, he would fail and seem to rally from time to time. He lingered but finally died on April 23, 1915, at the age of twenty-seven, aboard a French hospital ship, in the company of a school friend. He was buried the same day on the nearby island of Skyros, where a memorial was later raised in his honor.

Brooke's memory, however, lived on, sometimes in ways that were flattering and meaningful, other times in ways that were distorted and tasteless. The poet who wrote with conviction about fair England and the soldier's duty and privilege to serve was mourned and eulogized by many, not the least of whom was Winston Churchill, who had recognized the value of Brooke's verse. Beyond his work, there were other matters, more difficult to pinpoint but significant nevertheless, that contributed to his fame. His background, his education, and even his dashing good looks (he was called the "fair-haired Apollo," to his embarrassment) represented what was best about "the Empire," and much of the British approach to this war was intimately involved, of course, with "the Empire" and all it implied. It is too bad, in a way, that this fine poet and remarkable person has had to bear these burdens, for the excessive publicity obscures what is best about his work and life. Paul Fussell has rightly called World War I an "ironic" war; by that he means that the gestures and ideals of the participants appear almost ludicrous in the context of the brutal efficiency of the new century. There is much that is ironic about World War I's most famous poet, too, for today Brooke is often admired, often condemned, but in both cases, usually for the wrong reasons.

Analysis

Anyone who wishes to be objective in his evaluation of Rupert Brooke's short poetic career must acknowledge Brooke's weaknesses as well as his strengths. There is the untempered voice of boyish spontaneity, the popularizer of mindless and almost laughable patriotic sentimentalism, the friendly versifier of late Georgian poetry that did little but describe nature redundantly. This Brooke penned such lines as "There was a damned successful Poet; There was a Woman like the Sun./ And they were dead. They did not know it" ("Dead Men's Love"); he probably deserves ridicule for having done so. On the other hand, fortunately, there is also the exuberant and mature voice of a craftsperson, the defender of the noble sentiments of a nation in crisis, and the innovative artist who sought freshness and vitality even as he worked within traditional forms. This Brooke deserves acclaim.

The best approaches to understanding and appreciating the poetry of Brooke are to reveal the themes of place and sentiment that dominate his works, and to recognize the fascinating way in which he blends structural integrity and fluency, which appears spontaneous, passionate, and bordering on the experimental.

"The Old Vicarage, Grantchester"

Perhaps the work that most reveals these traits is "The Old Vicarage, Grantchester." Written in Berlin in 1912, this unusual poem, sometimes flippantly comic and other times grossly nostalgic, shows Brooke's tendency to idealize the past, or the "other place," wherever and whenever he was not. Written in octosyllabic couplets, it can be praised for the clarity and tension of its best lines; it can also be condemned for the immature slackness of its worst. A homesick traveler, Brooke sits at a café table in Berlin, conscious of the activity, much of it repulsive, about him. He begins with a graceful recounting of the natural splendor of Grantchester and its environs, but these pleasant thoughts are rudely interrupted by the guttural sound of the German language spoken around him—"*Du lieber Gott!*"—which sets up an immediate and abrupt passage in which the "here" and "there" are effectively juxtaposed.

The sudden introduction of a phrase, in Greek, which means "if only I were," is a nice touch (linking classical and British civilization), followed by repetition of his desire, to be "in Grantchester, in Grantchester." There is a long catalog of reasons why one would wish to be "in Grantchester," detailing the natural splendor of the place and much more. Among the many pleasures, the most notable are the educational tradition (especially a reverence for classics), familiar and comfortable personalities, and the respect for truth and decorous behavior that may be found there.

It is true that this poem is extended far too long and becomes tediously redundant; it is just as true that some of the lines cause the reader to cringe, often because Brooke seems not to have considered the veracity of his assertions ("And men and women with straight eyes,/ Lithe children lovelier than a dream"), at other times because his slickness is only cute ("Ah God! to see the branches stir/ Across the moon at Grantchester!"). Still, one finds "The Old Vicarage, Grantchester" to be solid and mostly complete, if slightly flawed. First, Brooke manages to describe Grantchester fully, with sufficient detail to make the reader understand why the poet is moved to such excess and to sympathize with him. This is not only a celebration of pastoral elegance but also a characterization of the people of Grantchester verging on a statement of values tending toward thematic richness. The vocabulary of fiction employed here is no accident, as the poem has many qualities of the introductory chapters of a novel, complete with protagonist and dramatic action. Second, there is an irony in some of the passages that establishes a tone distinctly superior to juvenile "romanticizing."

In short, "The Old Vicarage, Grantchester" represents the best and worst of Brooke; not surprisingly, it is the kind of poem that leads to conflicting and confusing evaluations of his work. Those who praise him for his sensitive descriptions of his homeland, those who see in the poem evidence of wit and sparkling phrasing, and those who cringe at his excessive sentimentality will all find here numerous examples to support their contentions.

1914, AND OTHER POEMS

Whereas "The Old Vicarage, Grantchester" is vintage Brooke, he is best known for his sonnets, particularly those he wrote during 1914, shortly before his death, which glamorized the fate of martyred soldiers. Brooke evidently found great satisfaction in the sonnet form, and obviously the long relationship was liberating rather than inhibiting, for he showed thematic and structural flexibility while remaining true to the principles of sonneteering. In addition to his evocation of place, Brooke treated in his sonnets such diverse subjects as death, memory, time, psychic phenomena, growing up, lust, and, of course, the pain and pleasure of idealized love as found in the grand traditions of the sonnet. He wrote in the Petrarchan manner, complete with the requisite imagery of the distant and taunting enamorata; he mastered the English form and the difficult closing couplet of the Shakespearean sonnet; and he exhibited the logical strength and confidence so apparent in the Miltonic brand. When bored, he tried variations, such as introducing a sonnet with the couplet (as in "Sonnet Reversed"); his experiments are never disruptive, but suggestive of the strength of the form, and anticipatory of later twentieth century inventions (E. E. Cummings, for example, might be mentioned here).

The five "1914" sonnets reflect Brooke's facility in the sonnet form, while at the same time incorporating sentiments that touched his countrymen profoundly. All deal with the transcending reward that awaits those who make the supreme sacrifice for home and country during the Great War. Again, depending on one's perspective, the sonnets are either inspiring and gallant calls to arms for a generation of martyrs, or naïve and morbid musings that typify the tragic waste of the conflict. The first, "Peace," alludes, ironically, to the new life evident in those whose existence had turned stale, who now benefit from clarity of purpose. Those who must die lose little except "body" and "breath," and are glad to escape their environment. The second sonnet in this sequence, "Safety," can be linked with "Peace," in that those who are sacrificed are referred to as "we." Again the comforting thought recurs that a soldier's death (what might be called a "good death") is to be embraced, not feared, for it presumes the existence of a condition beyond suffering and fear, beyond time, even.

The next two sonnets of 1914, "The Dead" (I) and "The Dead" (II), refer to the martyrs in the third person, but the philosophy remains much the same. In the first, the poet calls for public recognition of an honorable departure from life: "Blow out, you bugles, over the rich Dead!/ There's none of these so lonely and poor of old,/ But, dying, has made us rarer gifts than gold." Ancestral dignity is the rationale for these extreme sentiments; "holiness," "honor," and "nobleness" are evoked as those who pour out "the red sweet wine of youth" are finally able to realize their true "heritage." In the second sonnet of this pair, the celebration is of a pastoral bent, not only in the description of those youths who exist so intimately with the natural world (". . . Dawn was theirs,/ And the sunset, and the colours of the earth."), but also in the elegiac sestet, where the world of the dead is little changed in its excellence.

In "The Soldier," Brooke writes in the first person. Perhaps it is this immediacy ("If I should die, think only this of me") that made the sonnet so touching for his countrymen. More likely it is the sentiments expressed that captured the tragedy of a proud nation losing its best young men in war and somehow finding solace in the loss. Some might even call the poem overbearing, chauvinistic. In the opening lines, the poet asserts that mourning should be brief, for wherever he may lie, that spot becomes "for ever England," where the "rich earth" is more enriched by "a dust whom England bore, shaped, made aware." In the sestet, lest the reader think that only the physical is to be exalted, Brooke suggests that the English soul, "this heart," or "pulse in the eternal mind" will inhabit the universe, much to our advantage.

Georgian influence

Brooke's poetry, then, is by turns admirable and condemnable. Another way to account for this baffling but intriguing trait is to place his work in relationship to what is called the Georgian Revolt. Brooke's role in this curious, little-understood era was a significant one: First, he was a close friend of Edward Marsh, whose Georgian anthologies set the tone for the period and who was eventually chosen to write Brooke's official biography; second, Brooke contributed to the anthologies and worked diligently to publicize the "Georgian" productions; third, the nature of Brooke's public and artistic reputation is as debatable as the confused reputation of "Georgian" poetry.

What "Georgian" has come to mean, of course, is the overly romantic, intellectually slack, structurally contrived efforts of a few "waspish" poets who refused to accept the birth of the twentieth century. The original plan of Marsh, Brooke, and others had been to provide a forum through which a new, energetic brand of modern poetry could transcend the stifling dominance of what was being called Edwardian poetry. The early volumes of Georgian work reveal this kind of energy, at least in comparison with later volumes after the war, when many of the best contributors had either died (Brooke and Isaac Rosenberg, among others), lost interest (Robert Graves, Siegfried Sassoon), or gone their own ways (Ezra Pound, D. H. Lawrence). Unfortunately, the later examples of Georgian poetry are frequently used by critics to describe the whole movement; for poets and critics of the late 1920's and 1930's, who demanded rock-hard language and precise imagery, there was nothing to do but to attack the Georgians with a vengeance.

OTHER MAJOR WORKS
PLAY: *Lithuania*, pb. 1935 (one act).
NONFICTION: *John Webster and the Elizabethan Drama*, 1916; *Letters from America*, 1916; *The Prose of Rupert Brooke*, 1956; *The Letters of Rupert Brooke*, 1968; *Friends and Apostles: The Correspondence of Rupert Brooke and James Strachey, 1905-1915*, 1998 (Keith Hale, editor).

BIBLIOGRAPHY
Delaney, Paul. *The Neo-Pagans: Rupert Brooke and the Ordeal of Youth*. New York: Free Press, 1987. In 1911, Virginia Woolf half-derisively gave Brooke and his carefree circle the label "neo-pagans." In this balanced appraisal, Delaney focuses on the flaws in the group's philosophies that undermined their optimism about the future, causing conflicts and fragmenting their relationships. Contains notes and references, a bibliography, and an index.
Hale, Keith, ed. *Friends and Apostles: The Correspondence of Rupert Brooke and James Strachey: 1905-1914*. New Haven, Conn.: Yale University Press, 1998. This collection of letters records the friendship and love shared by Brooke and Strachey, who first met at the age of ten. They were both eighteen and students at Cambridge University when they renewed their acquaintance, which marks the beginning of the collection.
Hamilton, Ian. *Against Oblivion: Some Lives of the Twentieth-Century Poets*. London: Viking, 2002. Contains an entry on Brooke, examining his life and works.
Jones, Nigel H. *Rupert Brooke: Life, Death, and Myth*. London: Richard Cohen Books, 1999. William Butler Yeats called Rupert Brooke "the most beautiful man in England." Jones draws on Brooke's previously unpublished letters to reveal what the publisher calls the "unsentimental truth." *The Times* of London comments, "Brooke

is sharply perceived, his inner corrosion convincingly described and analyzed."

Lehmann, John. *The Strange Destiny of Rupert Brooke*. New York: Holt, Rinehart and Winston, 1981. In this highly praised combination of biography and literary criticism, Lehmann explores Brooke's psychological history and explains why Brooke's friends expressed conflicting judgments about his character and abilities. Contains an index and a brief biography.

Read, Mike. *Forever England*. Edinburgh: Mainstream, 1997. This biography allows Brooke to speak for himself through the inclusion of poems and other writings. The work also provides a well-rounded picture of prewar England, providing detailed background to various persons and places alluded to in the texts.

Rogers, Timothy. *Rupert Brooke: A Reappraisal and Selection from His Writings, Some Hitherto Unpublished*. London: Routledge & Kegan Paul, 1971. Rogers says that Brooke has often been judged unfairly; the poetry has created the myth, and the myth has obscured the best in Brooke's work. Along with his collection of representative prose and verse, Rogers provides critical commentary, arguing persuasively that the charge of dullness frequently leveled at Brooke is unwarranted. A bibliography concludes this slight volume.

Turner, John Frayn. *The Life and Selected Works of Rupert Brooke*. Rev. ed. Barnsley, South Yorkshire, England: Pen & Sword Military, 2004. An updated biography of Brooke, a poet of World War I, that looks at his life and his works.

Robert Edward Graalman, Jr.

W. D. EHRHART

Born: Roaring Spring, Pennsylvania; September 30, 1948

PRINCIPAL POETRY
A Generation of Peace, 1975
Rootless, 1977
Empire, 1978
The Awkward Silence, 1980
The Samisdat Poems, 1980
The Outer Banks, and Other Poems, 1984
To Those Who Have Gone Home Tired, 1984
Just for Laughs, 1990
The Distance We Travel, 1993
Beautiful Wreckage: New and Selected Poems, 1999
Sleeping with the Dead, 2006

OTHER LITERARY FORMS

In addition to winning critical acclaim with his poetry, W. D. Ehrhart has distinguished himself in the fields of memoir and personal commentary. He has published four volumes on his experiences during and after the Vietnam War as well as an investigative account and oral history of how the war affected the members of his boot camp platoon. He has published hundreds of personal essays and short opinion pieces on various topics in newspapers and magazines, many of which appear in his 1991 collection *In the Shadow of Vietnam: Essays, 1977-1991*.

Ehrhart has also made his mark as an editor and critic. He has edited two anthologies of Vietnam War poetry and has coedited an additional anthology of Vietnam War poetry and an anthology of Korean War literature.

ACHIEVEMENTS

While he has never enjoyed great commercial success, W. D. Ehrhart has been widely credited with establishing the American experience in Vietnam as a subject for poetry and, as Donald Ringnalda has written, is generally considered the "poet laureate of the [Vietnam] war." He has especially been in demand as a speaker and lecturer at academic conferences and universities. He served as a visiting professor of war and social consequences at the William Joiner Center, University of Massachusetts at Boston (1990), as writer-in-residence with the National Writers' Voice Project of the Young Men's Christian Association in Detroit (1996), and as a guest-in-residence at the University of Illinois at Champaign-Urbana (1998). In 2001, he held a research fellowship with the American Studies Department, University of Wales, Swansea, United Kingdom. He has received a grant from the Mary Rinehart Foundation (1980), fellowships in prose and in poetry from the Pennsylvania Council on the Arts (1981, 1988), the President's Medal from Veterans for Peace, and a Pew Fellowship in the Arts for Poetry (1993). He was also featured in episode 5, "America Takes Charge," of the Public Broadcasting Service's series *Vietnam: A Television History* and was invited to edit a special issue of the journal *War, Literature, and the Arts* (Fall/Winter, 1997).

Biography

William Daniel Ehrhart was born in Roaring Spring, Pennsylvania, but spent his formative years in Perkasie, Pennsylvania, where his father was a minister. The third of four sons, Ehrhart excelled in school, but the escalating conflict in Vietnam left him feeling honor-bound to postpone college in favor of military service. Reminding his parents that they had not reared him "to let somebody else's kids fight America's wars," he secured their reluctant permission to enlist in the Marine Corps at age seventeen, immediately following his high school graduation in June, 1966.

Ehrhart served in Vietnam with an infantry battalion from 1967 to 1968 and was wounded in the battle for Hue during the Tet Offensive of 1968. Discharged in 1969 with the rank of sergeant, he went on to Swarthmore College, where he became active in the antiwar movement and wrote his first published works before his graduation in 1973.

While still at Swarthmore, Ehrhart gained national recognition as a poet in *Winning Hearts and Minds* (1972), a collection of Vietnam War poetry dedicated to the cause of ending the United States' involvement. Eight of Ehrhart's early poems appeared in this collection.

After college, Ehrhart went to sea as a merchant marine and later tried both newspaper reporting and high school teaching along with earning an M.A. in creative writing at the University of Illinois at Chicago in 1978. He married in 1981, and in 1985, he made his home in Philadelphia, Pennsylvania. He earned a Ph.D. in 2000 from the University of Wales at Swansea, United Kingdom. Although he has occasionally taken short-term teaching assignments, he bills himself as an "independent scholar and teacher," earning his living primarily through his writing and his speaking engagements.

Analysis

H. Bruce Franklin, in 1995, spoke for the critical consensus in praising W. D. Ehrhart for his "concision and avoidance of the mannerisms that have made 'poetry' seem like a coterie activity." Ehrhart's "distinctive flat voice speaking in a deceptively plain style," Franklin contends, gives his poetry a "visceral power" and forms the perfect stylistic complement to the "rare fusion of personal and historical vision" for which he has been widely praised. A constant theme throughout Ehrhart's poetry is the personal and collective disillusionment his generation suffered as a result of the U.S. intervention in Vietnam. Many of his poems are unabashedly polemical, and the great majority are written in free verse, Ehrhart's intention being to reach the widest possible audience. As Vince Gotera has pointed out, however, Ehrhart's apparent simplicity and earnestness belie a self-conscious artistry that involves a carefully considered selection and arrangement of language and even occasional forays into traditional poetic techniques and forms. Although he first came to prominence with his antiwar poetry, Ehrhart has not confined himself to that theme. His later poems, on a wide range of subjects, reveal a refreshing capacity for self-ironic reflection and an unabashed appreciation for the moments of grace, love, and contentment he continues to find in his own life.

A GENERATION OF PEACE

A Generation of Peace first established Ehrhart as a truth-teller par excellence and as an insightful interpreter of how the American cultural narrative failed the United States in Vietnam. His Vietnam experiences are crystallized in a series of seemingly simple and straightforward poetic vignettes illustrating the existential character of the war. "Guerrilla War," for example, bespeaks his frustration at finding himself unable to distinguish between friend and foe. The poem concludes with the honest admission that "After a while,/ You quit trying."

"Hunting" turns on the realization that, contrary to the American mythos that brought him to this point, Ehrhart has "never hunted anything in [his] whole life/ except other men." However, "such thoughts," he affirms, are quickly eclipsed by more immediate concerns, such as "chow, and sleep,/ and how much longer till I change my socks."

One of the most widely praised and culturally resonant poems to come out of this collection is "A Relative Thing," a title that Ehrhart intended as a play on the adage, "You can pick your friends but not your relatives." The poem strikes a tone of bitter recrimination over the willful ignorance of the generation that sent its sons to fight in Vietnam and bears dramatic witness to the brutal realities behind much of the sanitizing rhetoric of the era. "We have been Democracy on Zippo raids,/ burning houses to the ground," the speaker complains, and made the "instruments/ of your pigeon-breasted fantasies."

"Making the Children Behave" likewise challenges the previous generation's vision of American rectitude and stands in opposition to a pervasive tendency among veteran-authors to focus on American trauma to the exclusion of the Vietnamese point of view. The poem culminates in an ironic epiphany occasioned by the speaker's earlier sense of cultural and even racial superiority. When the people in the villages through which he passed "tell stories to their children/ of the evil/ that awaits misbehavior," he wonders, "is it me they conjure?"

Rootless, Empire, and The Samisdat Poems

The chapbooks *Rootless* and *Empire*, along with *The Samisdat Poems*, contain further reflections on the war's continuing effects on Ehrhart's life and the life of the country. The poem "Letter," for example, is addressed to the North Vietnamese soldier who almost killed Ehrhart in the battle for Hue during the Tet Offensive. The backdrop to the poem is the United States' 1976 centennial celebration, for which "we've found again our inspiration," the speaker wryly observes, "by recalling where we came from/ and forgetting where we've been." The poem ends with the speaker's fervent hope that Vietnam will "remember Ho Chi Minh/ was a poet" and not let their victory "come down/ to nothing."

These collections also contain reflections on perennial human themes, such as relationships, aging, and even the consolations to be found in nature. "After the Fire" is especially representative of Ehrhart's ability to celebrate the experience of love in poignant and even explicit imagery. "Turning Thirty," in fresh language, bespeaks the confusion of finding oneself suddenly older but not necessarily wiser.

To Those Who Have Gone Home Tired

A maturing of Ehrhart's vision as a public poet, one committed to addressing a growing political and popular amnesia over Vietnam, is evident in *To Those Who Have Gone Home Tired*. A restlessness and a self-ironic sense of frustration creep into many of the poems. The title poem is a far-ranging and bitter recrimination over the rapaciousness and brutality that Ehrhart sees as continuing to characterize post-Vietnam American life. "The Invasion of Grenada" likewise bespeaks his despair at popular and political appropriations of the Vietnam experience. Rejecting monuments and commemorative gestures, the speaker declares that he only wanted "a simple recognition" of the limits of U.S. power and an "understanding/ that the world . . . is not ours." What he really wanted is "an end to monuments."

The collection also contains some of his finest and most moving poems on subjects other than war. "Gifts" and "Continuity" express Ehrhart's love for his wife, while "New Jersey Pine Barrens" and "The Outer Banks" recount idyllic retreats into the world of nature. Just under the surface, and often explicitly noted, is an anxious sense that the saving graces of love and nature are only transitory and never unalloyed for someone who has committed himself to the cause of truth-telling. From the world's standpoint, he realizes, he is too readily dismissed as a "farmer of dreams" ("The Farmer") and is even considered boorish for his persistent refusal to accommodate himself to the world as it is ("Sound Advice").

The Distance We Travel

Inspired by his own trip back to Vietnam, *The Distance We Travel* is remarkable for illustrating Ehrhart's continuing capacity for reexamination and self-ironic reflection.

His frustration now is directed at a culture that has appropriated the Vietnam experience for both political manipulation and popular entertainment ("For a Coming Extinction"). As the title poem and at least two others suggest, Ehrhart's former bitterness has been mitigated by the openness and friendliness he has found among the postwar Vietnamese. The result seems to have been a modicum of peace with his past, a resolution reinforced by two of his most revealing poems about his present joys, "Making Love in the Garden" and "Star Light, Star Bright."

Mostly Nothing Happens

One of Ehrhart's longest poems, running to 156 lines, *Mostly Nothing Happens* first appeared in two separate journals and was later reissued as a pamphlet in 1996. It also appears in *Beautiful Wreckage*. A frankly autobiographical and personal statement, the poem places Ehrhart's present life squarely within the ironic context of his past and explores America's still unresolved legacy of racial tension. The backdrop is Ehrhart's refusal to give up on the American dream of brotherhood. He continues to live in an integrated inner-city neighborhood in the hope that his child would not "reach the age of seventeen/ with no one in her life/ who isn't white." The realization that so many of the angry young African American men he must pass day after day have no inkling of his good intentions and even resent his presence leaves him feeling understandably anxious. This anxiety occasions a poignant reflection on the first African American friend Ehrhart ever made and how this man's gentle strength helped him get through Marine recruit training. His friend, however, later died in Vietnam—an ironic fate that Ehrhart seems to hold up as an example of how the war itself only helped to exacerbate the legacy of racial disharmony and distrust he now confronts. The result, he realizes, is a depressingly familiar feeling: "Every day I'm always on patrol."

Beautiful Wreckage

A retrospective as well as a collection of new poems, *Beautiful Wreckage* stands as a fine introduction to Ehrhart's poetry and themes. The title poem speaks to the issue of strictly factual accuracy versus authenticity in a larger literary sense.

The collection also contains some of his finest occasional poems reflecting on his life and on the manners and mores of contemporary American life. "Not for You" is a painfully honest statement of frustrated hopes and expectations. "Prayer for My Enemies" is an ironic statement of the hypocritical pretense that Ehrhart sees as endemic to organized religion. "Rehobeth, One Last Time" shows how our self-indulgent tendency toward serial monogamy has affected a friend's life. Other poems suggest that he has made peace with his parents and with his own past ("Visiting My Parents' Grave," "What Goes Around Comes Around"). "A Meditation on Family Geography and a Prayer for My Daughter" expresses his fervent wish that his daughter will grow up to find "a place in the world/ surrounded by people who care."

Sleeping with the Dead

Sleeping with the Dead, a collection of eleven poems, takes a look at various ways that death occurs and how people respond when confronted with death. "What Better Way to Begin" describes an anticipatory scene on "Millennium Eve" in which a father and daughter prepare to witness an explosion of fireworks in Philadelphia, the city of "brotherly love." The choice of place in this poem is ironic because the father and daughter appear to feel a sense of doom rather than a sense of patriotism while watching "the bombs bursting in air." Through images of explosive red skies and mutilated body parts, Ehrhart connotes the lasting impressions of war violence. Ehrhart's often-repeated theme of American disillusionment is evident as the daughter—who coincidentally shares the name of Ehrhart's real-life daughter—clutches her father's hand "till the last bomb's blunt concussion/ fades away as if it never were." Even though war violence may be necessary to protect a nation, Ehrhart emphasizes how its aftermath can rob one's patriotic zeal and inevitably kill an aspect of the human spirit.

"All About Death" gives a vivid account of how powerless people are in controlling their own mortalities. Ehrhart personifies death as a malicious being who "rips your heart out through your throat/ and walks away laughing." This thirty-two-line, free-verse poem is a rant about death, and the venomous tone that the speaker uses suggests that he has witnessed an incidence of senseless death. To make the accusation that "Death feels/ sorry for nothing and no one" further underscores the disdain in the speaker's tone. The speaker ends the poem by recalling how his wife "still cries out in her sleep for her [deceased] mommy." Although the level of diction in the poem conveys an adult perspective, the choice of the word "mommy" suggests that death has the ability to make people feel as though their autonomy is stripped away when death occurs, regardless of their age.

"Gravestones at Oxwich Bay" and "The Orphan" explore the feeling of emptiness that often lingers among family members after a loved one's death. Beginning with the death of an infant daughter, "Gravestones at Oxwich Bay" memorializes the sequential passing of a family. For the mother's death to be remembered as "earth exchanged for heaven," Ehrhart emphasizes the old adage that parents are not supposed to outlive their children. Although "The Orphan" also makes a poignant statement about the agonizing feeling of emptiness that results after death, the poem employs a child/adult perspective. For this "orphan" to feel as though "home [is] long gone," Ehrhart implies that a parent's death often engenders a feeling of abandonment and that death is no easier to accept even if it occurs at an age when one is expected to be prepared.

In "Home Before Morning" and "Seminar on the Nature of Reality," Ehrhart pays homage to two people whom he describes as having displayed bravery in the face of death. "Home Before Morning" describes the unyielding work of a wife and mother who never stopped working, even when her body began to shut down. The poem is also infused with a bit a political protest as Ehrhart chastises "the posturing of presidents/

and statesmen who have never heard the sound/ of teenaged soldiers crying for their mothers." By juxtaposing the image of leaders making unconscious decisions to send young men into battle, with the idea of a dying mother sacrificing herself "to be an advocate for broken souls," Ehrhart illustrates that those who are revered are often the ones less worthy of praise. In "Seminar on the Nature of Reality," Ehrhart provides a similar account of the fearlessness with which a person confronts death. While Ehrhart may suggest a sense of powerlessness in writing, "when things are very large or very small/ they don't behave the way we think they should," he emphasizes a metaphysical mood, as well as an inevitable aspect of the human psyche—to decipher between image and reality.

"All About Love," "Manning the Walls," and "Kosovo" explore present-day threats of death and destruction. "All About Love" conveys a sense of disconnect between the people and the policies that are supposed to protect a society. Both "Manning the Walls" and "Kosovo" suggest that the threat of mass destruction is not limited to originating with foreign terrorists, and that a nation must first look at the enemies that lie within its own borders.

"Sleeping with the Dead," the last poem in the collection, explores the theme of lost love, which also can cause one to feel a sense of death. The poem begins with the speaker confessing in a somewhat sarcastic tone that he never really loved the person whom he claims "almost drove me mad/ to let go." The speaker's confession initially appears to be more of a victim's declaration of independence against the power that love had over him nineteen years ago. Although he appears regretful for succumbing to love's power, the speaker accepts responsibility for letting go of his love. Ehrhart underscores the power of love to awaken the emotional side of human nature when the speaker states that this now-lost love once made him feel like he had been "raised from the dead/ after all those dead [he] slept with/ every night."

OTHER MAJOR WORKS

NONFICTION: *Vietnam-Perkasie: A Combat Marine Memoir*, 1983; *Going Back: An Ex-Marine Returns to Vietnam*, 1987; *Passing Time: Memoir of a Vietnam Veteran Against the War*, 1989; *In the Shadow of Vietnam: Essays, 1977-1991*, 1991; *Busted: A Vietnam Veteran in Nixon's America*, 1995; *The Madness of It All: Essays on War, Literature, and American Life*, 2002.

EDITED TEXTS: *Demilitarized Zones: Veterans After Vietnam*, 1976 (with Jan Barry); *Carrying the Darkness: American Indochina, The Poetry of the Vietnam War*, 1989; *Unaccustomed Mercy: Soldier-Poets of the Vietnam War*, 1989; *Retrieving Bones: Stories and Poems of the Korean War*, 1999 (with Philip K. Jason).

MISCELLANEOUS: *Ordinary Lives: Platoon 1005 and the Vietnam War*, 1999.

BIBLIOGRAPHY

Beidler, Philip D. *Re-writing America: Vietnam Authors in Their Generation.* Athens: University of Georgia Press, 1991. Argues that Ehrhart is best understood within the cultural context of his generation and sees his work as an attempt to reinstate the values and ideals the country failed to live up to in Vietnam.

Gotera, Vince F. *Radical Visions: Poetry by Vietnam Veterans.* Athens: University of Georgia Press, 1994. Remains the best overall introduction to Ehrhart's themes and technique. Gotera establishes Ehrhart as a serious artist and acknowledges his influence as a critic and editor.

Metres, Philip. *Behind the Lines: War Resistance Poetry on the American Homefront Since 1941.* Iowa City: University of Iowa Press, 2007. Discusses antiwar poetry in general, with chapters on the Vietnam War that provide perspective on Ehrhart's writing. Ehrhart recalls audience response to his reading of "A Relative Thing."

Ringnalda, Donald. *Fighting and Writing the Vietnam War.* Jackson: University Press of Mississippi, 1994. Argues that Ehrhart is one of a number of Vietnam-veteran writers whose disregard of literary convention reflects the unconventional nature of the war itself and forms a fitting strategy for challenging residual conventional wisdom.

Rottman, Larry, and Basil T. Paquet, eds. *Winning Hearts and Minds: War Poems by Vietnam Veterans.* New York: McGraw-Hill, 1972. Ehrhart debuted in this anthology. One of his most striking Vietnam poems, "Hunting," first appeared here.

Ryan, Maureen. *The Other Side of Grief: The Home Front and the Aftermath in American Narratives of the Vietnam War.* Amherst: University of Massachusetts Press, 2008. Examines Vietnam war literature primarily from its depictions of life in the United States during and after the war. Contains some references to Ehrhart.

Smith, Lorrie. "Against a Coming Extinction: W. D. Ehrhart and the Evolving Canon of Vietnam Veterans' Poetry." *War, Literature, and the Arts* 8, no. 2 (1996): 1-30. A lucid and insightful survey of Ehrhart's career and of his influence within the field.

Tal, Kali. *Worlds of Hurt: Reading the Literatures of Trauma.* New York: Cambridge University Press, 1996. Places Ehrhart squarely within the "literature of trauma" school. Tal sees Ehrhart as bearing an intensely personal witness to his traumatic experience and as resisting any and all attempts at appropriating or generalizing upon his experience.

Edward F. Palm
Updated by Theresa E. Dozier

PHILIP FRENEAU

Born: New York, New York; January 2, 1752
Died: Near Freehold, New Jersey; December 18, 1832

PRINCIPAL POETRY
The American Village, 1772
"The Rising Glory of America," 1772 (with H. H. Brackenridge)
"The British Prison-Ship," 1781
The Poems of Philip Freneau: Written Chiefly During the Late War, 1786
A Journey from Philadelphia to New-York, by Robert Slender, Stocking Weaver, 1787
Poems Written Between the Years 1786 and 1794, 1795
Poems Written and Published During the American Revolutionary War, 1809
A Collection of Poems . . . Written Between the Year 1797 and the Present Time, 1815
The Poems of Philip Freneau, 1902-1907, 1963 (3 volumes; F. L. Patee, editor)
Poems of Freneau, 1929 (H. H. Clark, editor)
The Last Poems of Philip Freneau, 1946 (Lewis Leary, editor)

OTHER LITERARY FORMS

Philip Freneau (frih-NOH) is best remembered today for his poems. In his own time, however, such was hardly the case. Freneau's contemporaries knew him best for his satirical, sometimes vituperative essays. Freneau first used his satirical skills as a prose writer in *Father Bombo's Pilgrimage to Mecca* (1770), which he wrote with Hugh Henry Brackenridge while the two were undergraduate classmates at Princeton (then College of New Jersey). In the introduction to the 1975 edition of the book, Michael D. Bell argues convincingly that this brief volume, more than half of which is by Freneau, is the first American novel.

After the outbreak of the American Revolution, Freneau put his satirical pen to work for American independence by contributing prose (and some poetry) to Brackenridge's *United States Magazine* in 1779. During 1781 and 1782, he helped Francis Bailey publish *Freeman's Journal*, a liberal and, of course, anti-British newspaper. During 1790 and 1791, he edited the *Daily Advertiser* in New York. Freneau's next publishing venture is what some would consider his most famous; others would call it his most notorious. From October of 1791 until October of 1793, he edited *The National Gazette* in Philadelphia, which was at that time the center of the national government. In this newspaper, Freneau supported Jeffersonian politics and opposed the Federalist position of John Fenno's *United States Gazette*, which operated under the financial control of

Philip Freneau
(Library of Congress)

Alexander Hamilton, the principal voice of Federalism.

Following Thomas Jefferson's temporary withdrawal from politics, which concurred with loss of financial support for *The National Gazette*, Freneau returned to his New Jersey estate and set up a press of his own. There he published almanacs; yet another newspaper, *The Jersey Chronicle*; and another collection of his poetry (1795). In 1797, he and his expanding family relocated in New York, where Freneau began one more newspaper, *The Time Piece and Literary Companion* (March, 1797, to March, 1798). In his later years, he made contributions to such other newspapers as Charleston's *City Gazette* (1788-1790, and also 1800-1801), the Philadelphia *Aurora* (1799-1800), the *New-York Weekly Museum* (1816), and Trenton's *True American* (1821-1824).

Achievements

Philip Freneau's contribution to the development of American satirical journalism is considerable. In *The Political Activities of Philip Freneau* (1902), Samuel E. Forman presents a scholarly discussion of Freneau's role in the political arena of the early American republic. While serving as secretary of state, Jefferson declared that Freneau's *Na-*

tional Gazette "has saved our constitution, which was galloping fast into monarchy" (*The Writings of Thomas Jefferson*, edited by Paul L. Ford, 1892). In his "Tomo Cheeki, the Creek Indian," a series of essays written for the *Jersey Chronicle* and printed on his own press at Mt. Pleasant, New Jersey, Freneau celebrated the unsullied national life of the American Indian, which contrasted sharply with the corrupted, unnatural life of whites transplanted from Europe. He also used his newspapers to condemn slavery and to advance temperance (not abstinence, but control).

Freneau's major contribution to American letters, however, is his poetry. He has been called the poet of the American Revolution, the first American poet of any real significance, the founder of American poetry, and the first herald of Romanticism in America. None of these titles is entirely correct. Although he styled himself poet of the Revolution by publishing a collection of his poems in 1809 as *Poems Written and Published During the American Revolutionary War* (two-thirds of the poems in the volume have nothing to do with the war), Freneau must share the title of poet of the Revolution with at least one other poet, Phillis Wheatley, America's first African American to publish a book. Her *Poems on Various Subjects, Religious and Moral* appeared in 1773 and contains many poems that predict the movement toward independence; Wheatley continued to devote her pen to American independence in succeeding years by publishing such substantial poems as "To His Excellency General Washington" and "Liberty and Peace."

Certainly, Freneau can no longer be considered America's first significant poet but must join the growing list of poets whose reputations continue to be reclaimed or to be established for the first time. These recently recognized early American poets now include Anne Bradstreet, Edward Taylor, and Wheatley, as well as Freneau. The existence of this enlarged list of important early American poets assuredly calls into question the notion that Freneau is the founder of American poetry. Despite Lewis Leary's assertion, however, that "in the strict sense he had no descendants" (*Soundings: Some Early American Writers*, 1975), Freneau does participate significantly in the American experience of nature and in the struggle for freedom and identity, as well as in America's awakening Romanticism. Even though Freneau founded no school of poetry, his poems display characteristics and foreshadowings of Edgar Allan Poe, Ralph Waldo Emerson, James Fenimore Cooper, and Herman Melville.

Although Freneau must share several of his formerly attributed titles, he is no less significant as a writer of good poetry. To be sure, he is a transitional figure, but his significance does not begin and end as a figure of transition. This critical commonplace, that Freneau was a transitional figure and nothing more, may have predisposed many to find Freneau's poetic ideas desultory and inconsistent. Perhaps these readers have not yet discovered how to read Freneau, for as Richard C. Vitzthum has ably shown in his provocative and balanced work, *Land and Sea: The Lyric Poetry of Philip Freneau* (1978), Freneau created personal and highly internalized poetic symbols, thereby manifesting his most significant contribution to the Romantic movement. Freneau's poetry is, indeed, intensely personal, and when the keys to this personal intensity are revealed, his poems speak a universal tongue.

Biography

Shortly after Philip Morin Freneau was born, the family moved from New York City to Mt. Pleasant, New Jersey, where Freneau reached adolescence. Even though his father died in 1767, his mother, Agnes, managed to send her son to Princeton, then known as the College of New Jersey, in 1768. Freneau's classmates included such notables as Hugh Henry Brackenridge and James Madison; also in attendance during Freneau's tenure were William Bradford (later attorney general of the United States) and Aaron Burr. The curriculum of the college at that time was not structured to prepare men for the ministry but was designed to shape cultured gentlemen; in a word, Freneau was not trained to be a dogmatist, a factor that was to have profound significance on his development as a poet.

After leaving Princeton, Freneau tried teaching for a time, first in Flatbush, Long Island, and later at Somerset Academy in Maryland, where his former college classmate, Brackenridge, was principal. For the next two years, from 1773 to 1775, it is believed that Freneau studied theology. Later in 1775, while in New York, the poet wrote and published patriotic, satirical poems about the British; the first, short version of the gothic poem "The House of Night" also appeared that year. From 1776 to 1778, he lived and traveled in the Virgin and Caribbean islands. In July, 1778, while attempting to return to the United States, Freneau was taken prisoner by the British but was soon released. During the next two years, the young author wrote poems and essays for Brackenridge's *United States Magazine*. On May 25, 1780, Freneau shipped out on the *Aurora* from Philadelphia and found himself taken prisoner by the British a second time. This occasion was not destined to be the relatively uneventful one of his first capture. Indeed, he was kept a prisoner for almost two months and later wrote about the cruelty shown him and other prisoners in "The British Prison-Ship," which he published as a broadside in 1781.

For the next few years, Freneau sailed as supercargo or captain of several ships sailing from the American mainland to various islands of the Caribbean. In 1786, Francis Bailey, formerly publisher of Brackenridge's *United States Magazine*, printed the first edition of Freneau's collected poems, *The Poems of Philip Freneau: Written Chiefly During the Late War*. As was the case with his 1809 poetry collection, only about half of these poems actually address issues of the war. In 1788, Bailey published, *The Miscellaneous Works of Mr. Philip Freneau Containing His Essays and Additional Poems*.

By 1790, however, Freneau was back on land, where he married Eleanor Forman, whom he had been courting for several years. The following October, the Freneaus moved to Philadelphia, where the poet had been invited to serve in two capacities: as a part-time translator for the State Department under Jefferson and as editor of the *National*

Gazette. Freneau carried out the duties of these two positions with energy and distinction for the next two years; following the financial collapse of *The National Gazette*, brought on in large part by an epidemic of yellow fever in Philadelphia, the Freneaus returned to Mt. Pleasant. There the poet set up his own press, published much poetry and prose, and apparently tried farming for a while. By 1802, to support his family better, Freneau had returned to sea, probably as a captain. He stopped sailing for good, however, in 1807 at the time of Jefferson's Embargo Act. Later, in 1809 and then again in 1815, he supervised the printing of several collections of his poems. He and his family lost their home to fire in 1818 with the unfortunate result that many of his manuscripts and letters were destroyed. In 1824, the family moved to a small farm near Freehold, New Jersey, where the poet died in 1832 in a snowstorm while apparently trying to find his way back to his home.

Analysis

Philip Freneau's poetry gave rise to no school, and it fired no tradition. At all points, however, it celebrates the American quest for freedom—freedom of the individual to choose a political and intellectual identity, to pursue creative and artistic imagination, and to discover religious or spiritual commitment. Even America's rugged natural terrain seemed to promise limitless possibilities of achieving social and cultural independence. The principal subjects of Freneau's poems, then, include politics, the imagination, theology, and nature. His poems reveal the inner struggle of a man who refused to settle into the security of dogma (whether of a particular church or of societal codes) and who determined to find his own explanations for the human predicament. This determination to search for his own answers anticipates the attitude of later writers from the American Renaissance onward.

Political poetry

Jefferson's statement that Freneau "saved our constitution" readily identifies the trenchant role this citizen of the new republic played in politics. In addition to his numerous, biting essays that strike out against British cruelties and Hamilton's Federalism, Freneau wrote poetry dealing with various controversial political issues. In "The British Prison-Ship," Freneau exposes British inhumanity to American prisoners. Among Freneau's many political poems is a particularly strong indictment of slavery; "To Sir Toby" is as forceful a condemnation of traffic in human cargo as any of its time. After isolating the central motive for the practice of slavery—greed—the poet then describes the plight of the innocent victims of this avarice as the unwitting and certainly unwilling participants in a veritable hell on earth. In this description, Freneau makes effective use of his classical training; the pictures of the black man's torture call up horrible scenes "that Vergil's pencil drew." The captains of the slave ships become "surly Charons," while the slave masters who put to torture the new ranks of "ghosts" are "beasts, . . . Plutonian scourges, and despotic lords."

THE IMAGINATION

Freneau's poems on the force of the imagination may seem to be light-years away from his political poetry; such, however, is hardly the case. His poems on politics and the imagination merely represent two sides of the same coin whose mint is freedom. Those poems dealing with politics address problems of freedom in the actual world; those centering on the imagination treat of the ideal world produced by artistic creativity whose freedom is apparently boundless. It is fitting that one of this poet's earliest works is devoted entirely to the subject of the imagination; "The Power of Fancy" was composed in 1770 while Freneau was still an undergraduate at Princeton. In this piece, the young poet delineates the fancy as "regent of the mind," the mental faculty that derives its power from divine inspiration. By the power of fancy, the mind can set out on a cosmic journey, exploring distant stars, the moon, and even hell. From this journey through the cosmos, the fancy then takes the poet out into the Atlantic and on to such exotic sites as the Caribbean, the Pacific, and the Mediterranean. In the final lines of the poem, the young Freneau calls the fancy "the muses' pride" wherein "reside/ Endless images of things." These images are of "Ideal objects such a store,/ The universe could hold no more."

The sort of imagination Freneau describes in "The Power of Fancy" clearly owes much to Plato's theory of ideal forms; it is the function of the poet, so Freneau maintains, to tap this realm of forms for his own poetic images. The fancy then serves the poet as a mode of memory and is closely aligned with Lockean associative psychology. The view of the fancy or imagination that Freneau advances in this poem looks back rather than forward; it more nearly approximates the operation of the imagination explored by Mark Adenside in *The Pleasures of Imagination*, an immensely popular book-length poem first printed in English in 1744, than it points ahead toward the Romantics of the early nineteenth century. The mode of fancy that Freneau depicts in "The House of Night," however, looks to the future; written some nine years later than "The Power of Fancy," this poem suggests an affinity for some of the poems of John Keats. In the later poem, Freneau maintains that the power of fancy can in sleep play a "wild delusive part so well/ you lift me into immortality,/ Depict new heavens, or draw scenes of hell"; Keats's immortal nightingale sings a similar strain.

Other Romantic elements occur in "The House of Night," especially those projecting gothicism. Freneau achieves some gothic effects by use of the element of surprise. At one point in this poem about a young man's encounter with the personification of death (a gothic effect in itself), for example, the youth (as persona) describes darkness in terms of Apollo and his chariot of the sun. Rather than a blazing chariot, "darkness rode/ In her black chariot." Some lines of the poem strongly suggest Poe. Seduced by Death into attending him as he approaches his own "death," the youth describes his predicament in unsettling lines. In such phrases as "sad chamber," languishing "in despair," and breathing "loathsome air," one might fully expect to find Poe's "The Raven" or in such short stories as his "The Fall of the House of Usher" or "Ligeia."

THEOLOGY AND NATURE

The power of the imagination enabled Freneau to explore much more than his tendency to create strange, even perverse images and characters; indeed, in his poetry, he appears to pursue the construction of a personal theology. This pursuit is always punctuated by the poet's awestruck fascination for and appreciation of nature. These last two important subjects of Freneau's poetry, theology and nature, can therefore most profitably be examined together.

The pictures Freneau draws of nature are not always attractive. "The Hurricane" depicts an actual storm at sea that Freneau experienced on a voyage to Jamaica in 1784. The poem opens with this arresting couplet: "Happy the man who, safe on shore,/ Now trims, at home, his evening fire." Rather than being safe and enjoying the warmth of the hearth, Freneau finds himself exposed to a merciless cold storm at sea. At one point, he presents a vividly terrifying image of the small ship on whose fragile deck burst "mountains . . . on either side." He draws a picture of "death and darkness," which engulf the ship with tempests raging "with lawless power"; in such a pass, "What friendship can . . . be/ What comfort?" The dark and doom of this unhappy predicament foreshadow the destruction of Ishmael's ship, the *Pequod*, in Melville's *Moby Dick: Or, The Whale* (1851).

The contrast the poet establishes in "The Hurricane" between the security of the land and the peril of the sea is identified by Richard C. Vitzthum as a major key to the personal symbolism that Freneau develops in his poems; but while "The Wild Honey Suckle" and "The Indian Burying Ground," both wholly landlocked poems, do develop less precarious scenes, these poems of the land also resound with poignant notes of regret at life's transience. "The Wild Honey Suckle" celebrates the beauty of that plant's white flower, which is nevertheless doomed to a brief span of life. The lives of men correspond to the short duration of the flower; indeed, from birth to death, as Freneau writes in one of the most effective couplets in American literature, "The space between, is but an hour,/ The frail duration of a flower." "The Indian Burying Ground" describes the somber, sitting position of the dead, but Freneau sees promise of great spiritual and intellectual hope in such a posture. To him, the sitting position bespeaks "the nature of the soul,/ Activity, that knows no rest." Although "life is spent," so the poet explains, the old ideas that supported and breathed life into these honored dead are not gone.

"ON THE UNIVERSALITY AND OTHER ATTRIBUTES OF THE GOD OF NATURE"

The one poem of the Freneau canon that most clearly articulates his attitudes toward his religious consciousness is the often-overlooked piece "On the Universality and Other Attributes of the God of Nature." Written in 1815 when Freneau was sixty-three, the poem represents a crystallization of his theology. It is arranged into seven quatrains of iambic tetrameter. A reading aloud reveals that its fairly regular rhythm echoes common speech; the only variations of the iambic pattern occur in the occasional trochees and one spondee (in the twentieth line). In each case where a variation occurs, the word "all" appears and always receives a primary stress (emphasized word or syllable); "all" occurs fourteen times. These variations do indeed prevent the rhythm from becoming monotonous, thus holding the listener's attention.

The variations accomplish more, however, than merely holding one's attention. To be sure, Freneau's repeated use of the word "all" underscores the poem's emphasis on the universal; the persistence of this word then serves as a sort of incremental repetition that restates the poem's concern with the universal attributes of God in each of the seven stanzas; "all" appears twice in each of the first two, only once in each of the next two, but twice again in the fifth, and then three times each in the climactic sixth and seventh stanzas, establishing a pattern that enhances the meaning of the poem. The poem opens with the rhetorical question, "All that we see, about, abroad,/ What is it all, but nature's God?" The next couplet maintains that this God of nature may be seen in God's meaner works of the earth, such as human beings, animals, and plants, as well as in the heavens: "In meaner works discover'd here/ No less than in the starry sphere." Implicit in these lines is the idea of the Great Chain of Being, whereby creation may be viewed as a great ladder, the lowest rungs of which include elements of inanimate matter, while the highest hold the higher animals, and finally humans, closest to God; but more seems to be at work here.

In 1785 or 1786, Freneau came across a book by the Swedish scientist, mystic, and scholar of the Bible Emanuel Swedenborg; the poet records his experience of reading Swedenborg in the poem "On a Book Called Unitarian Theology." He remarks that God "Illumes all Nature" and "Bids towards itself all trees and plants aspire." Swedenborg had himself outlined in his *Principia rerum naturalium* (1734) an elaborate doctrine of series and degrees that he claimed accounted for each distinct link in a universal chain stretching from inorganic substance to humans and thence to God. Regarding this doctrine of degrees, Freneau appears to have changed his mind little between 1786 and 1815.

In the second stanza, Freneau asserts that God "lives in all, and never stray'd/ A moment from the works he made." If one includes the notion of an "absentee God" as a necessary tenet of a Deist, then at this point Freneau clearly denies his sympathy with Deism. The God whom he describes "Bespeaks a wise creating cause;/ Impartially he rules mankind." This last line suggests Freneau's strong support of religious freedom, for an impartial God is hardly selective about how he is worshiped. The poet expresses his unqualified commitment to religious freedom in "On the Emigration to America" (written in 1784), in which he describes the political and religious conditions in Europe as "half to slaves consigned"; Europe herself is a place "Where kings and priests enchain the mind." In "Reflections on the Gradual Progress of Nations from Democratical States to Despotic Empires" (written in 1799), he quips of priests per se that they "hold the artillery of the sky."

The last stanza of "On the Universality and Other Attributes of the God of Nature" contains one of the simplest and at the same time one of the finest lines in American poetry. The line states the thesis on which Freneau bases his theology: "He all things into *being* loved." In the Swedenborg piece, he draws a parallel picture of God as "One Power of Love" who "Warms into life the changeful race of man." This idea of God as a God of warmth and love is far distant from the cold, Deistic Clockmaker who left his machine to run itself down. Freneau's God, who is by virtue of his "attributes divine" unlimited and therefore universal or ubiquitous, brings into existence "all things"; this achievement he brings about out of unselfish love. "Things" take on form, then, as less perfect renderings of him. Freneau's God "never stray'd/ A moment from the works he made." Quite contrary to the Deist Clockmaker, the poet's God "still presides" over all he has created, and "For them in life, or death provides."

The line "He all things into *being* loved," then, is hardly simple. Contained within its eight syllables is the whole of Freneau's sophisticated and humanitarian theology. Although his identification of God as "of Nature" seems to align him with Deism (or, as some would undoubtedly hold, with pantheism), his insistence on a God of love denies this classification. His assertion that God provides for all in death may suggest to some a belief in an afterlife of heavenly bliss. Such is not the case, however, for in one of his last poems, "On Observing a Large Red-Streak Apple," Freneau defines the afterlife of the apple as the "youngsters . . . three or four" who will rise "from your core." This sort of afterlife whereby continuation is accomplished through successive generations resembles more closely Greco-Roman ideas of afterlife than it does Deism. Surely Freneau's classical training served him in arriving at his position. It is probably more accurate to label Freneau a unitarian than a Deist, though one senses that he would himself resist all labels.

Certainly his theology is liberal and not limited by dogma. So, also, his attitudes toward politics, the creative imagination, and nature are unencumbered by a dogmatic or didactic perspective. Rather, his poems describe the career of a man who found the world about him fascinating and who consequently used his poetry to record his experience of that world. Freneau's poetry is intensely personal, heralding the individuality that characterizes Poe, Nathaniel Hawthorne, Emerson, Melville, Henry David Thoreau, and Walt Whitman.

Other major works

LONG FICTION: *Father Bombo's Pilgrimage to Mecca*, 1770 (with Hugh Henry Brackenridge).

NONFICTION: *Letters on Various Interesting and Important Subjects*, 1799, 1943.

MISCELLANEOUS: *The Miscellaneous Works of Mr. Philip Freneau Containing His Essays and Additional Poems*, 1788; *The Prose of Philip Freneau*, 1955 (Philip M. Marsh, editor).

BIBLIOGRAPHY

Andrews, William D. "Philip Freneau and Francis Hopkinson." In *American Literature, 1764-1789: The Revolutionary Years*, edited by Everett Emerson. Madison: University of Wisconsin Press, 1977. The writings of Freneau and Hopkinson are examined as expressions of the political events of the time, particularly the war for independence. Freneau's bitter invective is contrasted with Hopkinson's witty urbanity, and Freneau's dedication to poetry as art is contrasted with Hopkinson's view of poetry as a hobby. Includes suggested readings and index.

Cray, Robert E., Jr. "The 'Horrors of These Hulks.'" *Naval History* 20, no. 1 (February, 2006): 42-48. Discusses Freneau's imprisonment in a British prison ship and his recovoery. Poems discussed include "The British Prison-Ship" and "Tomb of the Patriots." Also examines prose recounting the capture of the ship *Aurora*.

Elliott, Emory. "Philip Freneau: Poetry of Social Commitment." In *Revolutionary Writers: Literature and Authority in the New Republic, 1725-1810*. New York: Oxford University Press, 1982. Examines Freneau as a poet-teacher of morality. His changing directions are understood as moves to strengthen power of instruction through poetic forms. Several poems are analyzed to illustrate Freneau's faith in poetry as social commitment. Includes notes, select bibliography, and index.

Leary, Lewis. "Philip Freneau." In *Major Writers of Early American Literature*, edited by Everett Emerson. Madison: University of Wisconsin Press, 1972. Asserts that from early political verse to flights of fancy, Freneau was caught between destructive forces. After the Revolutionary War, his talents were released for light verse and humorous satire. As he grew older, his poems grew bitter and disillusioned. Although not a great poet, he had talent. Includes bibliography and index.

McWilliams, John P., Jr. *The American Epic: Transforming a Genre, 1770-1860*. New York: Cambridge University Press, 1989. This book uses Freneau's reaction to Timothy Dwight's *The Conquest of Canaan* (1785) to show contemporary criticism of attempts to write the American epic. Although Freneau did not himself attempt an epic poem, his influence on others to make the attempt was considerable. Includes notes and an index.

Marcus, Greil, and Werner Sollors, eds. *A New Literary History of America*. Cambridge, Mass.: Belknap Press, 2009. Contains an essay on Freneau and *The National Gazette*, looking at Freneau's influence on literature in the United States.

Ronnick, Michele Valerie. "A Note on the Text of Philip Freneau's 'Columbus to Ferdinand': From Plato to Seneca." *Early American Literature* 29, no. 1 (1994): 81. A discussion of Freneau's "Columbus to Ferdinand" as it was first published in *United States Magazine* with two lines that were left out of all subsequent editions.

Schaefer, Todd M., and Thomas A. Birkland, eds. *Encyclopedia of Media and Politics*. Washington, D.C.: CQ Press, 2007. Contains an essay on Freneau that examines his political role as well as his literary endeavors.

Vitzthum, Richard C. *Land and Sea: The Lyric Poetry of Philip Freneau.* Minneapolis: University of Minnesota Press, 1978. A book-length analysis of Freneau's poetry, examining themes of land and sea.

Wertheimer, Eric. "Commencement Ceremonies: History and Identity in 'The Rising Glory of America,' 1771 and 1786." *Early American Literature* 29, no. 1 (1994): 35. An examination of the thematic obsession with imperial beginnings in the poem "The Rising Glory of America" by Freneau and Henry Brackenridge.

John C. Shields

ROY FULLER

Born: Failsworth, Lancashire, England; February 11, 1912
Died: London, England; September 27, 1991

PRINCIPAL POETRY
Poems, 1939
The Middle of a War, 1942
A Lost Season, 1944
Epitaphs and Occasions, 1949
Counterparts, 1954
Brutus's Orchard, 1957
Collected Poems, 1936-1961, 1962
Buff, 1965
New Poems, 1968
Off Course, 1969
To an Unknown Reader, 1970
Song Cycle from a Record Sleeve, 1972
Tiny Tears, 1973
An Old War, 1974
From the Joke Shop, 1975
The Joke Shop Annexe, 1975
An Ill-Governed Coast, 1976
Poor Roy, 1977
Re-treads, 1979
The Other Planet, 1979
The Reign of Sparrows, 1980
More About Tompkins, and Other Light Verse, 1981
House and Shop, 1982
The Individual and His Times: Selected Poems, 1982
As from the Thirties, 1983
Upright Downfall, 1983 (with Barbara Giles and Adrian Rumble)
Mianserin Sonnets, 1984
New and Collected Poems, 1934-1984, 1985
Subsequent to Summer, 1985
Outside the Cannon, 1986
Consolations, 1987
Available for Dreams, 1989
Last Poems, 1993

Other literary forms

Roy Fuller was a competent novelist and may well be considered a poet-novelist, much like Thomas Hardy. His principal novels are *The Second Curtain* (1953), *The Perfect Fool* (1963), *My Child, My Sister* (1965), and *The Carnal Island* (1970). He wrote several children's novels, including *Savage Gold: A Story of Adventure* (1946) and *With My Little Eye: A Mystery Story for Teenagers* (1948). He also edited *Byron for To-day* (1948) and *Fellow Mortals* (1981), an anthology of animal verse. His autobiography was issued in a number of volumes: *Souvenirs* (1980), *Vamp Till Ready: Further Memoirs* (1982), and *Home and Dry: Memoirs III* (1984), reissued in complete form as *The Strange and the Good: Collected Memoirs* (1989).

Achievements

Roy Fuller was honored for his literary accomplishments, becoming a fellow of the Royal Society of Literature and a Companion of the Order of the British Empire in 1970. In that year, he won the Queen's Gold Medal for Poetry. Two years previously, he had won the Duff Cooper Memorial Prize for his *New Poems*, and in 1980, he received the Society of Authors Cholmondeley Award. In 1990, he was awarded an honorary doctorate of letters by the University of Kent at Canterbury.

Biography

Roy Broadbent Fuller was the elder son of Leopold Charles Fuller of Oldham, England, an industrial town in Lancashire, in the northwest of England, and of Nellie Broadbent. His father was manager of a rubber-proofing mill but died when Roy Fuller was only eight. Two years later, his mother and her two sons moved to Blackpool, a nearby seaside town, where Fuller received his education at Blackpool High School. He left there at age sixteen, the minimum leaving age then being fourteen, and was articled (apprenticed) to a local firm of solicitors (attorneys). He became briefly involved in left-wing politics and always retained left-wing sympathies. His northern upbringing, with its culture of wry, antiestablishment humor, became one of the distinguishing features of his poetic voice.

He completed his articles in 1934, passing the necessary exams to qualify him as a lawyer. He moved south for his first post, at a law firm in Ashford, Kent, in the southeast of England. There he met Kathleen Smith, whom he married in 1936. Their only child, John, was born January 1, 1937. Later John was to become a well-known poet and academic in his own right. Just before the outbreak of World War II in 1939, the family moved to London, where Roy Fuller joined the Woolwich Building Society, one of the largest mortgage lending societies in the United Kingdom.

In 1941, he enlisted in the Royal Navy, in which he served until 1946. He was one of the first technicians to work with the recently installed systems of radar. In 1942, he was posted to Kenya, an experience that propelled him into writing poetry in a much more systematic way than before, though he had published a largely unnoticed volume of poems in 1939. His two volumes written during the war, *The Middle of a War* (1942) and *A Lost Season* (1944), brought him to public attention. In 1944, he was relocated back to London, becoming a lieutenant in the Royal Navy volunteer reserve. He worked at the Admiralty as a technical adviser to the director of naval air radio.

Fuller then resumed his legal career with the Woolwich, remaining with it until his retirement. He wrote several legal volumes on Building Society law and from 1958 to 1969 served as chairman of the legal advice panel of the Building Societies Association. On his retirement in 1969, he was made director of the Woolwich, a post he held until his death, and vice president of the Building Societies Association.

Fuller was thus one of the few modern poets who have systematically and successfully pursued a career outside the academic or artistic world. His commercial role did not prevent him from writing profusely or from becoming a respected poet, novelist, essayist, and reviewer. Between 1945 and 1969, he wrote seven adult and two children's novels, produced six volumes of poetry, and edited three volumes of other people's poetry. Shortly before his retirement, he was voted Professor of Poetry at Oxford University, a post he held until 1973.

He continued to be extremely active after his retirement, not only writing poetry and another novel and producing a lengthy series of memoirs, but also serving as a governor of the British Broadcasting Corporation (BBC) and as a member of the Arts Council as chairman of its literature panel. He also was chairman of the Poetry Book Society. He continued to live in London until his death in 1991.

Analysis

Roy Fuller was respected as an accomplished poet and man of letters, who sought not only to raise the technical standards of poetry in his day but also to reinstate its moral voice and significance in a culture that he saw as constantly betraying itself. As a poet he fought against cultural sloppiness, using a voice typical of the great British ironists such as Alexander Pope and Lord Byron, but perhaps with more self-deprecation and sensitivity than most ironists.

The war poet

Fuller's first volume of verse, titled merely *Poems*, attracted little notice. Two poems in it, however, are worthy of note: "To M. S. Killed in Spain" and "To My Brother." Both reflect the growing sense of war in the Europe of the late 1930's, his friend killed in the Spanish Civil War, and his brother touring Nazi Germany. The latter poem's central image is an edition of Alexander Pope's poems his brother had given him, Pope becoming symbolic of the ordered world Fuller feels is now shattering. Its influence is that of W. H. Auden, a poet he continued to admire for his intelligence, discipline, and formal skills.

It is in his war poetry that Fuller first found his true voice, ironically, as World War II produced very few British poets of note. In contrast to World War I, World War II was not shocking. Fuller's depiction of it reflects personal boredom, the squalid world of military quarters and docks, and good-byes. The experience that really opened him was his being drafted to East Africa. The impact of a foreign culture and landscape forced his poetry to assume a new directness, as did the experience of living in close quarters with very ordinary young men, with the need to communicate in terms of their concrete realities.

"The Green Hills of Africa" depicts both a native village in striking detail and the debilitating effect of modern civilization. A similar pessimism informs "The Plains." Again, a masterful ability to depict a scene with a few vivid images is followed by a train of thought on the tawdriness of the cycle of killing and being killed. In the wake of the lion come the jackals and vultures. His concern for the animals is paralleled by his concern for the Africans. The narrative "Teba" shows the contradictions of a rapidly evolving society. Fuller's anti-idealism is again reflected in "The Petty Officers' Mess," possibly the most accomplished poem in the two volumes of war poetry. Fuller proceeds with an image of caged monkeys, through sailors' arguments to wider political questions, then ironically reduces these back again to the level of the monkeys' own scrapes and fights.

THE 1950'S

Returning to civilian life, Fuller wrote his next volume, *Epitaphs and Occasions*. His "Dedicatory Epistle" shows a new, easy ironic tone and verse form using iambic tetrameter couplets influenced by Pope and Auden. For all its lightness of tone, however, there is a note of purpose:

> The poet now must put verse back
> Time and again upon the track
> That first was cut by Wordsworth when
> He said that verse was meant for men.

This mixture of tautness, technical brilliance, ironic tone, and yet artistic seriousness was shared by a number of younger poets in the 1950's, particularly Donald Davie and Philip Larkin. The group came to be known as the Movement, representing a reaction to the florid Romanticism and gesturing of Dylan Thomas and other poets of the 1930's and 1940's.

Similar poems are "Meditation," often anthologized with its throwaway ending:

> ... perhaps we shall, before
> Anything really happens, be safely dead.

In "Obituary to R. Fuller," actually quoted at his memorial service forty-two years later, his self-deprecation is comic. "The Divided Life Released" talks of the reality of wartime life and the unrealities of postwar suburban life, a dichotomy parallel to that of the poet and the lawyer, which Fuller managed to come to terms with creatively.

Counterparts and *Brutus's Orchard* followed, both containing powerful poems that break through the typical understatement, self-deprecating irony, and avoidance of emotion typical of the Movement style. "Rhetoric of a Journey" continues the theme of the uprooted, divided poet, but anchors it far more autobiographically in a moving statement. "Ten Memorial Poems," on Fuller's mother's death, is a confessional series, in places reminiscent of Alfred, Lord Tennyson's *In Memoriam* (1850). The feeling is that of the poet coming to full maturity in his control, depth, and focus.

"Images of Autumn" expresses Fuller's feeling of cultural helplessness. Poetry is no longer a public art form; the public no longer can hear the poet, who is now unheard and invisible. What is particularly difficult is that the poet is not writing just out of personal need but because he desires revelation of some "social truths." "Poet and Reader" closes with:

> All art foresees a future,
> Save art which fails to weigh
> The sadness of the creature,
> The limit of its day,
> Its losing war with nature.

Such rejection forces him into self-regarding stances: "Poem out of Character" is typical. It finishes by deconstructing his own poetry as gesture in the face of universal truth.

In "Elementary Philosophy," the despair of a godless philosophy is heard in tones that echo Thomas Hardy. Another of Hardy's themes, and also of William Butler Yeats, is the growing dichotomy of body and mind. From the middle of *Brutus's Orchard*, Fuller becomes much more aware of his own sexuality as he feels his body aging. "The Perturbation of Dreams" and "Mythological Sonnets" are powerful expressions of midlife angst.

THE 1960's

"Faustian Sketches," the final section of Fuller's *Collected Poems, 1936-1961*, continues this awareness. In "On the Mountain," his own failing physical powers are symbolized by the decline and fall of the Roman Empire. The ironic surface tones of the earlier poems give way to deeper and more tragic ironies, with the poet's full range of emotions being engaged. The sonnet sequence *Meredithian Sonnets*, which closes the *Collected Poems*, well illustrates this.

Buff contains Fuller's third sonnet sequence, *The Historian*, which contains thirty-five sonnets, ranging over the ironies of history. "All history is the history of pain," he wrote elsewhere. "To X" is another sequence, of roundels this time, a difficult traditional form.

The decade began for Fuller with a recognition of his pivotal place in modern British poetry, with his *Collected Poems*; it closed with his *New Poems*, published shortly before his retirement from his business duties. Many of the poems in this volume are concerned with art and the artist. "Those of Pure Origin" is a striking, long philosophical poem, inspired by a quotation from the German poet Friedrich Hölderlin. Its clear, relaxed voice and well-controlled stanzaic free verse seem a model for philosophic discussion in verse.

LATER YEARS

Fuller's retirement merely released him into a prolific old age, although not adding unduly to his reputation. The same self-deprecating tone is heard in "To an Unknown Reader" in *Tiny Tears*: "a whole lifetime's remorseful exposure/ Of a talent falling short of its vision?" He continues to experiment in verse form; "At T. S. Eliot's Memorial Service" is written in couplets first used by Tennyson in "Locksley Hall."

From the Joke Shop probably illustrates best how prolific Fuller continued to be. It contains sixty-three poems written between late summer and early spring. Every poem is composed of three-line iambic stanzas, but the run-on lines and verses annul any sense of a mechanical form. The collection contains many poems reminiscent of "In Memoriam" and shows Fuller as a man of culture, not breaking any new territory in terms of what he has to say, but very stimulating in the flexibility of his poetic voice. "The Joke Shop" is his poetic imagination, with its need to "amuse" an audience.

If poems are jokes, they are also sparrows. Fuller sees himself as a minor poet in *The Reign of Sparrows*. What is striking here is the technical brilliance he has achieved, from cinquains to elegiac pindarics, as well as the ability to find significance in the most trivial everyday event. *Subsequent to Summer* (1985) continues the formal brilliance in this sequence of forty-nine quasi sonnets, each poem consisting of seven unrhymed couplets. It is effortless verse, philosophical poetry at its best. This fascination with the sonnet is akin to Robert Lowell's. In *Available for Dreams*, there is a tremendous variety of sonnet forms, becoming almost free verse, just as in Lowell's diary-like *Life Studies* (1959).

After Fuller's death, his son John discovered a large number of unpublished poems, which he edited as *Last Poems*. The American poet Wallace Stevens features prominently: Fuller's autumnal flowering has often been compared to that of Stevens, as to Yeats and Hardy. The final section, *Later Sonnets from the Portuguese* (echoing Elizabeth Barrett Browning's sequence), consists of some forty-four sonnets.

Fuller is praised for sustaining the quality of British poetry during the relatively lean period of 1950-1960. He went on to outwrite all the other Movement poets, using his intelligence, wit, and formal skills to make significant comments on the cultural and everyday life of the later part of the twentieth century. He may not take the reader out of that life, but he does fully engage with it in significant detail.

OTHER MAJOR WORKS
LONG FICTION: *The Second Curtain*, 1953; *Fantasy and Fugue*, 1954 (pb. in U.S. as *Murder in Mind*, 1986); *Image of a Society*, 1956; *The Ruined Boys*, 1959 (pb. in U.S. as *That Distant Afternoon*, 1957); *The Father's Comedy*, 1961; *The Perfect Fool*, 1963; *My Child, My Sister*, 1965; *The Carnal Island*, 1970; *Stares*, 1990.

NONFICTION: *Owls and Artificers: Oxford Lectures on Poetry, 1969-1970*, 1971; *Professors and Gods: Last Oxford Lectures on Poetry*, 1973; *Souvenirs*, 1980; *Vamp Till Ready: Further Memoirs*, 1982; *Home and Dry: Memoirs III*, 1984; *The Strange and the Good: Collected Memoirs*, 1989; *Spanner and Pen: Post-war Memoirs*, 1991.

CHILDREN'S LITERATURE: *Savage Gold: A Story of Adventure*, 1946; *With My Little Eye: A Mystery Story for Teenagers*, 1948; *Catspaw*, 1966; *Seen Grandpa Lately?*, 1972; *The World Through the Window: Collected Poems for Children*, 1989.

EDITED TEXTS: *Byron for To-day*, 1948; *New Poems*, 1952 (with Clifford Dyment and Montagu Slater); *Supplement to New Poetry*, 1964; *Fellow Mortals*, 1981.

MISCELLANEOUS: *Questions and Answers in Building Society Law and Practice*, 1949; *The Building Societies Acts: Great Britain and Ireland, 1957-1961*, 1962.

BIBLIOGRAPHY

Austin, Allan E. *Roy Fuller*. Boston: Twayne, 1979. This compact volume contains chapters on early, middle, and late poetry up to *From the Joke Shop*. An excellent, comprehensive volume.

Hamilton, Ian. *Against Oblivion: Some Lives of the Twentieth-Century Poets*. London: Viking, 2002. Contains a chapter on Roy Fuller, describing his life and poetry.

Orr, Peter, ed. *The Poet Speaks*. London: Routledge & Kegan Paul, 1966. Fuller proves forthright in talking both about himself and his work.

Powell, Neil. *Roy Fuller: Writer and Society*. Manchester, England: Carcanet Press, 1995. A full biographical account of Fuller's life and writings with a lengthy bibliography.

Smith, Steven E. *Roy Fuller: A Bibliography*. Aldershot, England: Scholar Press, 1996. A good bibliography with a full index.

Tolley, A. T., ed. *Roy Fuller: A Tribute*. Ottawa, Ont.: Carleton University Press, 1993. A far-ranging collection of biographical pieces celebrating Fuller's life and assessing his contribution to modern literature.

David Barratt

IVOR GURNEY

Born: Gloucester, England; August 28, 1890
Died: Dartford, England; December 26, 1937

PRINCIPAL POETRY
Severn and Somme, 1917
War's Embers, 1919
Poems, 1954 (Edmund Blunden, editor)
Poems of Ivor Gurney, 1890-1937, 1973 (Leonard Clark, editor)
Collected Poems of Ivor Gurney, 1982 (P. J. Kavanagh, editor)
Eighty Poems or So, 1997
Rewards of Wonder: Poems of Cotswold, France, London, 2000

OTHER LITERARY FORMS

Besides being a poet, Ivor Gurney (GUR-nee) is recognized as a gifted songwriter and composer of instrumental music. Of special interest are fine settings of poems by William Shakespeare, William Butler Yeats, Sir Walter Raleigh, Ben Jonson, John Clare, A. E. Housman, Wilfred Owen, John Masefield, and Edward Thomas. Gurney's musical work often exhibits the same erratic genius that distinguishes his poems, but this promising career was cut too short by the debilitating effects of military service and mental illness.

ACHIEVEMENTS

Ivor Gurney considered himself unjustly neglected and "one of Five War Poets." Both judgments are gradually being accepted by students of early twentieth century literature. His reputation is benefiting from the general recovery in critical esteem and cultural interest of the World War I poets. His work is associated with that of Wilfred Owen, Rupert Brooke, Siegfried Sassoon, Robert Nichols, Isaac Rosenberg, and others, as part of a significant chapter in modern literary history: the terrible interlude in which a conventional Georgian quietism was being replaced by new virtuosities of shock and disillusionment born in the trenches of war-ravaged Europe. Gurney's own poetry shares in that transformation of thought and technique. In many ways the most enigmatic and inconsistent of those soldier-poets and still the least known, he forged out of his own waywardness innovations in diction, rhythm, and tone that often surpass the others in interest and effect. None evokes more intricately the modernist pathos of "two ditches of heart-sick men;/ the times scientific, as evil as ever, again."

Gurney is also important as the first twentieth century writer to exhibit strongly the influence of Gerard Manley Hopkins, whose vigorous and technically daring verse appeared posthumously in 1916 and 1918. Specific resemblances of theme, language, and style suggest that Gurney responded immediately to the qualities in Hopkins now acknowledged as that Victorian poet's most energizing contribution to the voice of modern literature.

Since Edmund Blunden's 1954 edition of the poems, including many previously unpublished pieces of great merit, Gurney has been discussed in several studies of the war poets and represented in anthologies of modern verse. What more Gurney might have achieved were it not for his rapid psychological disintegration is not certain. There is justice, however, in William Curtis-Hayward's estimate that in Ivor Gurney "what we have is the ruins of a major poet."

Biography

The two pressing facts of Ivor Bertie Gurney's life and poetry were his grisly experiences as a signalman and gunner in the trenches during World War I and his subsequent (though not necessarily consequent) decline into insanity. He was already suffering "beastly nervousness" before the war and actually hoped that the rigors of military life might stabilize his mind. The conditions he endured in the battlefields of Europe would have shaken the steadiest constitution, yet Gurney's vivid poems and letters of this period are remarkably poised and ironic. There was even a kind of jauntiness about his amused image of himself as a "neurasthenic musician" in soldier's garb. He resorted seriously to poetry at this time as a substitute for music and as a therapeutic outlet for troubled feelings and observations. Some of these verses appeared in English magazines, and two small volumes, *Severn and Somme* and *War's Embers*, were published. After being gassed in 1917, however, Gurney went home disabled and soon began to be sporadically afflicted by the melancholic derangement that would haunt the rest of his life. Following several generally shiftless years of unhappiness and encroaching mental disorder, he was sent permanently to the asylum in Dartford, Kent. There he continued to compose poems and verse fragments of eccentric brilliance, mostly expressing baffled resentment and spiritual anguish or intensely reliving grim wartime experiences.

Counterpointing the fierce inspirations of war and madness were two other important influences in Gurney's life: natural beauty and music. His heart was always in the delightful rural byways of his native Gloucestershire, where his elemental need for country beauty and for rich associations rooted deep in local history was nourished. Nevertheless, it took the refining crucibles of battle and mental torment to transform the Severn and Cotswold landscape in Gurney's poetry into a sustained metaphor of joy and timeless sanity. Likewise, it was war and then psychological debility that turned his hand to poetry from his first love, music. He left the Royal College of Music to enlist in a Gloucestershire infantry regiment, and after the war was ultimately unable to resume the career that had been expected of him. Still, Gurney's accomplishment in music remains impressive. When he died of tuberculosis at Dartford in 1937, it was just a month too soon to see the tribute to his music in a special issue of *Music and Letters*. Nature and music, then, had formed his determination to "let beauty through" in the face of all that seemed ugly, brutal, and discordant in the world. Both recur as subjects in his poetry.

Among Gurney's acquaintances were many familiar names from the literary and musical circles of the day: Walter de la Mare, Ralph Vaughan Williams, Lascelles Abercrombie, John Masefield, Sir Edward Marsh, Herbert Howells, and others. Neither his sufferings nor his work was neglected by influential friends during his lifetime, although sad petitioning verses and letters from the asylum years sometimes accused "England" of shameful ingratitude. Altogether, it was Gurney's fate to make poetry out of the sorrows and rare consolations of a stricken consciousness.

ANALYSIS

Ivor Gurney's most interesting poetry falls generally into three types or styles. In two of these his accomplishment is often of the highest quality. To some extent, the three modes represent a development in his manner and technique, though the trend toward increasing originality, urgency, subjectivity, and disruptiveness is far from consistent. If there is any chronological pattern, it perhaps reflects the emergence and then the fragmentation of a unique artistic personality.

SPARE LYRICS

The first category of poems consists of lucid lyrics notable for a spare and laconic modernity of expression. Usually short, these terse, cool pieces demonstrate a precise control of form and tone. Typical verses in this sardonically beautiful vein include "The Love Song," "Generations," "Old Tale," "The Songs I Had," "When I Am Covered," "To His Love," and even the sinister "Horror Follows Horror." As some of these titles suggest, Gurney's style here is songlike—a reflection of his strong musical talents and disposition. His thought, however, almost always has an elusive quality.

"GENERATIONS"

In the Blakean parable "Generations," for example, "The plowed field and the fallow field" alike sing a "prudent" song of fatalistic indifference to life's vicissitudes. The method of this poem is both unromantic and economical, with a disarmingly steady naturalness of idiom. Its amoral vision nevertheless seems to be slyly undermined by the poet's use of ambiguous connotative diction ("prudent," "reckoning," "power," and "brooding"), together with shifting values of the word "best." Rhythmic regularity reinforces this ambivalence of tone, and of course the relation of inanimate to human destinies remains an unasked question. Gurney's other poems of this type have much the same redolent simplicity. He achieves on these occasions the ironic distance that has since been considered the predominant perspective of twentieth century verse.

"To His Love"

One of the finest war poems of this sort is the elegiac "To His Love," addressed with subtle but bitter irony to a dead comrade's beloved. It is ostensibly a nostalgic reminiscence and a conventional tribute to the commemoration of patriotic sacrifice. This poem too, however, is discreetly ambivalent. The phrasing and imagery actually signal bleak indignation at the untruths about war and death that are perpetrated by sentimental attitudes and rituals. In particular, attention is increasingly focused on the soldier's shattered body itself ("You would not know him now . . .") and on the significance of burying as quickly as possible ("Cover him, cover him soon!") what is left of their friend ("that red wet/ thing").

The real meaning of those sickeningly dehumanized remains is obviously not what the state and customary sentiment demand. Hence the compulsion to conceal the ghastly evidence under "violets of pride" in memorial rites that transmute the soldier's memory into a romantic glorification of war. Without openly offending the bereaved, the sustained ironic potential of words such as "pride" illustrates Gurney's ability to let tone control the fury underlying a placid surface. A similar duality is expressed in the offhandedness and coy enjambment of "But *still* he died/ *Nobly*." Here the tone captures and undermines the cavalier outlook of those who pass over the ugliness of death in battle by summarily glamorizing it. The same effect is achieved in the brusque logic of the immediately following clause ("so cover him over/ with violets . . ."), which dismisses the victim by automatically according him the standard "poetic" formalities of interment amidst royal purple violets. Burial deep under "thickset/ Masses of memoried flowers" removes and idealizes a gruesome reality that, the poem implies, should in fact be confronted. Moreover, habitual sentiments and ceremonial gestures tend to supplant authentic personal expression of grief and dissipate any sense of official responsibility. The flowers must be especially "thick-set" in "Masses" (a pun on the eucharistic service) to conceal sufficiently the horror beneath from anyone who might rightly be angered or disillusioned by it. The unusual adjective "memoried" is richly connotative, hinting that the violets bring memories of happier days, are commemorative of military honor, reminding one of death, and perhaps capable themselves of remembering generations of other soldiers misrepresented and exploited even in death for the sake of pride.

Memory is indeed the poem's dominating idea. What impression of the dead should be retained? One possibility is the pastoral image of blithe youth in Gurney's opening stanzas, but that seems "useless indeed." Likewise, to make the soldier's death an instrument of nationalistic propaganda or romantic self-delusion is to perpetuate falsehoods that have, as his embittered fellows know, no connection with what really happened to him. The poem's final irony is the realization that even those aware of the truth yearn to escape it. A better use for a profusion of memorial flowers, it is urged, would be to hide from the poet himself "that red wet/ Thing I must somehow forget." It is nevertheless strongly implied that such immediate, excruciating knowledge cannot, and hence must not, be forgotten or betrayed. This complex and poignantly developed theme, found in other Gurney poems too, suggests the unsettling insights that England was being afforded by the war poets.

PERSONAL NARRATIVES

The second strong vein in Gurney's verse is much more personal, tumultuous, and distinctive. The poems of this sort tend to be descriptive narratives that powerfully realize scenes, events, or sensations—usually stirring impressions connected with battle or with nature. Emphatic irregular rhythms and densely packed language show the influence of Hopkins and, to some extent, of Walt Whitman. Gurney first read these poets in the trenches, where, inevitably, his own manner was already being reforged into a more vigorous utterance.

The result was the emergence of a dramatic diction and syntax suited to the emotions and violent physicality of his new experiences: "wading/ Three feet of water past fire to the bones/ For Hell cold east of snow-sleeting Chaulness." The language energetically struggles with and overleaps grammar and traditional usage. It abounds in compound words, alliteration, striking inversions, breathless rhythms, onomatopoeia, and strikingly compacted visual and sensory effects. In many of the war poems, raw, brutal, shocked action and feeling are reenacted with physical and psychological realism.

Sometimes it is sound that the thickly textured language indicates ("the thud of boots/ On duck-board wood from grate on rough road stone"); elsewhere it is a visual image ("Moonlight lying thick on frost spangled fleet foot sward"), and still elsewhere a terrible revelation of mental anguish. Occasionally, Gurney juxtaposes styles, as in the black drollery of "The Silent One." There the "finicking accent" of an officer in the trenches is incongruous amid battle's "flashes" and "bullets whizzing." The poet-soldier is politely invited by his superior to crawl ahead to almost certain death. "Darkness, shot at: I smiled, as politely replied—/ 'I'm afraid not, Sir.'" Instead he keeps flat, thinking about music and swearing "deep heart's deep oaths/ (Polite to God)."

"CANADIANS"

In general, the war poems seek to catch directly the feel and mentality of battlefield life itself—the hours of waiting, the marching, the brief respites, and of course the squalor and violence. More than anything else, Gurney captures the pity and degradation. In "Canadians," the reader keenly senses the "infinitely grimed" faces, numbed weariness, and brutalization of "slouching" men "Dead past dead from the first hour" in a desolate place. A fifteen-line sentence of especially elliptical and interrupted syntax suggests the jumbled association of ideas raised in a fellow soldier's mind by such "iniquity of mere being," and biblical echoes and other religious allusions extend the situation's moral significance and lead the speaker to a bitter final reflection. He concludes that these Canadian volunteers, supposedly having come "finely" and freely and recklessly, must actually be victims that "Fate had sent for suffering and dwelling obscenely/ Vermin eaten, fed beastly, in vile ditches meanly."

The disillusionment felt by the poem's evidently Christian speaker enhances the force of the protest; to suggest that only a malevolent impersonal Fate could contrive such misery is to deny the right of Europe's Christian nations to make war in this fashion. That does not, of course, necessarily reflect Gurney's own view. As in the case of "Generations," discussed earlier, ideas different from the writer's own opinions may sometimes be dramatized in this way. In any event, the poem depicts one witness's emotional and intellectual reaction to the sordidness of modern mechanical warfare. The effect, as in other verses on related topics, is to deglamorize utterly a species of conflict that, ironically and ominously, makes men seem "Cave dwellers last of tribes."

Nature poems

Gurney employs the same densely textured style for other subjects—notably in poems evoking "the love of Earth in me." What distinguishes those nature poems is an extraordinary fidelity to concrete particulars. Again like Hopkins, he is fascinated with specificity—real things that can be seen and named in catalogs of precise images. Poems such as "Cotswold Ways," "The Dearness of Common Things," "The Escape," and "Looking Up There" are typical. In such verses, Gurney is drawn especially to creation's counterpointing of "strange" and "queer" beauties. He works at "breaking to sight" the hidden richness of "small trifles,/ Real, beautiful" and even of sensually tactile things such as the fabric of clothing. "How hard beauty hurts men," he cries, "with commonness and pangs and hurts them!"

There is also a dynamic vitalism, as in lines such as "The stars are sliding wanton through trees" or "The line of blue faint known and the leaping to white." The nature poems also express a personal devotion born of the need for engrossing antidotes to the distresses of battle and psychological suffering. Music figures similarly in the poems, occasionally being linked to the harmonies of nature; in one moment of dark humor, moreover, Gurney describes how he "learnt the machine gun, how it played/ Scales and arpeggios."

The poetry of this second type, then, divides Gurney's admirers from his detractors. The style is often undeniably knotted and cryptic—here and there virtually to the point of unintelligibility. Punctuation is haphazard, grammar deliberately tortured, allusions cryptic, and psychological impressionism pursued with such verisimilitude as to defy confident interpretation. The effect is to concentrate wonderfully Gurney's strenuous dramatization of consciousness, however, and to capture with distinctiveness what Hopkins would have called the "inscapes" of objects, action, or feeling. The peculiarity is not just the price paid for visual, aural, and semantic richness; it actually inheres in what Gurney is determined to elicit from the difficult materials of his experience. Success with such techniques is bound to be erratic, and there is a limit to what the power of suggestion by itself can express, but there are some splendid achievements in Gurney too. Indeed there is more than enough to justify the trouble of attending patiently to the poems—reading them aloud wherever possible—and perhaps valuing them as much for what they bravely attempt as for their relatively few sustained, unquestionable triumphs.

FLEXIBILITY IN VERSIFICATION

In formal versification, Gurney shows the flexibility that might naturally be expected of a musician. This is true of both the generally early simpler poems and the more rhetorically emphatic idiom of his second style. There is little inclination toward free verse or even blank verse and extraordinary versatility in rhyme patterns and cadences. Gurney's rhymes are usually rigid, yet remarkably unobtrusive—except when he attempts audacious pairings such as "coolish" with "foolish" or, within one line, "clangour" with "anger." Successful half-rhymes contribute to this effect of naturalness. The finely modulated poem "When I Am Covered," which may be Gurney's own epitaph, has four tercets that repeat twice an *aba bab* arrangement, while the following stanza from "To Crickley" shows the cumulative effect of more forceful rhyming:

> Then to you—deep in Hells now still-burning
> For sleep or the end's peace—
> By tears we have not saved you; yearning
> To accusation and our hopes loss turning.
> What gods are these?

The poet's rhythms, on the other hand, mark a decisive break from tradition. They tend toward the irregularity of passionate speech rather than the more or less consistent stress patterns of metrical law. Like Hopkins, he strove for the authentic accents of "speaking in high words," and wrote few pieces in standard rhythm that do not have a rather trivializing sing-song quality. The "To Crickley" stanza may serve also to illustrate Gurney's irregular cadence; each of the five lines is rhythmically different, only the last being standard, and the remaining stanzas of the same poem exhibit still other variations.

A MIND AT WAR WITH ITSELF

In turning to the third of the characteristic types of poem written by Gurney, technical analysis is difficult and perhaps out of place. Fascinating and moving as these strange poems are, they are bound to be incidental to the development of Gurney's critical reputation. Their form can be described as a peculiarly loose and discursive soliloquy sometimes reminiscent of William Wordsworth's procedure in *The Prelude: Or, The Growth of a Poet's Mind* (1850). Most of these poems date from the asylum years and are in fact repetitive and fragmentary. They tend also to be obsessive autobiographical laments in which Gurney strives courageously to make sense of his pain, disappointment, and shame. One or two, such as "The Lock Keeper," are more even and detached, though they do not surpass in power and pathos the ungainly personal utterances.

All the poems of this type do contain occasional lines or passages with the lucid beauty or Hopkinsesque strength of Gurney's other work, but the main interest of these pieces lies in their curiously gripping revelation of a sensitive mind at war with itself. For example, in "Chance to Work," addressed to the police authorities, Gurney begins with fervid recollections of a youthful joy in books, in music, in poetry, in love, and especially in natural beauty. Then come lines about strange illness, war, hospital, "evil forces," broken hopes, and the desperate therapy of hard physical exertion. Finally, there are the dreadful loneliness, suicidal longings, and complex recriminations of the asylum ward. The litany of real and imagined horrors concludes ruefully with the recurrent plea of Gurney's last years: "O if such pain is/ Not of account—a whole life's whole penalties/ To cancel... Grant pity, grant chance of Work." This poem, and others like it, are probably artistic failures, but they portray with unforgettable authenticity the hell of what is too readily called maddened consciousness.

A few excellent representative poems that have not already been cited are "Memory, Let All Slip," "Half Dead," "Darkness Has Cheating Swiftness," "Moments," and "What Evil Coil." Taken as a whole, Gurney's best poetry represents an imaginative and technical accomplishment at least comparable to that of the better-known war poets. Doubtless he is less consistent, and much more often confusingly idiosyncratic. At the same time, his is in certain ways a more sensitive and stylistically original voice. One cannot help responding to what he called "the making's eager pain"—his urgent impulse to find adequate forms of utterance for thoughts and feelings that customary poetic modes would not accommodate. Admired more by fellow poets—Blunden, de la Mare, Jon Silkin, and others—than by academic critics, Gurney's verse is probably too frequently singular, febrile, disorderly, and experimental (and too notoriously that of a madman) for the popular or scholarly taste. He may have been right to cry with ghastly candor, "There is nothing for my Poetry, who was the child of joy./ But to work out in verse crazes of my untold pain." Yet Blunden is also correct in having said of him,

> He perished, one may say, war and consumption apart, from the merciless intensity of his spirit both in watching the forms of things moving apace in the stream of change and in hammering out poetic forms that should remain as their just representation and acclamation.

OTHER MAJOR WORK
NONFICTION: *Collected Letters*, 1991.

BIBLIOGRAPHY

Blevins, Pamel. *Ivor Gurney and Marion Scott: Song of Pain and Beauty*. Rochester, N.Y.: Boydell Press, 2008. This double biography looks at the life of the poet Gurney, who met Marion Scott while studying music and formed a partnership with her. Describes their lives separately and intertwined.

Gray, Piers. *Marginal Men: Edward Thomas, Ivor Gurney, J. R. Ackerley*. Houndmills, Basingstoke, Hampshire: Macmillan, 1991. An examination of Gurney, along with Edward Thomas, and J. R. Ackerley, that looks at his marginalized life and poetry.

Gurney, Ivor. *Collected Letters*. Edited by R. K. R. Thornton. Manchester, England: Carcanet Press, 1991. Invaluable source of biographical details of Gurney's life and friendships.

Hill, Geoffrey. "Gurney's 'Hobby.'" *Essays in Criticism* 34 (April, 1984): 97-128. Hill explores Gurney's poetry and music, oddly enough finding his poetry to be his self-proclaimed "hobby." Examines Gurney's irony as evidenced in his poetry, the same irony that Gurney claimed he detested, much like Walt Whitman, the poet Gurney considered to be his mentor.

Hipp, Daniel. *The Poetry of Shell Shock: Wartime Trauma and Healing in Wilfred Owen, Ivor Gurney, and Siegfried Sassoon*. Jefferson, N.C.: McFarland, 2005. This examination of three poets of World War I contains a section on Gurney and his works.

Hooker, Jeremy. "Honoring Ivor Gurney." *Poetry Nation Review* 7, no. 17 (1980): 16-19. Emphasizes the fact that Gurney's world was one of madness and incarceration, deeply affecting his poetry. Hooker honors Gurney as a poet and a man who, through a disintegrating life, managed to enliven the language with verse and was not fully appreciated in his period or in modern times.

Hurd, Michael. *The Ordeal of Ivor Gurney*. New York: Oxford University Press, 1978. The most quoted of all Gurney's sources, this book is an exhaustive study of his life and writings. In the course of the text, Hurd analyzes dozens of Gurney's poems while maintaining a chronological perspective. Supplemented by indexes and notes.

Moore, Charles Willard. *Maker and Lover of Beauty: Ivor Gurney, Poet and Songwriter*. Introduction by Herbert Howelles and decorations by Richard Walker. Rickmansworth, England: Triad Press, 1976. Although issued in a limited edition, this biographical volume on the poet-musician is one of the few sources available.

Pilkington, Michael. *Gurney, Ireland, Quilter, and Warlock*. Bloomington: Indiana University Press, 1989. A reference guide to the songs of Gurney and three other songwriters of these turn-of-the-century composers.

Waterman, Andrew. "The Poetic Achievement of Ivor Gurney." *Critical Quarterly* 25 (Winter, 1983): 3-19. Waterman's primary focus is to show how Gurney modernized himself and his perspectives in his poetry between the war years and his incarceration in a lunatic asylum. Gurney's musical talent is also critically explored.

Michael D. Moore

DAVID JONES

Born: Brockley, Kent, England; November 1, 1895
Died: Harrow, London, England; October 28, 1974
Also known as: Dai Greatcoat

PRINCIPAL POETRY
In Parenthesis, 1937
The Anathemata: Fragment of an Attempted Writing, 1952
The Tribune's Visitation, 1969
The Sleeping Lord, and Other Fragments, 1974
The Kensington Mass, 1975
The Roman Quarry, and Other Sequences, 1981

OTHER LITERARY FORMS

David Jones's other main creative outlet was painting, but he did write a number of essays and reviews connected to art and literature. A collection of these essays and reviews, many of which date back to the 1940's, appeared as *Epoch and Artist: Selected Writings* (1959), edited by his associate, Harman Grisewood. Other essays were collected after his death by Grisewood as *The Dying Gaul, and Other Writings* (1978).

ACHIEVEMENTS

David Jones's *In Parenthesis* gained instant recognition for the poet when it won the Hawthornden Prize in 1938. Before and immediately afterward, Jones's achievements had been in his modernist painting. Recognition of Jones as both artist and poet came with the award of a Civil List Pension in 1954 and the award of the Order of the British Empire in 1955. *The Anathemata* won the Russell Loines Award in 1954.

Further recognition came with the Bollingen Prize for Poetry in 1960, the Levinson Prize from *Poetry* magazine in 1961, and an award from the Society of Authors Travelling Fund in 1962. His *Epoch and Artist* won a Welsh Arts Council Award in 1959 and an honorary doctor of literature degree from the University of Wales in 1960. The next year, he was elected as a fellow of the Royal Society of Literature and to membership in the Royal Watercolour Society. In 1972, he won the gold medal of the Royal National Eisteddford on Wales in recognition of his promotion of Welsh culture and history. Perhaps his greatest honor came in 1974 (the last year of his life), when the Queen invited him to become a Companion of Honour, an order limited to just sixty-six notable men of letters and public figures.

Biography

Walter David Michael Jones was born in Brockley, Kent, the youngest of three children. His father, a printer who was also a lay reader in the Church of England, came from North Wales. His mother was a Londoner whose father was a barge builder at Rotherhithe on the River Thames. David attended the local parish church and was educated locally, early demonstrating a gift for drawing.

At the age of fourteen, he entered the newly formed Camberwell School of Art in south London, where he studied from 1909 through 1914. At the outbreak of World War I, despite his poor physique, he managed to enroll in the London Welsh Battalion of the Royal Welsh Regiment, which was made up of London Cockney boys and Welshmen. By this time, Jones had become interested in his Welsh roots, especially after visits to relatives in North Wales. During his service, Jones sustained wounds, contracted trench fever, and finished the war in a peacekeeping force in Ireland. He was demobilized in 1919. Many of Jones's war experiences found their way into his long poem *In Parenthesis*.

As a war veteran, Jones was granted a scholarship to the Westminster School of Art, a center of British modernism. He was particularly attracted to Eric Gill, a Catholic convert who was establishing a reputation as a modernist sculptor. When Jones left the school in 1921, he joined the Catholic arts community Gill had founded in southern England and became a Catholic, a move that created a breach between him and his father. He also fell in love with Petra, Gill's younger daughter. The couple got engaged but did not marry.

In 1924, Gill moved the community to mid-Wales, the first time Jones had actually lived in the country he had come to regard as his true home. Jones was developing his own style as a painter of both oils and watercolors. In 1928, Jones held his first exhibition in London. Gill moved the community to outside northwest London in the Chiltern Hills, where Jones met and fell in love with Prudence Pelham, an aristocrat. He also met Helen Sutherland, who became a much-needed patroness, even though he was painting prolifically from 1928 through 1932.

In 1932, he had a complete nervous breakdown. This began a series of depressive episodes that occurred throughout the rest of his life. He was not able to paint but instead worked on writing prose and poetry about his war experiences. He was again influenced by modernists, especially T. S. Eliot and James Joyce. By 1936, he presented the text of *In Parenthesis* to Faber & Faber, the publishing house where Eliot worked. The first print run of fifteen hundred copies enjoyed instant success, receiving praise from both Eliot and William Butler Yeats. Jones followed this work with a series of poetic meditations on the Catholic Mass.

During World War II, Jones stayed in London and continued writing and painting. Much of his writing consisted of essays on art and literature in which he sought not only Catholic insights, but also ways back into Celtic and Roman history to work out a cultural history of Western Europe. The poetic outcome was *The Anathemata*.

Before *The Anathemata* could be published, Jones had another nervous breakdown in 1947 and entered a nursing home in Harrow in north London. After his recovery, he remained in Harrow. In the 1950's, Jones began to receive wider recognition through prizes and exhibitions, culminating in being named to the Queen's Birthday Honours List in 1955. In the 1960's, he was writing rather more than painting, but he was also fighting to keep chronic depression in check. His last major painting, *Trystan ac Esseult*, was done in 1963. Recognition and honors continued to come in, though by now modernism was giving way to other literary and artistic movements. Jones died quietly in 1974.

Analysis

David Jones's poetry is difficult to categorize, apart from saying that it is modernist and long. In some ways, it is not even poetry, as large sections are written in poetic prose and can be read more like a novel. Jones was inspired to use such a mix by medieval sources, in which the division between prose and poetry was more fluid than in the twentieth century. Like Eliot and Ezra Pound, he draws on whatever sources inspire him and quotes them, regardless of whether they are in English. Like Eliot, he relies on notes to explain the more private associations.

What is different is that Jones's poetry is much more grounded in his personal experiences as soldier and artist and in his identity as a Londoner, Welshman, and Catholic. His speech makes his poetry dramatic, and like other modernists, he writes much of his work as dramatic monologue. The voices are typically those of London Cockneys or Welsh bards. The matter is epic and mythic, his imagination having been grounded as much in Celtic and Germanic mythology as in Roman or Greek. Though never having been taught Latin, Greek, or Welsh, Jones is prepared to write in them. His knowledge of the traditional Latin rites of the Roman Catholic Church pervades all of his writing, and his is profoundly religious and spiritual poetry.

In Parenthesis

It could be claimed that *In Parenthesis* is the greatest war poem to have come out of World War I, but it is long, difficult, and appeared well after the other war poets had published their poetry. In addition, it is not quotable, though it is eminently readable, demanding to be read out loud, hence its success as a radio poem.

In Parenthesis is divided into seven parts, covering a period from December, 1915, to the Battle of the Somme in the summer of 1916, which becomes its climax. At all stages, it seems autobiographical. At first, the poet's persona is Private John Ball, named after a rebel priest who led an uprising against Richard II. At the end of the poem, Ball appears to be dying of wounds. The poet at times stands back from Ball and seems closer to some of the Welsh soldiers. The poet's stance is thus made more ambiguous.

Part 1, "The Many Men So Beautiful," follows a battalion of soldiers from their base camp in England to their embarkation. Parts 2 to 4 follow their journey through France to the front lines, showing how they accustom themselves to their conditions and survive through the winter. Jones's minutely detailed descriptions of the front lines is akin to Robert Graves's war memoir *Goodbye to All That: An Autobiography* (1929).

Part 5, "Squat Garlands for White Knights," details the battalion's removal from winter quarters southward to an unknown destination. Parts 6 and 7 deal with their new deployment and the ensuing battle, in which most of the battalion are massacred. Ball survives with a few others but is critically wounded. The poem ends with his waiting to be carried off the battlefield by stretcher-bearers.

THE ANATHEMATA

By contrast, *The Anathemata* is not specific as to time or place. Its ambition is to trace the rise and nature of western civilization from a Christian, and especially Catholic, point of view. Its focus is on "the matter of Britain" and the Mass. However, it incorporates other spiritual traditions and sees Britain not as an amalgam of Celtic and Saxon traditions. It is a more difficult work than *In Parenthesis* because of its historical circularity, and it demands a great deal of work from its readers. They need to grasp some quite obscure Welsh mythology, for example, and to be able to converse in several languages.

However, Jones's own control and grasp of what he is doing is profound. Once the sense of the speaking voice is internalized, it creates a momentum that carries the reader through the difficult and obscure passages into an experience that is singularly rare in modern poetry: a sense of being involved with the past and the present as a continuity.

The name of the poem means "things devoted to a deity," and it is one of the most profoundly moving religious poems of the modernist movement, comparable to Eliot's *Four Quartets* (1943). It is divided into eight parts, from "Rite and Foretime," dealing with the Greeks' first discovery of Britain, to "Sherthursdaye and Venus Day," which deals with the crucifixion of Christ. Section 5, "The Lady of the Pool," is set in London's docklands and at times echoes Jones's grandfather, the Thames barge builder.

THE SLEEPING LORD, AND OTHER FRAGMENTS

The Sleeping Lord, and Other Fragments is a collection that gathers most of Jones's other poems, some of which are unfinished. The title poem, written 1966-1967, deals with a Welsh version of the Arthurian legend and shows how deeply immersed Jones became in Welsh myth and prehistory and how he was able to detect traces of its spirituality in Catholicism. Normally Welsh Christianity is seen as ineluctably Protestant, so Jones is revealing new insights.

"The Tribune's Visitation" is set in Roman Palestine at the time of Christ. Jones developed a great sense of the continuity of the Roman world, and the Roman soldiers are shown as similar to those of World War I. Other poems included are "The Tutelar of the Place" and "The Hunt," the latter a reworking of another Welsh legend.

OTHER MAJOR WORKS

NONFICTION: *Epoch and Artist: Selected Writings*, 1959 (Harman Grisewood, editor); *David Jones: Letters to Vernon Watkins*, 1976; *The Dying Gaul, and Other Writings*, 1978 (Grisewood, editor); *Dai Greatcoat: A Self-Portrait of David Jones in His Letters*, 1980 (Rene Hague, editor); *David Jones: Letters to a Friend*, 1980; *David Jones, a Fusilier at the Front: His Record of the Great War in Word and Image*, 1985; *Inner Necessities: Letters of David Jones to Desmond Chute*, 1985.

BIBLIOGRAPHY

Alldritt, Keith. *David Jones: Writer and Artist*. London: Constable, 2003. This biography of Jones covers both his artistic and poetic lives in detail and traces Jones's philosophical and religious changes. Includes black-and-white plates of paintings.

Blamires, David. *David Jones: Artist and Writer*. Manchester, England: Manchester University Press, 1971. This is not a biography, but rather a critical analysis of Jones's work, both artistic and poetic. It is still one of the definitive books on Jones's achievement.

Blissett, William. *The Long Conversation: A Memoir of David Jones*. New York: Oxford University Press, 1981. This is a detailed recording of all the conversations the author had with Jones, from their first meeting in 1959 until Jones's death in 1974. It contains biographical material as well as a sense of Jones's wide-ranging literary and artistic interests and concerns.

Dilworth, Thomas. *Reading David Jones*. Cardiff: University of Wales Press, 2008. Provides Jones's poetry along with commentary, explanations, and biographical information. Notes the influence of his painting on his poetry.

Hague, Rene. *A Commentary on "The Anathemata" of David Jones*. Wellingborough, England: Christopher Skelton, 1977. This is a detailed commentary on the complete text of Jones's greatest poem, written by a very old acquaintance, who had discussed the work with Jones.

Matthias, John, ed. *Introducing David Jones: A Selection of His Writings*. Boston: Faber and Faber, 1980. While this is mainly a selection of Jones's three major long poems, it does contain a valuable introduction by Stephen Spender, a contemporary of Jones, and a long introduction by the editor.

Miles, J., and D. Shiel. *David Jones: The Maker Unmade*. Cardiff, Wales: Poetry Wales Press, 1995. A full-length analysis of his poetry with a particular emphasis on its Welsh roots.

Robichaud, Paul. *Making the Past Present: David Jones, the Middle Ages, and Modernism*. Washington, D.C.: Catholic University of America Press, 2007. Examines Jones's treatment of medieval mythology in his poetry and how his poetry relates to modernism.

David Barratt

CHRISTOPHER LOGUE

Born: Portsmouth, Hampshire, England; November 23, 1926
Also known as: Count Palmiro Vicarion

PRINCIPAL POETRY
Seven Sonnets, 1954
Count Palmiro Vicarion's Book of Limericks, 1955
Devil, Maggot, and Sons, 1956
The Man Who Told His Love: Twenty Poems Based on Pablo Neruda's "Los cantos d'amores," 1958
Count Palmiro Vicarion's Book of Bawdy Ballads, 1959
Patrocleia: An Account of Book Sixteen of Homer's "Iliad" Freely Adapted into English, 1959
Red Bird, 1959
Songs, 1959
Songs from the Lily-White Boys, 1960
Pax: Episodes from the Iliad, Book Nineteen, 1963
Logue's A.B.C., 1966
The Words of Christopher Logue's Establishment Songs Etcetera, 1966
The Girls, 1969
New Numbers, 1969
The Isle of Jessamy, 1971
Twelve Cards, 1972
Abecedary, 1977 (with Bert Kitchen)
War Music: An Account of Books Sixteen to Nineteen of Homer's "Iliad," 1980
Ode to the Dodo: Poems, 1953-1978, 1981
Lucky Dust, 1985
Kings: An Account of Books One and Two of Homer's "Iliad," 1991
The Husbands: An Account of Books Three and Four of Homer's "Iliad," 1994
Selected Poems, 1996
Logue's Homer—War Music, 2001
All Day Permanent Red: The First Battle Scenes of Homer's Iliad Rewritten, 2003
Cold Calls: War Music Continued, 2005

OTHER LITERARY FORMS

At the beginning of his literary career, while in Paris, Christopher Logue (lohg) did a certain amount of hack work for Olympia Press, including a pornographic novel, *Lust* (1954). On returning to London, he worked for the satirical magazine *Private Eye*, and a number of his pieces have been compiled in *Christopher Logue's True Stories from Private Eye* (1972) and *Christopher Logue's Bumper Book of True Stories* (1980).

Logue became engaged in writing film and theater scripts and in translating. His translation *The Seven Deadly Sins* (1986), unfortunately, did not gain the approval of the Bertolt Brecht estate. He also became interested in children's literature, writing children's verse and editing a number of anthologies of children's verse, including *The Children's Book of Children's Rhymes* (1986).

Achievements

As an antiestablishment poet, Christopher Logue has probably found it more difficult to achieve recognition in the mainstream literary world of Britain. However, his experiments with public verse reading, including the first public poetry reading at the National Film Theatre in 1958, did create something of a stir in London in the 1950's, when new forms of drama were also beginning to gain a following. His main recognition came first from writing for *Private Eye* from the 1950's through the 1970's, when it became the leading British satirical magazine and much feared by politicians and establishment figures and before crippling libel cases tamed it.

Logue was a middle-aged man before he won any major awards. In 1990, he won the Bernard F. Conners Prize for Poetry from the *Paris Review* for his poem "Kings." In 2002, *Logue's Homer—War Music* was shortlisted for the Griffin Poetry Award. His reworking of Homer's *Iliad* (c. 750 B.C.E.; English translation, 1611) had caught the public eye, however, and for *Cold Calls*, the fifth volume of the enterprise, he received the Whitbread Poetry Prize for 2005 and was also nominated for the Whitbread Book of the Year. In 2007, he received national recognition by being made a Companion of the British Empire.

Biography

Christopher Logue was born to a middle-class Roman Catholic couple living in the port city of Portsmouth, in southern England. Their only son, he was sent away to a private Catholic school in Bath run by the Christian Brothers, then briefly attended Portsmouth Grammar School. In 1943, when Logue was seventeen, he joined the army as a paratrooper. After an accident in which he lost sight in one eye, he was transferred to the Black Watch. In 1945, he was sent to Palestine. While there, he served a sixteen-month prison term for possession of classified documents. Up until this time, he had shown no interest in books or writing, but in prison, he began reading.

After release in 1948, he drifted back to London, then moved on to Paris in 1951, finding himself in the literary world of Samuel Beckett, Henry Miller, and Alexander Tocchi, a Scottish novelist. To earn money, he wrote for the pornographic market under the pseudonym Count Palmiro Vicarion. Two novels and two volumes of poetry brought him his first earnings from publications. He also edited a new literary magazine, *Merlin*.

Returning to England in 1956, he found work as a scriptwriter and actor in the Royal Court Theatre of Kenneth Tynan and in British films under director Ken Russell. He also starting writing for *Private Eye*, then in its infancy as a satirical review of British cultural and political life. Satire was a main literary genre of the time, and Logue's antiestablishment stance fitted in perfectly.

However, Logue became drawn to poetry, especially poetry as performance and as poster art, which he saw as a main vehicle of the left-wing views he espoused. He helped reestablish the tradition of public poetry readings accessible to ordinary people in pubs, clubs, and theaters. He published small volumes of verse that gained a reputation among more avant-garde reviewers. He became very active in the Campaign for Nuclear Disarmament and was imprisoned several times on marches and demonstrations. In the 1970's, he suffered bouts of depression.

Logue had remained unmarried, despite developing an interest in children's literature, especially verse for children. However in 1985, at the age of fifty-eight, he met and married a somewhat younger woman, the critic and biographer Rosemary Hill, settling down in Camberwell, an inner suburb of south London.

He worked on a project that had long fascinated him. A British Broadcasting Corporation commission in 1956 got him interested in reworking the *Iliad*, the ancient epic poem by the Greek poet Homer. Logue's version, as it evolved, was not a translation, as Logue had never learned Greek and he added material. Although a pacifist, he focused on the battle scenes of the original text. The first volume in Logue's version was *Patrocleia*, from book 16 of Homer's epic. He followed this with numerous other titles. Together, these works earned him the title of Britain's best living war poet.

Analysis

Christopher Logue's poetry has developed from its first Romantic-modernist beginnings under the inspiration of Ezra Pound, William Butler Yeats, and T. S. Eliot, to a fully fledged mock heroic. His first two volumes of poetry contain work that is by and large modernist but with occasional Romantic flashes. In this, it is not strikingly original in any way, but it does suggest someone trying to move away from the formalism of the Movement poets of the time, while refusing to get drawn into what he felt was the too comfortable Romanticism of the later Yeats. "For My Father" is one early poem in which the poet has struck an authentic voice. Real dialogue lies at its heart. The influence of Pablo Neruda can be seen in the collection *Red Bird* as well as *The Man Who Told His Love*.

As early as 1959, however, *Songs* shows the poet breaking away from the erudtion and allusiveness of his first poems. Logue was beginning to find the voice that made him famous as a public poet, declaiming in a popular style on the issues of the day in the idiom of the day, a voice that perhaps culminated in the 1969 Isle of Wight Festival, where he gave public poetry readings before some 100,000 people and singer-songwriter Bob

Dylan performed. The biggest influence on these 1959 poems was German Marxist dramatist Brecht. Logue abandoned the academic style of poetry, and his language became dramatic, strident, racy, and satiric.

As time went by, Logue adapted this style to both comic and children's verse. He used some forms of children's verse in his poetry for adults; for example, he adapted the rhyming ABC for adult satiric verse as in *Abecedary*. At the same time, Logue had a developing interest in Homer's great epic poem, the *Iliad*. Early attempts to put this into English verse, not as a translation but as a new, culturally relevant version, include *Patrocleia* and *Pax*. These two attempts were reprised and enlarged in *War Music* in 1980. The volume dealt with the episodes in the *Iliad* in which Achilles re-enters the war on the Greek side, enraged by the death of his partner, Patroclus. Two further volumes, *Kings* and *The Husbands*, were then packaged with *War Music* and reissued as one volume under the title *Logue's Homer—War Music* in 2001. Two further volumes followed: *All Day Permanent Red*, which got its title from a Revlon lipstick advertisement, and *Cold Calls*. The enterprise closely parallels that by the contemporary West Indian poet, Derek Walcott, whose *Omeros* (1990) is likewise based on a work by Homer but set in the Caribbean.

NEW NUMBERS

New Numbers is probably the most representative of Logue's populist poetry. Its opening poem is typical in that it brashly refuses to behave like a poem, challenging the audience with "This book was written to change the world." In other words, the volume is intended to be politically charged and dynamic, not merely of academic or aesthetic interest. It is absurdist in language and imagery. None of the poems have titles, and they are divided from each other only by small spaces, giving the sense of continuity and creating a cumulative effect.

One of the longer ones, "I have to tell you about Mr Valentine," is an allegory of the search for the ideal love preventing enjoyment of the real and actual grace of life as it is to be found in its fullness. The figures at times are cartoon-strip figures, grotesque, with fragments of dialogue thrown in. They capture the culture of the 1960's, with hippies, beatniks, and the search for Eastern mysticism. Each topic is treated with sympathetic absurdity. Many seem takeoffs of stories from the gutter press. The language is demotic, colloquial, and begging to be read aloud. This is the Brechtian ideal done in English.

SELECTED POEMS

Selected Poems, published in 1996, has become the most available collection of Logue's poetry, as many of the earlier volumes have gone out of print. The collection draws from earlier volumes but does not identify the collection in which each poem was originally published. However, the earliest poem, "Professor Tucholsky's Facts," is from *Songs*, the first of Logue's populist collections. Some poems were selected from

Ode to the Dodo and *Songs from the Lily-White Boys*. Others have not been published anywhere else, including the last poem in the collection, "From Book XXI of Homer's *Iliad*," which was a discarded experiment for *War Music*. The collection also presents work from *Singles* (1973), a series of lyrics set to music. The final lyric contains the lines "Last night in Notting Hill// I saw Blake passing by...." These poems are reminiscent of William Blake's *Songs of Innocence and of Experience* (1794) because of their lyric and ironic quality and also in that they comment on contemporary London.

Other selections are made from *New Numbers* and *The Girls*. *Urbanal* (1975) is possibly the best poem of the volume, an urban elegy not unlike Robert Lowell's. It references Blake again, beginning with a lament for a thirty-year-old tree taken down because it is inconvenient to a neighbor. It takes on a tragic note, the poet/tree identification being deeply felt. The fact that there are very few poems representing the 1980's and 1990's show how much of Logue's creative writing was being put into the Homer project.

COLD CALLS

Cold Calls, billed as the penultimate volume of *Logue's Homer*, covers book 5 of the *Iliad*, going back before the original *War Music* to where Achilles, the great Greek hero, is still sulking in his tent, refusing to help his side. It covers the battle in the plains before Troy, where the Trojans sweep the Greeks back to their ships and threaten to burn them, despite suffering heavy losses themselves.

The style is clearly dramatic and, in fact, does better read aloud. Dialogue, commentary, and narrative mingle in a fast-paced, easily understandable style vastly different from traditional translations. There are detailed descriptions of the blood-thirstiness of the fighting, mingled with the gods' frequent interventions as they take sides. The volume is just forty-four pages long and needs almost no notes. The gods, especially Aphrodite, are made to seem very fallible, very human. However, it is difficult to see the poet as a pacifist. The soldiers are made to seem ridiculous at times, but only from a political point of view.

OTHER MAJOR WORKS
LONG FICTION: *Wand and Quadrant*, 1953; *Lust*, 1954.
SHORT FICTION: *Christopher Logue's True Stories from Private Eye*, 1973; *Christopher Logue's Bumper Book of True Stories*, 1980; *Private Eye's Oxford Book of Pseuds*, 1983 (with Kathryn Lamb).
SCREENPLAY: *Savage Messiah*, 1972.
TELEPLAYS: *Antigone*, 1962; *The End of Arthur's Marriage*, 1965.
NONFICTION: *Prince Charming: A Memoir*, 1999 (autobiography).
CHILDREN'S LITERATURE: *The Crocodile*, 1976 (of Peter Nickl; illustrated by Binette Schroeder); *Puss in Boots*, 1976 (illustrated by Nicola Bayley); *Ratsmagic*,

1976 (illustrated by Wayne Anderson); *The Magic Circus*, 1979 (illustrated by Anderson).

TRANSLATIONS: *Friday*, 1972 (of Hugo Claus); *The Seven Deadly Sins*, 1986 (of Bertolt Brecht).

EDITED TEXTS: *The Children's Book of Comic Verse*, 1979 (illustrated by Bill Tidy); *London in Verse*, 1982; *Sweet and Sour: An Anthology of Comic Verse*, 1983 (illustrated by John Glashan); *The Children's Book of Children's Rhymes*, 1986 (illustrated by Tidy).

BIBLIOGRAPHY

Bainbridge, Charles. "The War in Heaven." Review of *Cold Calls*. *The Guardian*, October 8, 2005, p. 18. Examines both *Cold Calls* and the entire *War Music* project, finding Logue's translation successful in part because of the vigor and energy he brings to the story.

Carne-Ross, D. S. *Classics and Translations: Essays*. Edited by Kenneth Haynes. Lewisburg, Pa.: Bucknell University Press, 2010. Contains an essay examining Logue's *Patrocleia* as a translation. Carne-Ross, a radio producer and classicist, helped Logue begin his work.

Leddy, Michael. "*All Day Permanent Red*: The First Battle Scenes of Homer's *Iliad* Rewritten." Review of *All Day Permanent Red*. *World Literature Today* 78, nos. 3/4 (September-December, 2004): 100-102. Praises the action in the poem and Logue's ability to make the reader see it happen.

Logue, Christopher. "Logue in Vogue." Interview by Liz Hoggard. *The Observer*, January 22, 2006. Logue gives a full-length interview after publication of *Cold Calls*, discussing his life and writing.

Ramsden, George. *Christopher Logue: A Bibliography, 1952-1997*. London: Stone Trough Books, 1997. The only fully annotated bibliography of Logue's many publications, small and large, and critical and journal articles.

Underwood, Simeon. *English Translators of Homer from George Chapman to Christopher Logue*. London: Northcote House, 1998. Fits Logue into the English tradition of Homer translation, comparing him to Alexander Pope especially.

David Barratt

WALT MCDONALD

Born: Lubbock, Texas; July 18, 1934

PRINCIPAL POETRY
Caliban in Blue, and Other Poems, 1976
One Thing Leads to Another, 1978
Anything, Anything, 1980
Burning the Fence, 1981
Working Against Time, 1981
Witching on Hardscrabble, 1985
The Flying Dutchman, 1987
After the Noise of Saigon, 1988
Rafting the Brazos, 1988
Night Landings, 1989
The Digs in Escondido Canyon, 1991
Where Skies Are Not Cloudy, 1993
Counting Survivors, 1995
Blessings the Body Gave, 1998
All Occasions, 2000
Climbing the Divide, 2003
Great Lonely Places of the Texas Plains, 2003
A Thousand Miles of Stars, 2004
Faith Is a Radical Master: New and Selected Poems, 2005

OTHER LITERARY FORMS

Walt McDonald's short stories have appeared widely in literary magazines, anthologies, and in the collection *A Band of Brothers: Stories from Vietnam* (1989). As a scholar and critic, he has published essays in many journals and reference works, and he coedited *A "Catch-22" Casebook* (1973) with Frederick Kiley and *Texas Stories and Poems* (1978) with James P. White.

With archivist Janet M. Neugebauer, McDonald has also published art books, including *All That Matters: The Texas Plains in Photographs and Poems* (1992) and *Whatever the Wind Delivers: Celebrating West Texas and the Near Southwest* (1999). These volumes present McDonald's poetry alongside historic photographs from the Southwest Collection, creating a strong aesthetic effect and an engaging interpretive social history.

Achievements

In addition to his poetry collections, Walt McDonald has published more than nineteen hundred poems in periodicals, and his works have appeared in more than sixty anthologies and textbooks. *The Flying Dutchman* won the Elliston Poetry Prize, *After the Noise of Saigon* won the Juniper Prize, and *Blessings the Body Gave* won the Ohio State University Press/*The Journal* Award in Poetry. In 1999, McDonald was named poet laureate of Lubbock, Texas (a lifetime honor), and he served as poet laureate of Texas in 2001. He has received two creative writing fellowships from the National Endowment for the Arts and six awards from the Texas Institute of Letters, including the Lon Tinkle Memorial Award for excellence sustained throughout a career. He won the A. C. Greene Literary Award in 2002, the Texas Book Festival Bookend Award in 2004, and the Western Writers of America's Spur Award in 2005. Four of his books—*Whatever the Wind Delivers*, *All That Matters*, *The Digs in 2Escondido Canyon*, and *Rafting the Brazos*—have won the Western Heritage Award from the National Cowboy Hall of Fame.

Biography

Walter Robert McDonald was born in Lubbock, Texas, to Vera Graves McDonald and C. A. McDonald, a veteran of World War I who had worked as a cowboy in his youth and later as a commercial painter. After earning his B.A. from Texas Tech University in 1956, McDonald was accepted into U.S. Air Force pilot training. Since his class would not begin for another year, he stayed at Texas Tech and completed his M.A. in English. In 1959, he married Carol Ham.

After pilot training, McDonald taught English at the Air Force Academy. Later he attended the Writers' Workshop at the University of Iowa, where he studied fiction writing with R.V. Cassill and Vance Bourjaily. At this time he had no interest in poetry and did not take a single poetry-writing class. After completing his Ph.D. in 1966, he returned to his teaching assignment at the Air Force Academy. In 1969, he was sent to Vietnam, where he served as a ground officer at Tan Son Nhut and Cam Ron from late 1969 to early 1970. After a medical discharge from the Air Force, McDonald returned to Texas Tech in 1971, where he started the creative writing program and remained as its director until 2000. He served as poetry editor for the Texas Tech University Press (1975-1995) and as Paul Whitfield Horn Professor of English and poet-in-residence until his retirement in 2002.

Although McDonald customarily writes in the first person, he is not the speaker in his poems. As he told interviewer Darryl Tippens,

> Always I'm writing poems, not autobiography. In the sense that poems expose some of my interests, obsessions, the regions of the mind I keep prowling, sure. But almost *only* in that sense. . . . I'm not there, frank and undisguised, in a poem or a short story. Experience is valuable for what it is; then the writing takes over.

In other words, he is not the soldier or the pilot, the cowboy or the hardscrabble rancher, who speaks from the pages. However, he does share a part of those characters' history and culture, and the common experience makes the poems rich and real.

Analysis

Though early in his career Walt McDonald was considered a Vietnam poet, he is best known as a Southwest regionalist. In an interview with Fred Alsberg, he suggested that his regions are not so much real places as "regions of the mind," "cluster[s] of images or obsessions that a writer draws on over and over, for poems." What he is describing is more accurately an intellectual complex than any particular place on the map. Thus as the term "region" applies to McDonald's work, "Texas" and "Vietnam" are rightly understood as regions, but so are "flying" and "family life."

Caliban in Blue, and Other Poems

Informed by his years as a pilot, service in Vietnam, and literary study, the poems in McDonald's first book, *Caliban in Blue, and Other Poems*, are carefully crafted, allusive, and detached. After reading the book, poet Donald Justice asked, "Where's Texas in your poems, Walt?"—a question that would prove to be a turning point. Though *Caliban in Blue, and Other Poems* was an excellent book, its foremost critical importance may reside in what it lacked: Texas.

McDonald responded with four collections in five years in which Vietnam recedes, replaced by increased attention to family relationships and southwestern scenes and culture. The ironic detachment of *Caliban in Blue, and Other Poems* erodes: The voice becomes more engaged, less critical, more forgiving of the human condition; literary allusions grow less frequent and less schoolish, more casually effective; the vignettes gain narrative continuity; the voice seems more aware of joy.

Burning the Fence

Burning the Fence culminates this transition, in that it establishes the trajectory of craft and theme that McDonald's later work would follow. All his "regions" are here: family, the mountains, flying, Texas, and Vietnam. Most important, however, *Burning the Fence* highlights a sophisticated merging of the physical and spiritual. "Tornado Alley," a poem ostensibly about a family's yearly storm preparations, becomes in its final line —"We search the sky. There's time"—a comment on the fragile comfort humans take in putting off death. "First Solo" warns a new pilot, "Give everything you have to the runway./ You will have all night to dream," clearly a statement about how to live one's life as much as how to land one's plane. Finally, the collection's title poem features a quasi-personified fence doing its best to resist burning. As the flames "waver within cracks" and the posts "hold in their flames," the fence is "unwilling to stop being fence," just as humans resist their own material and temporal limitations.

Hardscrabble Country of Texas

By the early 1980's, McDonald had mastered his method and charted his regions, the most frequented of which is the Texas hardscrabble country. Hundreds of his poems not only portray the region's countryside and culture but also exploit its metaphoric richness. By attending to everyday particulars, McDonald discovers its grandeur as well, portraying what critic Michael Hobbes has called the poet's "hardscrabble sublime." His apparently simple vignettes of common tasks consistently suggest truths about how to be human in a difficult world—Texas or elsewhere.

That often means acting on faith. In "Starting a Pasture" (from *Rafting the Brazos*), the narrator, against common sense and in spite of the real or imagined jeers of his neighbors, fences a new pasture in dry cotton country. The poem is at once a self-deprecating monologue and a testament to the stubbornness necessary to exist in a harsh environment. "Living on Buried Water" (from *After the Noise of Saigon*) portrays similar determination, lightened by persistent faith. The arid conditions naturally trigger poems about finding wells—often by "Witching with sycamore." "Sometimes a twig drags down to water," the speaker tells us, "and we risk digging." "We haven't found it," he confesses, but ends with an affirmation: "we believe it's here."

In "Digging for Buried Water" (from *The Flying Dutchman*), the narrator has risked shoveling a well and has struck water, resulting in a near-religious ecstasy. At the signs of success, the diggers begin scooping "like a rescue team in a cave-in/ delirious, convinced we hear tapping." "Rigging the Windmill" (from *Witching on Hardscrabble*) relates the story of a narrator whose labor has been successful, but its difficulty has suggested questions both practical and theological. He wonders "how many cows/ it will water, how many angels dance/ in whirlwind, how many times/ a pump goes around before breaking." "Wind and Hardscrabble" (from *The Flying Dutchman*) further reflects on the tenuous life. Only the cattle, untroubled by human doubt, do not worry the brutal heat—so long as the wind keeps turning the windmill's blades. The final image is one of Canaan-like abundance:

> Parched, they wade still pastures
> shimmering in heat waves
> and muzzle deep in stock tanks
> filled and overflowing.

Cattle may not realize the fragility of life, but cattlemen do. "The Witness of Dry Plains" (from *Rafting the Brazos*) portrays an arid world in which "a hawk rises high in the heavens," sees a rabbit, and dives, "wings stiff and wide, totally silent." McDonald often refers to nature "red in tooth and claw," but that situation is, it would seem, part of the sublimity. The death of the rabbit and the salvation of the hawk are a single act—a part of that balance in which humans are not simply observers but participants: "All is as it will be, in a desert./ Even the trees are balanced."

It takes a determination to stay. According to "Living on Open Plains" (from *Rafting the Brazos*), the only source of water, the Ogallala water table, is dropping three feet every year, but the narrator has no intention of leaving. Looking out into the dark evening, he claims, "wherever others on the road a mile away/ are going, we are here." To live on hardscrabble, people must be willing to accept "whatever the wind delivers." In the poem by that title (from *The Flying Dutchman* and the later *Whatever the Wind Delivers*), the narrator and his wife accept the dust, "the earth we live on, the dust our fingers/ string new fences on, holding each other/ one more night with loving words."

FLYING

McDonald has returned to his "flying" region throughout his career, often with vignettes that find power simply in their clear telling of a story. In "Ejecting from Jets" (from *Night Landings*), Kirk, the pilot, has become inverted and ejected "downward like a dart." In a flatly stated but horrific final image, his head is found crushed in his helmet, and "under the burned fuselage,/ the bones of his hand/ squeezing the trigger like a gun." Strong as this poem is, McDonald often reaches for a greater metaphorical resonance. A similar situation occurs in "For Dawes, on Takeoff" (from *The Flying Dutchman*), but with a different effect:

> They found his head
> stuck to his helmet.
> In trees downrange, they found his arms
> flung out from the body as if asking why.

The image of Kirk is one of desperation, but the image of Dawes, though similarly horrific, suggests greater philosophical significance: In death, Dawes asks the most important question, "Why?" "First Solo in Thunderstorms" (from *Night Landings*) works toward a more subtle thematic weight. The pilot, flying at night in hard weather, reflects that there is nothing to be done but fight the panic and believe that "storms like our lives/ have to end, that wings never/ level enough could hold me,/ that only a turbine was burning." Flying here clearly becomes a metaphor for human lives: frail, tenuous, demanding of faith in the face of doubt.

VIETNAM

Though the theme of Vietnam temporarily disappeared from McDonald's poems after *Caliban in Blue, and Other Poems*, it eventually returned in a few poems in each volume. Many of these present a soldier's straightforward emotional observations: "The Children of Saigon" (from *Night Landings*) and "The Food Pickers of Saigon" (from *After the Noise of Saigon*), for example, portray destitute Vietnamese eking out a living on the waste of American military bases. Poems such as "The Last Still Days in a Bunker" (from *Night Landings*) and "War Games" (from *After the Noise of Saigon*) create realistic scenes of the danger shared by many soldiers. More often, however, the Vietnam experience is felt as a subtle but controlling presence, one of several psychic forces.

By using that region in this more understated manner, McDonald achieves powerful compression and is able, often with a single term or phrase, to trigger a complex psychological response. In "After the Noise of Saigon" the Vietnamese landscape never appears—the poem is ostensibly about hunting in the mountains. However, the simple phrase "after the noise of Saigon" suggests a complex of meaning that informs the way readers understand the narrator's actions in pursuit of a wounded cougar. As the speaker states, "These blue trees have nothing/ and all to do with what I'm here for/ after the noise of Saigon." Because of the suggestiveness of the lines—and because, too, no doubt, his poems gain a cumulative effect as the volumes progress—such minimalism turns rich in the reading. Readers understand on a visceral level how hunting allows the speaker to work through his Vietnam experience, to handle "the simple bitter sap that rises in me/ like bad blood I need to spill/ out here alone in the silence." The bitterness that in the poems in *Caliban in Blue, and Other Poems* might have vented from a detached distance is here an emotional force that leads to a hard-won self-knowledge.

"For God in My Sorrows"

The potential pitfall of working and reworking the same regions is monotony. However, while McDonald's poems do use the language of his regions, or intellectual complexes, they are not merely about those regions. Texas and flying and Vietnam are less the subjects of McDonald's poems than they are languages in which to consider what it means to be human.

As critic Tippens has suggested, place for McDonald is "vehicle rather than tenor, and what he ultimately reveals through geography is timeless, universal, and spiritual." Other critics, too, have noted a tendency to deal more directly with religious questions in the later work. "For God in My Sorrows" (from *Blessings the Body Gave*) is nothing short of an impassioned plea: The speaker is reaching beyond that which can be seen, not to the stars but to "whatever scattered them." He seems to find his answer:

> When I close my eyes, magically,
> it's here. This, this is what I need,
>   without lights or cities
> man-made and dying, somehow to know I'm known.

Though close study of McDonald's work reveals intricate and sophisticated religious thinking throughout his career, this poem is arresting in its directness: The poet is not simply alluding to a story from the Bible or making observations about life that imply a Judeo-Christian understanding of evil and good. He is directly asking the most basic and speculative of theological questions. Further, he is doing so not in a narrative, but in something very close to a purely lyrical meditation.

CLIMBING THE DIVIDE

While McDonald's regions continue to provide the structure for his vignettes, in *Climbing the Divide*, the poet is most concerned with family, the tapestry of generations, the cycles of life, the inevitability of aging and death, and the timelessness of these cosmic realities. Everyday occurrences symbolize universal truths. In "Breathless for Twenty Seconds," the mysteries of a home movie starring the narrator's mother taken by his father before "the war" are juxtaposed with stanzas about her final illness: the lines ". . . Whatever/ our mother tried to tell us/ that last hour before she died, we'll never know. . . ." introduce immediate contemplation of the film itself, silent and brittle, yet nonetheless establishing the father's adoration of the mother despite the mystery of what went on during filming. Images of the "shaky ladder" on which the mother stands and "blank spots blinking by" suggest the tenuousness of one's actual control and perception in even the happiest of circumstances and the fast-approaching forgetfulness of eternity: "then nothing but the screen's bright light, the plastic clicking/ until I flick the switch."

As do most of McDonald's poems, "The War in Bosnia, the Beach at Kitty Hawk" includes more than one of his regions in creating his poetic tapestry. A cycle of seashells, from sea to beach to indoors as decorations, parallels the narrator's collecting of shells with his grandchildren. He reflects on his own collection of shells in Vietnam and on a son now flying in Bosnia. The idea of protectorship is rife in this collection, the shifting of it from one generation to the next and the bittersweet helplessness of letting it go. The poet reaches into past and future, emphasizing the timelessness of this cycle. In the single-stanza "The Gulls of Kitty Hawk," a highly metaphoric offering, gulls are stern, protective angels forever on guard, worshiping the eternal cycle, "the ebb and flow of boats," that makes their presence necessary. "That Night and Others Like It" addresses the enormity of time and brings in a religious aspect. The moon is "round like wagon wheels," a "Comanche moon, moon of ten thousand years of people/ huddled and wondering, drawing models of the moon," a cryptic symbol of eternity then and now. American ancestors rode on rickety wagon wheels, "warped and split wood," trusting in the heavens, "God's own book of stars," as their accustomed guide, the family Bible, had been destroyed in a fire. Their moon is "a huge, blank ball pockmarked over Lubbock." Though the place in which they find themselves is bleak, wild, and strange, they take comfort in the eternal wheel, the cycles of life and nature, which they recognize and trust instinctively. Though an astronaut, a personal friend of the narrator, later visits the moon and once there engages in such mundane human activities as taking golf swings, the orb remains mysterious yet visible, as it has over many centuries.

In "Fencing the Hardpan," universal cycles appear in the commonplace as the task of digging fencepost holes becomes an excursion into ancient ocean: "Who could believe this hot/ and dusty desert was a sea, crushed underfoot/ millions of years before Noah?" The "posts sunk in centuries and packed to hold four rolls of barbed wire in the wind" conjure the idea of cosmic yet ignorant building on what has passed and the layers and repetition of eons of which each human is a part, driven by "... hunger for God or fodder, pain in the heart/ or the scrotum, ovary and thumb squeezing hard/ to make an egg or fence, a fresh start/ on limited range under heaven, a home."

A Thousand Miles of Stars

Echoing the cycles, relinquishment, aging, and death of earlier works, this volume expands more fully into McDonald's regions and inserts a note of urgency not as apparent before. Even poems not overtly relating to these themes, such as war remembrance pieces, carry stronger hints of the endgame. In "October Compost," cooking imagery and compost create a paean to the solidarity of marriage, and in "Woodworker's Saturday Nights" and "Hoping to Break the Chain," which decry domestic violence, the reader glimpses a loss of power and strength and the accompanying fear.

In "Practice During the Cuban Missile Crisis," the narrator and other "boys" in pilot training fly above the field where the "men" who play professional football practice. The youths "who'd never been to war" flying over the adults playing a game provides a contrast, and people's ignorance of what the future holds and the youths' possible primary role in it parallels humanity's helplessness in sacrificing its most preciously protected members, those just beginning to soar, who are at "full power and climbing" yet already headed for that "red sun in the west." The narrator has survived that particular era but now is headed inevitably toward that red sun, which is growing nearer and nearer.

The ranch motif in "Harvest" presents the short, idyllic life of beef cattle, oblivious to their fast-approaching fate in the slaughterhouse. As "Artists of the cud and tongue,/ they carved delicious marble/ and waddled off to wade and lap the lake,// not bothered by wind or showers,/ the shout of cowboys by the corral,/ the final blast of air brakes,/ trucks from the slaughterhouse/ backed tight to loading docks." The cattle, like humans, are the architects or "artists" of their own demise, creating their own tombstones with their teeth, hastening death by eating and lazily enjoying life while blissfully ignoring its evitable end. Although this raises and allows the reader to answer the question, "What better way to go?" it nevertheless presents a chilling prospect.

In "All Salty Summer," the narrator wonders if his progeny will remember him, perhaps as he remembers and is curious about his own parents when he sees films and photographs of them. He concludes that despite hard work and generosity, all one has is materially and surely empty, like a "... conch/ washed up and hollow as a heart," and as much suffering and goodness as one may exhibit, all will be forgotten, unknown to future generations. Still, one should still fight the good fight and live one's life: "... Give,/ if we wish, just do./ The tomb takes care of time." Whether anyone remembers or not, and no one will, whatever has happened, has happened, and that is all that matters.

OTHER MAJOR WORKS

SHORT FICTION: *A Band of Brothers: Stories from Vietnam*, 1989.

EDITED TEXTS: *A "Catch-22" Casebook*, 1973 (with Frederick Kiley); *Texas Stories and Poems*, 1978 (with James P. White).

MISCELLANEOUS: *All That Matters: The Texas Plains in Photographs and Poems*, 1992 (with Janet M. Neugebauer); *Whatever the Wind Delivers: Celebrating West Texas and the Near Southwest*, 1999 (with Neugebauer).

BIBLIOGRAPHY

Beidler, Philip D. "Poets After Our War." In *Rewriting America: Vietnam Authors and Their Generation*. Athens: University of Georgia Press, 1991. Emphasizes the increasingly subtle and contextualized—but nevertheless important—role that Vietnam plays in McDonald's work.

Christianity and Literature 49, no. 2 (Winter, 2000). Edited by Darryl Tippens. This special issue focuses on McDonald's work. Includes an interview by Tippens, four articles on McDonald's poetry, and a selected bibliography.

Gotera, Vicente F. "Walter McDonald: After the (Machine) Noise of Saigon." In *Radical Vision: Poetry by Vietnam Veterans*. Athens: University of Georgia Press, 1994. Examines Vietnam poetry in relation to traditional American interpretive myths. Particularly insightful on the thematic place of technology in McDonald's work.

Hobbs, Michael. "Walter McDonald." In *Updating the Literary West*, edited by Thomas J. Lyon et al. Fort Worth: Texas Christian University Press, 1997. Useful article that introduces the concept of "hardscrabble sublime." Claims *Witching on Hardscrabble* is McDonald's best volume.

Hudgins, Andrew, and Janice Whittington, eds. *The Waltz He Was Born For: An Introduction to the Writing of Walt McDonald*. Lubbock: Texas Tech University Press, 2002. Contains sixteen essays on McDonald's religious themes, artistic techniques, regional topics, war themes, and general discussions. Also includes an interview with the poet.

William Jolliff
Updated by Mary Lang

WILFRED OWEN

Born: Oswestry, England; March 18, 1893
Died: Sambre Canal, France; November 4, 1918

PRINCIPAL POETRY
Poems by Wilfred Owen, 1920 (Siegfried Sassoon, editor)
The Poems of Wilfred Owen, 1931 (Edmund Charles Blunden, editor)
The Collected Poems of Wilfred Owen, 1963 (Cecil Day Lewis, editor)
Wilfred Owen: War Poems and Others, 1973 (Dominic Hibberd, editor)

OTHER LITERARY FORMS

Like many of the poets and artists of his time, Wilfred Owen professed a strong interest in the theater and supposedly drafted a play while recovering from shell shock in Craiglockhart military hospital in 1917, although no manuscript has appeared. Owen's letters, which have been collected, deserve mention for two reasons. First, the style reflects both the poetic temper of the man and the adherence to detail reflective of an age of correspondence that will probably never return. Second, and perhaps more important, Owen's letters record the transitions typical of most British soldiers who survived on the front for a long time: from resolve to do the soldier's duty, to disgust, fear, and depression, to the solemn acceptance of fate that extended service produced. One is fascinated by Owen's attempt to depict his life on the front for his naïve family and friends, as well as his ability to do so in spite of censorship.

ACHIEVEMENTS

Many commentators have emphasized that Wilfred Owen exhibited more potential to continue and enlarge the craft of poetry than any of the soldier-poets of World War I. He was a technician, an innovator, a "poet's poet" long before he was a proud soldier, a horrified combatant, and a victim. The kinds of criticisms applied to Rupert Brooke (immature, too much style, and too little substance) or Siegfried Sassoon (limited, more propaganda than art) have little validity when it comes to Owen. Indeed, in spite of his early death and limited canon, several twentieth century poets (among them W. H. Auden and Stephen Spender) have publicly stated their admiration for Owen's work or have used or expanded his methods. A notable dissenting voice is that of William Butler Yeats, who shocked many writers and critics by excluding Owen's work from his *Oxford Book of Modern Verse* (1936). Yeats defended his decision in a famous venomous blast, writing to Dorothy Wellesley that Owen was "unworthy of the poet's corner of a country newspaper. He is all blood, dirt, and sucked sugar stick ... (he calls poets, 'bards,' a girl a 'maid,' and talks about 'Titanic wars'). There is every excuse for him, but none for those who like him."

Wilfred Owen
(Library of Congress)

Owen's champions, however, far outnumber his detractors. It is true that all his work, from earliest to latest, is characterized by a kind of romantic embellishment, an intensity that borders on parody. This was more of a problem early in his career; as he matured, he assimilated the devices of John Keats, Percy Bysshe Shelley, and Lord Byron (among others), creating effective juxtapositions and dramatic tensions. This change was perhaps a result of the sophisticated and shocking material he found in his war experience.

Shocking the war poems are. Certainly among the most descriptive and horrifying of their era, they continue to penetrate minds supposedly benumbed by exposure to the twentieth century. In what became the preface to his first published volume of poetry, Owen wrote: "Above all, I am not concerned with Poetry. My subject is War, and the pity of War. The Poetry is in the pity." Indeed it appears true; of the many horrifying experiences suffered by the artists who recorded their experience in World War I (Robert Graves, Sassoon, Isaac Rosenberg, Edward Thomas, Brooke, and others), it is Owen's cries that are the loudest and most anguished. Owen seems to have been more outraged than most by the lamentable tragedy of fine young men lost in the struggle. What is surprising, however, is that the resultant verse is never self-indulgent, self-pitying; rather, Owen was able to focus his vision outward. He concluded sadly in the preface previously cited that "all a poet can do today is warn." Owen's disgust with the war he experienced and despised is readily apparent, but it goes beyond immediacy and is elevated to prophecy as well.

Another of Owen's goals, through all the years of fighting and suffering, was to cling to his artistic voice, to expand his abilities, to become a better poet. He sought new ways to use language, and his mastery of alliteration, onomatopoeia, assonance, and dissonance have been often cited. Perhaps his most consistently brilliant device was the use of slant rhyme (or "half rhyme" or "pararhyme" as it has been called), the subtle and effective mixture of vowel dissonance and consonant assonance most often effectively employed at the end of his lines (for example, "cold" and "killed").

The effect of Owen's expert use of form (he was a master of sonnets and elegiac mood) and his fluency (both traditional and experimental) was to suggest a poet who would have been very much at home with modernism, but who never would have forgotten his literary heritage. In fact, an observation often made concerning the poetry of Thomas Hardy, that his was the soul of the nineteenth century anticipating twentieth century innovations, applies equally well to Owen. That Owen was able to sustain his brilliance under the stress of battle makes the reader appreciate his achievement all the more.

Biography

Wilfred Edward Salter Owen was born in Oswestry, Shropshire, England, on March 18, 1893, the first child of Tom and Susan Owen. Owen's mother was a devout and cautious woman; his father was an active, rough-hewn, hardworking sort who was nostalgically attracted to the sea and those who sailed it. The early years of their marriage and Owen's childhood were sometimes difficult, characterized by several moves, frequent if not severe financial difficulties, and tensions produced by his parents' conflicting characters. Their union produced four children. Owen's younger brother Harold became a successful artist and devoted much of his adult life to chronicling the life of his more famous war-poet brother.

Owen was sent to Birkenhead Institute for his first years of schooling; his father approved of the discipline for which the school was noted, but Owen probably profited most from an adoring teacher and early exposure to the pleasures of literature. He also showed a great interest in religious matters, much to the delight of his mother. In 1907, the family moved to Shrewsbury, where Owen enrolled in the technical school. There he read diligently and began to compose serious essays (some on politics, some on art theory) and put down his first attempts at verse.

Somewhat confused about his future after his matriculation examination at London

University in 1911, Owen accepted an opportunity to become a lay assistant to the Vicar of Dunsden. His activities were many-faceted, from the intellectual (extensive reading and attending lectures) to the practical affairs of the parish (playing with children and assisting the poor). His poetry began to mature, not so much in its subject matter as in its increasing flexibility of language. For reasons that remain unclear, Owen became disenchanted with his commitment to the vicarage and left Dunsden. After a period of contemplation, during which he struggled with his health, he was offered, and he accepted, a post to teach English at the Berlitz School in Bordeaux. He enjoyed the experience and the climate was beneficial, even as the clouds of war gathered over Europe.

Because Owen was in France during the "exhilarating" first part of the war, a time when nationalism and enthusiasm for battle possessed young men like him in England, his wavering emotions regarding the conflict are understandable. He had left his job in late 1915 to assume a position as a private tutor to a well-to-do family in Merignac, France. His correspondence reveals a confused but honor-bound attitude toward his own responsibilities: appalled at the destruction and suffering so near by, confident and proud of his ability to serve, excited at the prospect of taking his gift for poetry into battle. He briefly investigated business opportunities, flirted with but rejected the idea of joining either the French army or the Italian cavalry, and in September, 1915, returned to England, where he enlisted with the Artists' Rifles.

During his training, he sought not only to become a fine soldier but also to become familiar with many people active in the literary circles of London. He met Harold Monro of the *Poetry Review* and lived briefly in a flat adjacent to the magazine's offices. Owen performed admirably as a soldier and claimed to enjoy his work, though he appeared uncomfortable, out of place with his peers. He was well liked, however, and in June, 1916, Second Lieutenant Owen was attached to the Fifth Battalion of the Manchester Regiment.

After a few months of polishing, Owen was sent with thousands of his fellows to the front. The Somme offensive, begun in July, 1916, had been stalled tragically for several months, and war planners had determined to begin another push as the new year began. Immediately, Owen was struck by the difference between the grotesque reality of the war zone and the appallingly inaccurate depictions of the war at home. These sentiments, together with supportive vivid details, were relayed home regularly. Still, he took comfort in his devotion to duty and in writing, criticizing, and discussing poetry, pleasures that he never neglected.

Writing and fighting with distinction for six months, Owen showed signs of suffering from the strain and was finally sent to Craiglockhart military hospital, where he was diagnosed as suffering from neurasthenia, or shell shock. His stay there was to be crucial, not only for his health but for his poetic and intellectual development as well. Owen participated in many of the therapeutic activities offered by the hospital. Also at Craiglockhart was Siegfried Sassoon, the distinguished soldier, poet, and most recently a virulent antiwar spokesperson. The two became friends and eventually Sassoon became audience and critic for the work that began to reveal Owen's growing artistry. Robert Graves, a friend of Sassoon and a regular visitor to the hospital, also encouraged Owen to continue his work. In December, Owen was dismissed and returned to London, where he pursued other contacts in the literary establishment. (Later, in 1920, Sassoon became responsible for collecting and publishing selections of Owen's poetry.)

In spite of his increasing disgust at the carnage of battle, amply evident in his poems of this time, Owen was compelled to return to the war, and during the summer of 1918, he was granted permission to cross to France. Participating in the heavy fighting preceding and during the armistice talks, Owen became a respected and competent soldier, winning the military cross. Invigorated artistically by his friendship with prominent writers during his recuperation, he sent poems and lively letters back to England. On November 4, 1918, one week before the armistice, Owen was killed while leading his troops across the Sambre Canal.

Analysis

Wilfred Owen's most memorable, and often cited, works reveal several characteristic traits. Romantic imagery dominates his work, regardless of whether it is war-inspired. Owen was a passionate disciple of Keats; he made pilgrimages to Keats's shrines and felt a personal affinity for the great Romantic poet. There is also brutal realism in Owen's war descriptions. Had Owen not been there himself, the reader might be tempted to believe the verse exaggerated, such is its power. The poetry is also characterized by the sensual glorification of male beauty and bravery, and the hideous waste of wartime slaughter. Such elements have prompted a plentitude of conjecture about Owen's personal relationships; but the sentiment with which he glorifies male qualities in his early years and the depth with which he expressed his concern for his fellows in his war years are not, in his case, cause for prurient speculation by the psychological critics. The simple fact concerning Owen's poetry is that he wrote about his comrades in ways that were never offensive and always eloquent.

"To Poesy"

Innovations and experiments with the potential of language give Owen's best work a quality that is more of the modernistic than the Edwardian or Georgian temper. In spite of its strength and ferocity, however, there is an equally noticeable fragility. Owen's earliest extant attempts at poetry (according to Jon Stallworthy, it is probable that his first efforts were burned by his mother at his death, at the poet's request) reflect a somewhat awkward sentimentalism. He laboriously expresses his adoration for the muse in "To Poesy." The poem, an odd beginning for one who would later write that he was "not concerned with poetry," contains a variety of religious, erotic quest images (none very effective) designed to signify the "purer love" of his aesthetic principles. Also noticeable at this time in Owen's poetic infancy are poems and fragments that either imitate Keats or illustrate his exultant emotions after having visited locales associated with Keats's life and work. Again, the sentiments are apparent, if hardly laudable artistically, as in "SONNET, written at Teignmouth, on a Pilgrimage to Keats's House." Its sestet begins: "Eternally may sad waves wail his death,/ Choke in their grief 'mongst rocks where he has lain." Still, the young poet shows signs of searching for more sophisticated methods. A revealing fragment from an early manuscript shows that Owen had penciled in lines to attract attention to the interesting effect of half-rhymed words, "tomb, home," "thou, below," "spirit, inherit."

"DULCE ET DECORUM EST"

The effect that one experiences when turning from Owen's earlier works to his mature verse is dramatic indeed. "Bent double, like old beggars under sacks,/ Knock-kneed, coughing like hags, we cursed through sludge," begins "Dulce et Decorum Est," one of his most often cited depictions of the reality of war. An interesting juxtaposition established at the beginning is that of the simple exhaustion of the troops who "marched asleep... lame... blind... drunk with fatigue," and the nightmarish, almost surreal atmosphere of the battle, lighted by "haunting flares," pierced by the "hoots" of artillery fire, and pervaded by the sickening presence of gas. The soldier who has donned his gas mask looks through "misty panes" at thick green light, as if submerged in a "green sea." The nightmare is unrelieved by the passage of battle as the persona sees "in all my dreams," without relief, a comrade who was unable to survive the attack, who lurches grotesquely, "guttering, choking, drowning."

After witnessing these events, the reader is drawn more intimately into the scene, as the persona uses the second person, asking directly if "you too" could imagine witnessing eyes "writhing in his face", and blood that "gargles from froth-corrupted lungs." As Owen builds the intensity and visceral detail of his description, he is preparing the reader for the ironic and bitter conclusion that uses a tag from Horace (*Odes*, 23 B.C.E., 13 B.C.E.; English translation, 1621), familiar to schoolboys and used to glorify the war effort: *Dulce et decorum est pro patria mori* (it is sweet and honorable and proper to die for your country). For Owen, however, the sentiments expressed in the phrase can now only be considered an "old lie" that cannot honestly be told to children anymore. Owen brilliantly half-rhymes in the last three lines the words "glory" (what children seek) and "mori" (what happens to them in war).

"STRANGE MEETING"

Another nightmare vision serves as the stimulus for a greatly admired work. "Strange Meeting" recounts a frightful reverie, an encounter between two soldiers in hell. Their confrontation, unified by dramatic dialogue, is inspired by the horrors of war, but it also serves as an occasion for Owen to comment on poetic principles and to prophesy (quite accurately and depressingly) on the nature of the new century.

Owen begins by describing his descent down "some profound dull tunnel," arriving at a shattered place where "encumbered sleepers groaned." He is surprised when one of these fellows jumps up; there is a moment of recognition not only between them but also of their mutual circumstance, standing "in Hell." Owen comforts his opposite in a dramatic understatement, suggesting that even here, dead, in hell, there "is no cause to mourn." Such was the gruesome reality above ground, alive, in battle. The stranger is in no mood to be assuaged, because he too had been a poet who ventured and strove for "the wildest beauty in the world." Thus, the poet's life is lost, but that loss is not to be lamented nearly as much as the loss of the truth he might have written, the "truth untold." The ultimate tragedy is not temporary, but lasting, as future generations will be unaware of the truth of war that the poet could have recorded. Instead of rejecting the past, those generations will embrace it, probably with devastating efficiency. Had he lived, the poet would also have battled, not with instruments of war, but with his "courage" and "wisdom." His would have been a war to dominate men's minds, fought when men wearied of bleeding and death, a soothing message of "truths that lie too deep for taint" that would have flowed from his "spirit."

Owen does not wish to end the poem at this abstract level, seeking instead to pull the reader back to the immediacy of war. Even though the setting is highly contrived, Owen provides a "surprise ending" that serves two purposes: to impress upon the reader the brutal infighting characteristic of many World War I battles, and to ridicule the notion of nationalism and emphasize the common humanity of all the war's combatants. The early "recognition," a foreshadowing device, had not been between friends but between enemies, as the poet-narrator had evidently slain the poet-prophet with a bayonet. Rather than continuing either the hostilities or the discussion, the soldier who had been thus murdered offers a simpler, but more final and disturbing alternative: "Let us sleep now. . . ."

"Arms and the Boy"

In other poems, Owen draws attention to the waste of young men slaughtered. "Arms and the Boy" (an ironic revision of the opening of Vergil's *Aeneid*, (c. 29-19 B.C.E.; English translation, 1553; "Arms and the Man I sing. . . .") is a three-stanza portrait of youthful innocence confronting the awful mysteries of the instruments of war. He emphasizes the apparent discomfort as a boy tests a bayonet "keen with hunger for flesh" and caresses a bullet that seeks "to nuzzle in the hearts of lads." These gestures are not natural for youngsters whose "teeth seem for laughing round an apple" (the immediate thought here is of a soldier's death-grimace). Moreover, the human animal was not designed for battle; there are "no claws behind his fingers supple." His appearance is of gentle, delicate demeanor, a face framed with "curls," as opposed to the brutish nobility of animals that possess "talons" and "antlers."

"ANTHEM FOR DOOMED YOUTH"

Similar sentiments, now supported by religious imagery, are expressed in "Anthem for Doomed Youth," a sonnet that illustrates Owen's fusion of the traditional elegiac mood with the realities of modern warfare. The opening question serves as an example: "What passing-bells for these who die as cattle?" The answer is that the only possible form of lamentation for the war dead is the cacophonous sounds of war, "the stuttering rifle's rapid rattle." Not only are religious ceremonies out of the question, but they would also be a "mockery." Here Owen shows the extent to which his disillusionment with organized religion had gone. Instead of the glow of holy candles, the poet finds light in "their eyes." They will wear no "pall," but will be recognized and remembered through the "pallor of girl's brows." The essence of this poem is that in such times as these, Christianity seems incapable of providing its traditional comfort. The memorial of the dead soldiers will not be "flowers" but memories held by "patient minds." Their legacy, sadly and not of their making, is but darkness, at "each slow dusk a drawing-down of blinds."

In a sense, Owen's poetic legacy can also inspire darkness for the reader. His work is highly educational, however, and thus valuable, especially when read in the context of World War I and in contrast to that of some of his fellow soldier-poets. The reader, ultimately grateful for the work that Owen left, is intrigued by what he might have become.

OTHER MAJOR WORKS

NONFICTION: *Collected Letters*, 1967 (Harold Owen and John Bell, editors); *Selected Letters*, 1998 (Bell, editor).

BIBLIOGRAPHY

Breen, Jennifer. *Wilfred Owen: Selected Poetry and Prose*. London: Routledge, Chapman & Hall, 1988. Breen does an excellent job of giving a brief analysis of Owen's major poems and supports her opinions by subjectively looking at his personal correspondence to gain insight for her analysis. Contains a limited bibliography.

Hibberd, Dominic. *Wilfred Owen: A New Biography*. Chicago: I. R. Dee, 2003. A fine biography, well-documented and engaging. Hibberd's detailed look at Owen's life discusses previously unexplored territory.

Hipp, Daniel. *The Poetry of Shell Shock: Wartime Trauma and Healing in Wilfred Owen, Ivor Gurney, and Siegfried Sassoon*. Jefferson, N.C.: McFarland, 2005. Contains a chapter on Owen, focusing on the topic of shell shock in his poetry.

Owen, Wilfred. *Wilfred Owen: Collected Letters*. Edited by Harold Owen and John Bell. New York: Oxford University Press, 1967. Follows the life of Owen from the time he was five until his death at the age of twenty-five, through his letters to his family and friends. Includes an index.

Purkis, John. *A Preface to Wilfred Owen*. London: Longman, 1999. A brief biographical and critical introduction to Owen and his work. Includes bibliographical references and an index.

Simcox, Kenneth. *Wilfred Owen: Anthem for a Doomed Youth.* London: Woburn, 1987. Begins with Owen's interaction with his family, focusing on his influential mother. His religious background is highlighted as Simcox reviews the major issues in Owen's poetry, amply augmented with examples from his primary works. Includes an index.

Stallworthy, Jon, ed. *The Poems of Wilfred Owen.* New York: W. W. Norton, 1985. An intensive study into the chronological sequence of 103 poems and 12 fragments by Owen. Factual footnotes allow readers a concise foundation from which to formulate their own explications.

_____. *Wilfred Owen.* New York: Oxford University Press, 1995. A full and sensitive illustrated biography of the short-lived poet and war hero. Appendixes offer genealogies, fragments of previously unpublished poems, a bibliography of Owen's library, and an index.

White, Gertrude. *Wilfred Owen.* New York: Twayne, 1969. Traces Owen's maturation as a poet from dreamy, romantic imagery to the harsh realities of World War I. Includes a bibliography and an index.

Robert Edward Graalman, Jr.

SÁNDOR PETŐFI

Born: Kiskörös, Hungary; January 1, 1823
Died: Segesvár, Hungary; July 31, 1849

PRINCIPAL POETRY
A helység-kalapácsa, 1844 (*The Hammer of the Village*, 1873)
Versek, 1842-1844, 1844 (*Poems, 1842-1844*)
Cipruslombok Etelke sírjáról, 1845 (*Cypress Leaves from the Tomb of Etelke*, 1972)
János Vitéz, 1845 (*Janos the Hero*, 1920; revised as *John the Hero*, 2004)
Szerelem gyöngyei, 1845 (*Pearls of Love*, 1972)
Versek II, 1845 (*Poems II*, 1972)
Felhok, 1846 (*Clouds*, 1972)
Összes költeményei, 1847, 1848 (*Collected Poems*, 1972)
"Széchy Mária," 1847
Az apostol, 1848 (*The Apostle: A Narrative Poem*, 1961)
Sixty Poems, 1948
Sándor Petőfi: His Entire Poetic Works, 1972

OTHER LITERARY FORMS

Sándor Petőfi (PEHT-uh-fee) wrote several short narrative pieces for the fashion magazines and periodicals of his day. "A szökevények" (the runaways) was published in the *Pesti Divatlap* in 1845. The following year, his melodramatic novella *A hóhér kötele* (*The Hangman's Rope*, 1973) was published in the same magazine. In 1847, he published two tales in *Életképek*: "A nagyapa" (the grandfather) and "A fakó leány s a pej legény" (the pale girl and the ruddy boy). "Zöld Marci," a drama written in 1845, was destroyed by the author when it was not picked up for theatrical production; the bombastic *Tigris és hiéna* (tiger and hyena) was withdrawn from production but published in 1847. The most valuable prose Petőfi wrote was the personal essay and brief diary entries relating to the events of March, 1848. "Úti jegyzetek" ("journal notes") was serialized in *Életképek* in 1845; in 1847, *Hazánk* published his "Úti levelek Kerényi Frigyeshez" (travel notes to Frigyes Kerényi). *Lapok Petőfi Sándor naplójából* (pages from the diary of Sándor Petőfi) appeared in 1848. In addition, his letters, published in the 1960 *Petőfi Sándor összes prózai muvei és levelezése* (complete prose works and correspondence of Sándor Petőfi), provide good examples of his easy prose style. Early in his career, Petőfi earned some money doing translations of works by such authors as Charles de Bernard, George James, and William Shakespeare. In 1848, Petőfi's translation of Shakespeare's *Coriolanus* (pr. c. 1607-1608) appeared. He also began a translation of *Romeo and Juliet* (pr. c. 1595-1596) but died before finishing it.

Achievements

Sándor Petőfi has been called Hungary's greatest lyric poet. He made the folk song a medium for the expression of much of the national feeling of the nineteenth century, establishing a new voice and introducing new themes into Hungarian poetry. Building on past traditions, he revitalized Hungarian poetry. Though a revolutionary, he did not break with all tradition, but rather sought a return to native values. Choosing folk poetry as his model, he endorsed its values of realism, immediacy, and simplicity. He also exploited to the fullest its ability to present psychological states through natural and concrete images, with an immediacy that had an impact beyond the poetic sphere.

Petőfi's poetry is the "poetry of Hungarian life, of the Hungarian people," according to Zsolt Beöty. However, although Petőfi drew on popular traditions, he did so with the conscious art of a cultivated poet. This combination of Romantic style and realistic roots gives his poetry a freshness and sincerity that has made him popular both in Hungary and abroad. More important, it has assured him a place in the development of Hungarian lyricism.

Petőfi's impact, however, goes beyond Hungary. He appeals to the emotions yet maintains a distance: His themes seldom lose their universality. For Petőfi, the revolutionary ideal of the nineteenth century applied equally to politics and poetics. Folk orientation and nationalism were equally an organic part of his poetry, and his revolutionary ideals were unthinkable without a popular-national input. Thus, he both mirrors and creates a new world, a new type of person, and a new society. He is an iconoclast and revolutionary only when he perceives existing values and systems as denying the basic value of human life. His endorsement of conventional values of family, home, and a just social order can be understood only in this context.

Style and form, matter and manner were never separate for Petőfi. A consummate craftsperson and a conscious developer of the style and vocabulary of mid-nineteenth century Hungarian poetry, he knew that in helping to create and enrich the new poetic language, he was bringing poetry to the masses. In exploring the language, he made poetic what had been commonplace.

Following in the footsteps of the great Hungarian language reformers and poets of the late eighteenth and early nineteenth centuries, Petőfi expanded the scope of poetry in both theme and language. Like William Wordsworth and Robert Burns in English literature, he placed emphasis on everyday themes and the common person. It would be unfair to the earlier molders of Hungarian poetry, from Mihály Csokonai Vitéz through Károly Kisfaludi, Dániel Berzsenyi, and Mihály Vörösmarty, to minimize their influence on Petőfi. To a great extent, they created a modern Hungarian poetic medium no longer restricted by the limitations of language. Simultaneously, they created a poetic language and encouraged the taste of the public for native themes and native styles. Classical and modern European influences had been absorbed and naturalized by these men. The German influence, strong for both political and demographic reasons, had also been greatly reduced. The intellectual and cultural milieu, in fact, changed so dramatically in these years that German- language theaters and publications were becoming Hun garian in language as well as sentiment. For example, *Hazánk* (homeland), a periodical to which Petőfi contributed regularly, was called, until 1846, *Vaterland*.

As a poet of a many-faceted national consciousness, Petőfi was always committed to the simple folk, to the common person. He did not categorically support the unlettered peasant in favor of the clerk, nor did he condemn the class hierarchy of earlier times without cause. He did condemn, however, inequity and petrified institutions that did not allow for the free play of talent. He endorsed human values above all.

Biography

Sándor Petőfi was born on January 1, 1823, in Kiskörös—a town located on the Hungarian plain—to István Petrovics, innkeeper and butcher, and his wife, Mária Hruz. Petőfi's father's family, in spite of the Serbian name (which Petőfi was to change when he chose poetry as his vocation), had lived in Hungary for generations. His mother, Slovak by birth, came from the Hungarian highlands in the north. Such an ethnic mix was not unusual, and the young man grew up in what he himself considered the "most Magyar" area of all Hungary, the region called Kis Kúnság (Little Cumania) on the Great Plains. Much of his poetry celebrates the people and the landscape of this region: Though not the first to do so, he was more successful than earlier poets in capturing the moods of the region known as the Alföld (lowlands).

Petőfi's father was wealthy, and desiring his sons to be successful, he determined to educate them. The young Petőfi was sent to a succession of schools that were designed to give him a good liberal education in both Hungarian and German, among them the lower gymnasium (high school) at Aszód, from which he graduated valedictorian. He was active in various literary clubs and, through the zeal of several nationalistic teachers, became acquainted with the prominent authors of the eighteenth century: Berzsenyi, József Gvadányi, and Vitéz, as well as the popular poets of the day, Vörösmarty and József Bajza.

The year spent at Selmec, in the upper division of the gymnasium, was marred by his father's financial troubles and by Petőfi's personal clashes with one of his teachers. As a result of these pressures, he yielded to his penchant for the theater and on February 15, 1839, when he was barely sixteen, ran away with a group of touring players.

Petőfi's decision to become an actor was not made lightly, for he knew the value of an education, and he made every effort to complete his studies later. The years that followed were particularly hard ones. Petőfi roamed much of the country, traveling mostly on foot. He took advantage of the hospitality offered at the farms and manor houses, and thus he came to know a wide spectrum of society. On these travels, he also developed his appreciation for nature, uniting his love for it with the objectivity of one who lives close to it. Since acting could not provide him a living, Petőfi decided to join the army, but he was soon discharged for reasons of ill health. In the months following, he became friends with Mór Jókai, later a prominent novelist but at that point a student at Pápa. Petőfi, determined to complete his studies, attended classes there. He joined the literary society and gained recognition as a poet: "A borozó" (the wine drinker), his first published poem, appeared in the prestigious *Athenaeum* in May, 1842, and he also won the society's annual festival.

Petőfi, then nineteen, considered himself a poet; he was determined that this would be his vocation. He planned to finish his studies, to become a professional man able to support himself and to help his parents and also to pursue his chief love, poetry. When a promised position as tutor fell through, however, he was once more forced to leave school and to make his living as an actor, or doing whatever odd jobs (translating, copying) he found. In the winter of 1843-1844, ill and stranded in Debrecen, he copied 108 of his poems, determined to take them to Vörösmarty for an opinion. If the verdict was favorable, Petőfi would remain a poet and somehow earn his living by his pen; if not, he would give up poetry forever. The venture succeeded, and this volume, *Poems, 1842-1844*, firmly established his reputation.

A subscription by the nationalistic literary society Nemzeti Kör provided Petőfi with some funds, and on July 1, 1844, he accepted a position as assistant editor of the *Pesti Divatlap*. From this time on, he earned his living chiefly with his pen. Besides submitting shorter pieces to a variety of journals, he published two heroic poems and a cycle of love lyrics. In March of 1845, he left the *Pesti Divatlap* to tour northern Hungary. A rival journal, *Életképek*, published the series of prose letters, "Journal Notes," in which Petőfi reported his impressions of the people and scenes he encountered. Two more volumes of poetry, *Pearls of Love* and *Poems II*, appeared. Although he became increasingly dedicated to *Életképek*, Petőfi continued to publish in a variety of journals.

In 1846, while campaigning for better remuneration for literary contributors to journals—founding the Society of Ten and even leading a brief strike-—Petőfi published another volume of poetry, *Clouds*, and a novella, *The Hangman's Rope*. In the fall, he took a trip to eastern Hungary, intending to publish a second series of travel reports. Early in the trip, however, he met Júlia Szendrey, and the travelogue, as well as his life, changed dramatically. He fell in love with her almost at their first meeting. They were engaged and, despite parental opposition, gained a grudging approval and were married a year later. Júlia was to provide the inspiration for Petőfi's best love lyrics. Sharing his political and national convictions, she encouraged his involvement in politics, even in the campaigns of 1848 and 1849. Petőfi's "Úti levelek Kerényi Frigyeshez" (travel notes to Frigyes Kerényi) thus became more than an account of the customs and sights of Transylvania and the eastern part of the country; they show the development of the relationship between Petőfi and Júlia, their courtship and marriage.

The year 1846 also marked the beginning of Petőfi's friendship with János Arany. Petőfi had been drawn to Arany when the latter won a literary prize with his epic *Toldi*

(1847; English translation, 1914). Feeling that they were kindred spirits, Petőfi wrote immediately—and also composed a poem in praise of the then-unknown man from Nagyszalonta. Later, after they met, their friendship deepened and, with it, Arany's influence on the younger man. Arany helped form the objective vein in Petőfi's poetry. Thus, the influence of a worthy mentor who could rein the excesses of his emotions helped Petőfi attain the perfection of the poems he wrote between 1846 and 1849.

Finally, Petőfi also achieved a measure of financial independence through a contract signed in August of 1846 with the publisher Gustáv Emich for the publication of his *Collected Poems*. This relationship assured Petőfi a regular, if modest, income and gave him a friend and adviser who would stand him in good stead in his last, troubled years.

After his marriage and brief honeymoon at Koltó, the hunting castle lent to him by Count Teleki, Petőfi and his wife returned to Pest in November of 1847. Several poems commemorate the weeks at Koltó, including "Szeptember végen" (at the end of September), regarded by many critics as one of the masterpieces of world literature. In Pest, too, Petőfi continued to write, contributing to various journals. His poetry of this period included political themes, and he became increasingly involved in the liberal movements that were sweeping the city. While the seat neither of the Diet nor of the king, Buda and Pest were still regarded by many Hungarians as the rightful center of the country. There was agitation to have the capital returned from Pozsony, now that the reason for its move, the presence of the Turks, no longer existed. Social, legal, and economic reforms were sought, and the cessation of certain military measures, such as the special occupation status of Transylvania and parts of the southeastern region of the country; simply, the Hungarian people desired the reunion of their artificially divided country.

As one of the leaders of the young radicals, Petőfi took part in these political activities, which were to culminate in the demonstrations of March 15, 1848. He had written his "Nemzeti dal" (national ode) the previous day for a national demonstration against Austria. During the day, when his poem, along with the formal demands expressed in the Twelve Points, was printed and distributed without the censor's approval as an affirmation of freedom of the press, Petőfi was in the forefront, reciting the ode several times for the gathering crowds. Through a series of negotiations, acceptance in principle of the program of reform was won. The revolution—as yet a peaceful internal reform—had begun.

When both public safety and national security seemed threatened by the invitations of the Croatian army of Count Josef Jellačić and similar guerrilla bands, Petőfi became a member of the Nemzetor (national guard), which he was to commemorate in one of his poems. He joined the staff of the *Életképek*, which had been edited by his friend Jókai since April, 1848. He published his diary on the events of March and April, 1848, a lively if fragmented account of his activities and thoughts in those days, and also a translation of Shakespeare's *Coriolanus*. In September, he undertook a recruiting tour, and in October, he joined the regular army. The War of Independence was in full force by this time, relations between the Hungarians and the Habsburgs having deteriorated completely. Even the fact that Júlia was expecting the couple's first child in December did not allow Petőfi to draw back from the struggle he had so often advocated in his poems.

Commissioned as a captain in the army on October 15, 1848, Petőfi was assigned to Debrecen. He had difficulties with the discipline and procedures of army life, however, until transferred to the command of General József Bem, a Polish patriot and skillful general who was winning the Transylvanian campaign. Through the first half of 1849, Petőfi participated in the Transylvanian campaigns, visiting his wife and son whenever a lull in the fighting or his adjutants' duties allowed. On July 31, 1849, he took part in the Battle of Segesvár and was killed by Cossack forces of the Russian army, which had come to aid the Austrians according to the agreements of the Holy Alliance. Petőfi's body was never found, because he was buried, according to eyewitnesses, in a mass grave. This fact, however, was not known until much later, and many rumors of his living in exile, in hiding, or in a Siberian labor camp were circulated in the 1850's, proof of the people's reluctance to accept his death. His widow's remarriage was severely criticized, though eventually the poet's death had to be accepted. His poetry, however, continues to live.

ANALYSIS

Antal Szerb remarked in his 1934 work, *Magyar irodalomtörténet* (history of Hungarian literature), "Petőfi is a biographical poet. There is no break between the experience and its poetic expression." Sándor Petőfi's poetry, although best analyzed from a biographical perspective, is not autobiographical; its themes and topics span a surprisingly broad range for a career compressed into such a few years.

THE HUNGARIAN TRADITION

In the early poems, written from 1842 to 1844, Petőfi had already established his distinctive style and some of his favorite themes. Although he was influenced both by classical poets (especially Horace) and by foreign poets of his own era—Friedrich Schiller, Heinrich Heine, the Hungarian-born Austrian poet Nikolaus Lenau, and probably the English poets Lord Byron and Percy Bysshe Shelley—Petőfi believed that Hungarian poetry must free itself of its dependence on foreign rules of prosody in order to reflect native meters and patterns.

In this, he was not the first: The tradition of medieval verse and song had survived and had been revived by previous generations of poets; the seventeenth century epic of Miklós Zrinyi had continued to inspire poets; the folk song, too, had been cultivated by earlier poets, notably Csokonai in the late eighteenth century and Kisfaludi in the early nineteenth century. What was new in Petőfi's approach was his conscious effort to establish a poetic style that put native meters and current speech at the center of his art.

Proof of his success is found not only in the immense and ongoing popularity of his poetry among all classes of the population, but also in the recognition accorded him by Arany, who was later to define the "Hungarian national meter" chiefly on the basis of a study of Petőfi's use of native rhythms.

Petőfi's early poems were written primarily in the folk-song style. In subject, they ranged from Anacreontics to love lyrics to personal and meditative poems. The love poems are light and playful exercises without great emotional commitment, but they present the people and locale Petőfi was later to make his own: the *puszta*, its people, plants, and animals. In "Egri hangok" (sounds of Eger), however, the Anacreontic is used for a serious and patriotic purpose, anticipating Petőfi's later use of this genre.

The poem grew out of a personal experience: Walking from Debrecen to Pest in February of 1844, in his gamble to be recognized as a poet or to abandon this vocation, he was welcomed by the students of the college. The poem opens with a quiet winter scene: On the ground, there is snow; in the skies, clouds; but for the poet everything is fine, because he is among friends in a warm room, drinking the fine wines of Eger. The mood is not rowdy but serene and content. Juxtaposing natural imagery and emotion in a manner reminiscent of folk song, he states: "If my good spirits would have seeds:/ I'd sow them above the snow,/ And when they sprout, a forest of roses/ Would crown winter." The mood here, however, only sets the stage for the patriotic sentiment that is the poem's real purpose. Petőfi moves on to consider the historical associations of the city of Eger, the scene of one of the more memorable sieges of the Turkish wars; thus, he examines the decline of Hungary as a nation. He does not dwell long on nostalgia, however, but turns back to the good mood of the opening scenes to predict a bright future for the country.

THE FAMILY

Petőfi's early poems about his family reveal the emotional depth of his best work. They are full of intense yet controlled feeling, but the setting, the style, and the diction remain simple; a realistic note is never lacking. Contemplating a reunion with the mother he has not seen for some time, he rehearses various greetings, only to find that in the moment of reunion he "hangs on her lips—wordlessly,/ Like the fruit on the tree."

The felicitous choice of image and metaphor is one of the greatest attractions of Petőfi's poetry. "Egy estém otthon" (one evening at home) and "István öcsémhez" (to my younger brother, István) reflect the same love and tender concern for his parents. The emotions are deep, yet their expression is restrained: He sees his father's love manifest in the grudging approval bestowed on his "profession" and his mother's love manifest in her incessant questions. Objective in his assessment of his father's inability to understand him, he knows that the bond between them is no less strong. His own emotions are described in a minor key, coming as a comment in the last line of the quatrain, a line that has the effect of a "tag," because it has fewer stresses than the other three.

The Hammer of the Village

Petőfi's two heroic poems use the same devices to comment on society—albeit in a light and entertaining manner. *The Hammer of the Village*, written in mock-heroic style, satirizes both society and the Romantic epic tradition, which by this time had become degraded and commonplace. Using a mixture of colloquialism and slang, the parody is peopled with simple villagers who are presented in epic terms. The characters themselves behave unaffectedly and naturally; it is the narrator who assumes the epic pose and invests their jealousies and Sunday-afternoon amusements with a mock grandeur. Thus, Petőfi shows his ability to use the heroic style, though he debunks certain excesses in the heroic mode then fashionable, presenting the life he knows best; he does this not by ridiculing simple folk but by debunking pretentiousness. Though popular, the poem understandably failed to gain the critical approval of the journal editors, whose main offerings were often in the very vein satirized by Petőfi.

Janos the Hero

In contrast, *Janos the Hero* received both critical and popular support. It has served as the basis of an operetta and has often been printed as a children's book—especially in foreign translations. Much more than a fairy tale cast in folk-epic style, the work has several levels of meaning and explores many topics of deep concern for the poet and his society.

The hero and his lover, his adventures, his values, and his way of thinking are all part of the folktale tradition. The epic is augmented by more recent historical material: the Turkish wars and Austrian campaigns, events that mingle in the imagination of the villagers who have fought Austria's wars for generations and who fought the Turks for generations before that. The characterization, however, remains realistically rooted in the village. The French king, the Turkish pasha, even the giant are recognizable types. The hero, Janos, remains unaffected and unspoiled, but he is never unsophisticated. His naïveté is not stupidity; he is one to whom worldly glory has less appeal than do his love for Iluska and his desire to be reunited with her.

The style of the poem reinforces this "obvious" level: It is written in the Hungarian Alexandrine, a ten- to eleven-syllable line divided by a caesura into two and two, or two and three, measures. The language is simple and natural, but, as in the folk song, the actual scene is merged with the psychological world of the tale. The similes and metaphors of the poem reflect the method of the folk song and thus extend the richness of meaning found in each statement. The use of the devices goes beyond their traditional application in folk song. Through the pairing of natural phenomena and the protagonist's state of mind, a higher level of meaning is suggested: The adventures of Janos become symbolic of the struggle between good and evil. Iluska becomes the ideal for which he strives as well as the force that keeps him from straying from the moral path; he does not take the robbers' wealth to enrich himself, nor does he accept the French throne and the hand of the princess. Helping the weak and unfortunate, he continues to battle oppression, whether in the form of an unjust master or the Turks or giants and witches who rule over the forces of darkness.

The images used by the lovers on their parting illustrate these principles quite well: Janos asks Iluska to remember him in these words: "If you see a dry stalk driven by the wind/ Let your exiled lover come to your mind." His words are echoed by Iluska's answer: "If you see a broken flower flung on the highway/ Let your fading lover come to your mind." The cosmic connections are suggested, yet nothing inappropriate on the literal level is said. Furthermore, the dry stalk is an appropriate symbol for the grief-stricken and aimlessly wandering Janos. The faded flower as a symbol of the grieving girl becomes a mystical metaphor for her; in the concluding scenes, Janos regains Iluska when he throws the rose he had plucked from her grave into the Waters of Life.

The realism of the folk song and the quality of Hungarian village life are not restricted to the description of character or to the imagery. The setting, particularly when Janos is within the boundaries of Hungary, is that of the Hungarian plain. He walks across the level, almost barren land, stops by a sweep well, and encounters shepherds, bandits, and peddlers, as might any wanderer crossing these regions. These touches and Janos's realistic actions—such as eating the last of the bacon that he had carried with him for the journey, using the brim of his felt hat for a cup and a mole's mound for a pillow, and turning his sheepskin cloak inside out to ward off the rain—reaffirm the hero's basic humanity. He is not the passive Romantic traveler in the mold of Heine or of Byron. He never becomes a mere observer; instead, he naturally assumes an active role and instinctively takes charge of his own life and of events around him. Even in the more mythical setting of the second half of the poem, his sense of purpose does not waver.

The years 1845 and 1846 were intensely emotional ones for Petőfi, and many of his works of this period suffer from a lack of objectivity and of emotional distancing. Love, revenge, and patriotism, a struggle between national priorities, the gulf between the rich and the poor—all sought a voice. The simple lyric of the traditional folk song was not yet strong enough to carry the message, and Petőfi sought a suitable medium of expression. In this time of experimentation, he found in the drama of the Hungarian people an objective correlative for his own emotions.

Clouds

The collection *Clouds* contains occasional poems in the world-weary mood of the previous year, but new forms and a new language show that to a great extent Petőfi had mastered the conflicting impulses of the earlier works. The best poems lash out against injustice, or they are patriotic poems that become increasingly militant in tone. In "A Csárda romjai" (the ruins of the Csárda), Petőfi takes a familiar landmark of the arid, deserted lowlands and makes it a metaphor for the decline of the country. The poem opens as a paean to these plains, the poet's favorite landscape because it reminds him of freedom; in succeeding stanzas, he seems to digress from the objective scene into sentimentality. He stops himself, however, before this train of thought goes too far; inasmuch as it is the ruin before him that has inspired these thoughts, the poem is also returned to the concrete scene. The ruin is of stone—a rarity here—so he seeks an explanation, which is soon given: A village or city once stood here, but the Turks destroyed it and left only a half-ruined church. A parenthetical expression brings the poem back to the idea of lost liberty ("Poor Hungary, my poor homeland,/ How many different chains you have already worn"), and the narrative is then resumed.

In time, an inn was built from the church, but those who once lodged there are now long dead. The inn has lost its roof, and its door and window are indistinguishable; all that remains is the sweep of the well, on top of which a lone eagle sits, meditating on mutability. In the final four lines, the scene is expanded to encompass the entire horizon, which serves to give it an optimistic and magical tone. The melancholy scene is bathed in sunshine and surrounded by natural beauty. The parallelism between the decline of the nation and the slow ruin of the church-inn has been established, and a note of optimism for the nation's future has been introduced, but precise development of this idea is only suggested. The point is not belabored.

"A NÉGY-ÖKRÖS SZEKÉR"

The poems of these years showed great variety; not all are in the meditative-patriotic vein. In "A négy-ökrös szekér" (the ox cart), for example, Petőfi returned to a more personal theme: a nighttime ride in an oxcart. The poem is set in the country; the speaker is on a visit home. With a group of young friends, he returns to the next village in an oxcart to prolong the party. The magic of the evening is suggested in the second stanza—"The merchant breeze moved over the nearby leas/ And brought sweet scents from the grasses"—but the refrain anchors the scene in reality: "Down the highway, pulling the cart,/ The four oxen plodded slowly." The poem remains a retelling of the evening, although a pensive note is introduced when the poet turns to his companion, urging that they choose a star "which will lead us back/ To the happy memories of former times." The poem then closes with the calm notes of the refrain.

"TÜNDÉRÁLOM"

The culmination of this process of revaluation and poetic development comes in "Tündérálom" (fairy dream). This lyric-psychological confession is written in iambic pentameter and eight-line stanzas with a rhyme scheme of *abcbbdbd* so that the *b* rhyme subtly connects the two halves. Its real theme, despite the poet's explicit statement that he has here conjured up "first love," is the search for happiness. As such, the poem fits Petőfi's preoccupations in 1845 and 1846. Although many of the trappings of Romanticism are found in the poem, the longing for an unattainable ideal is given its own expression. It is almost impossible to trace specific influences, yet the poem expresses some of the quintessential notions of the Romantic movement without ever quite losing touch with reality.

The poem owes its success partly to its images, through which the everyday world is constantly brought into contact with the ethereal without disturbing it in the slightest:

> I'm a boatman on a wild, storm-tossed river;
> The waves toss, the light boat shakes,
> It shakes like the cradle that is rocked
> By the violent hands of an angry nurse.
> Fate, the angry nurse of my life.
> You toss and turn my boat,
> You, who like a storm drove on me
> Peace-disturbing passions.

Throughout, the ambiguity between realistic phenomena and magical manifestations is maintained: The dreamer seems to imagine the latter, but the former are asserted. Thus, the mysterious sounds he hears are identified as a swan's song, and, as he leaps from a mountain peak into the sky to gain his ideal, he falls back to awake to a lovely yet earthly maiden. Thus, the idyll is again returned to reality.

The ambiguity can be sustained so successfully because it is the imagery that creates the mood, and Petőfi's sure handling of imagery never allows it to get out of control. The description of the progress of the idyll illustrates this well:

> Dusk approached. On golden clouds
> The sun settled behind the violet mountains;
> A pale fog covered this dry sea,
> The endlessly stretching plain.
> The cliff on which we stood glowed red
> From the last rays, like a purple pillow
> On a throne. But truly, this was a throne
> And we on it the youthful royal couple of happiness.

In a sense, this poem was for Petőfi the swan song of the purely internal lyric. Appropriately, it exhibits the best qualities of his subjective, Romantic early verse. It is melodious, and it unfolds the story in a series of rich and sensuous images. The objective world is completely subordinated to the imaginative one, but it is not ignored. Symbols abound, but they are suggestive, not didactic. The girl in the poem is Imagination and Inspiration; she is the ideal goal of those starting their careers. When she is lost, the ideal is lost, but Petőfi suggests in the closing lines that such an ideal can be held for only a moment. It must give way to reality; thus, it is not lost, only changed. The impractical dreams of youth are supplanted by the practical programs of adulthood which will implement these goals.

"Levél Várady Antalhoz"

Two more poems of this fertile period deserve mention: "Levél Várady Antalhoz" (letter to Antal Várady) and "Dalaim" (my songs). Each of these poems serves as an *ars poetica*. In the former, Petőfi states that the beauty of nature has revived him and cured him of his world-weariness, and he affirms his commitment to social and political causes. The six stanzas of "Dalaim" are a masterful expression of the variety of themes and moods found in Petőfi's poetry, from the landscape poetry of his homeland to joy, love, Anacreontics, patriotism, and the desire to free his homeland of foreign rule, as well as to the fiery rage that makes his songs "Lightning flashes of/ his angry soul."

"Dalaim"

"Dalaim," like "Tündérálom," serves as a transition to the final, mature phase of Petőfi's poetry, characterized by a harmonious fusion of the often divergent trends identified so far in his poetry. Personal experiences and national events play as important a part in the formation of this style as do the experimentations of his earlier years. Structure and mood, internal and external scenes merge as his themes become more complex and his subjects more serious. "Naïve realism" is supplanted by a deeper realism, and the personal point of view is gradually replaced by a conscious spokesman for the Hungarian people. The intense emotions of Petőfi's mature poems continue to be expressed in a restrained style, and even the deep love poetry addressed to his wife finds expression in a controlled style that continues to reflect the Hungarian folk song and the European traditions that influenced him at the beginning of his career.

"Reszket a bokor, mert"

The objective lyric style that marks the best of Petőfi's poetry had two inspirations. One was his wife, Júlia; the other was his friend and fellow poet Arany. Though Petőfi's love for Júlia was deep and passionate, the poetry in which he celebrates that love is both objective and universal.

The poems of his courtship and marriage show a progression from an emphasis on physical beauty to a desire for spiritual identification. The style remains that of the folk song and the direct personal lyric, but the imagery brings a wealth of associations to bear on the relationship. Most prominent are images of blessedness and fulfillment. In "Reszket a bokor, mert" (the bush trembles, because), the intensity of feeling is almost too much for the classic folk-song pattern, yet the poet retains the delicate balance between form and content. Written shortly after their meeting, before Petőfi had a firm commitment from Júlia, the poem is essentially a question posed through a range of associations: "The bush trembles, for/ A little bird alighted there./ My soul trembles, for/ You came to mind." In the following lines, the balance between the exterior, natural scene and the interior, psychological one is maintained. The beloved is likened to a diamond—pure, clear, and precious—and to a rose. This latter image receives emphasis and gains freshness as Petőfi uses the word *rozsaszálam*—that is, a single, long-stemmed rose. To the usual associations, grace and slenderness are added, along with the suggestion of something individual, unique.

The last stanza poses a question: Does Júlia still love him in the cold of winter, as she had loved him in the warmth of summer? Through the reference to the seasons, Petőfi not only retains the parallelism on which the poem is built but also refers to the actual moment from which the poem springs. All this, even the gentle note of resignation in these lines, leads to the statement: "If you no longer love me/ May God bless you,/ But if you do still love me,/ May He bless you a thousandfold." Júlia's answer was, "A thousand times," and from that time on, Petőfi seems to have had no doubt that her commitment to him was as complete as his to her.

"SZEPTEMBER VÉGEN"

The poems continue to chronicle the events and emotions of the courtship, marriage, and honeymoon. "Szeptember végen" (at the end of September) records a day of meditative peace touched by melancholy. The images raise it to extraordinary heights, and the skillful use of meter and mood, image and meaning makes it a masterpiece. It unites the virtues of folk poetry and the gentle philosophy of Petőfi's peaceful moments in an eternal tribute to his wife. Its three stanzas of eight lines each, written in dactylic tetrameter, a relatively slow and descending cadence, are meditative yet grand, suggesting that the poet's soliloquy is not merely a personal matter. The images reflect the scene at Koltó in the foothills of the eastern Carpathians and the autumn setting with its associations of death. The atmosphere created again depends on the union of the natural and the psychological. The poet addresses his wife, calling her attention to the contrast between summer in the garden and the snow already on the mountaintops. He, too, feels this contrast:

> The rays of summer are still flaming in my young heart,
> And in it still lives spring in its glory,
> But see, gray mingles with my dark hair;
> The hoarfrost of winter has smitten my head.

A line that rivals François Villon's "Où sont les neiges d'antan?" (Where are the snows of yesteryear?) introduces the next stanza: "The flower fades, life fleets away." This line gently leads the poem to the next topic, the brevity of life and the poet's premonition that he will precede his wife to the grave. Will she mourn him, or will she soon forget their love?

The gradual movement of the poem, revealing the manner in which one emotion fades into another, enables the poet to escape excesses of sentimentality and melancholy in spite of the topic. As always, realistic touches help bring the reader to accept the closing lines. On one level, the poem is a metaphysical statement concerning the enduring reality of love. On another, it is a deeply felt personal declaration of love set in a specific time and place. The poet's control of his material enables him to assert, without a trace of the maudlin, that life has no more durability than a flower, that permanence is to be found only in the love that endures beyond the grave. The themes of love, nature, and death are united in such a way that not one of them is slighted, not one of them is vague and impersonal.

"Rózsabokor a domboldalon"

Though his married years were also years of increasingly greater involvement in public affairs and politics, Petőfi continued to write beautiful love poems to his wife. In "Rózsabokor a domboldalon" (rosebush on the hillside), he returns to the happy, carefree tones of the folk song as he compares his wife's leaning on him to the wild rosebush hugging the hillsides. "Minek nevezzelek?" (what shall I name you?) also uses a lighter style, as the poet seeks to explain just what his wife means to him. A catalog of her ethereal charms and spiritual qualities tumbles forth, for he cannot summarize her essence in a word. The directness of his approach, as well as the seeming paradoxes in which the description is couched, again invites the reader to go beyond the surface to think about the thesis of the poem.

"Szeretlek, kedvesem"

Shortly before his death, Petőfi wrote "Szeretlek, kedvesem" (I love you, my dear). Again, there is what seems to be a breathless profession of love as Petőfi lists the ways in which he loves Júlia. The eighty lines of the poem constitute essentially one sentence. Its form, free verse in lines ranging from two to four measures, reflects this quality. The message is not frivolous, however, for he succeeds in conveying a depth of love that excludes all other feelings yet encompasses all. Theirs is a fully mutual relationship, as he states in the last line, for he has learned all he knows of love from her.

"Bolond Istók"

In Petőfi's objective poetry of the time, also, the mood of these years of married happiness is seen. The verse narrative "Bolond Istók" (crazy Steve) reflects this mood in its story of a wandering hero who finds a haven and a loving wife through his dedication and service. The objectivity and restrained style of the poem balance the hardships of the student with the sentimental overtones of the grandfather, who is disillusioned with his son. Even the romantic flight of the granddaughter to escape a marriage her father wishes to force on her is spared sentimentality. Tongue-in-cheek hyperbole is often the key: The deserted farm "seems to be still in the throes of the Tatar raids," and the old housekeeper and host seem about as civil as Tamburlaine's forces when Istók first comes upon them. The young man's optimism serves to offset this mood and also to introduce the new theme: the arrival of the granddaughter, whose plea for help is to bring hope and new life to the old farmstead. In time, he marries the girl, and in due course a cradle is rocked by the hearth. The cycle of life reasserts itself over the disruption caused by evil.

Other poems, such as "A vńdor" (the wanderer), "A kisbéres" (the hired man), and "A téli esték" (winter evenings), return to the theme of domestic bliss, as do two prose works written during this period: "A nagyapa" (the grandfather) and "A fakó leány s a pej legény" (the pale girl and the ruddy boy).

Friendship with Arany

Petőfi's friendship with Arany also reinforced the objective orientation of his poetry. The two men shared many of the same goals, though they did not always agree on the methods to be followed in achieving them. Poetically, too, they differed, yet the friendship was fruitful for both. In the years following their first exchange of letters, their correspondence ranged from their common concern with creating a national poetry, to their families, to a general exchange of information and ideas. The naturally more reserved as well as more pessimistic Arany was often shaken out of his soberness by the playful letters of Petőfi.

The two friends, occasionally joined by others, undertook several projects together. As a result of their collaborative efforts, Petőfi wrote "Széchy Mária" (1847) and began his translation of Shakespeare. It was in Petőfi's genre and landscape poems, however, that the influence of Arany's calmer, more objective style seems to have borne the richest fruit.

Patriotic poems

Nationalism, a sense of commitment to and concern for the Hungarian people, and patriotism, a commitment to the political institutions of a free and independent Hungarian nation, are themes found throughout Petőfi's poetry. Often, these concerns appear in an oblique way. Increasingly, after March 15, 1848, however, they became open topics of his poetry while continuing to influence the other genres in the same indirect fashion as earlier. As early as 1846, in "Egy gondolat bánt engemet" (one thought troubles me), Petőfi had expressed a desire to die on the battlefield in defense of liberty. The next year, he stated the obligation of the poet to sacrifice personal feelings in the interests of patriotic and human duty in "A XIX: Század költői" (the poets of the nineteenth century). After the events of March, 1848, Petőfi plunged into these responsibilities fully; it is perhaps this which gives his poetry the masculine quality not captured by Western European poets of his time: He calls for action with the conviction of one who is ready to be the first to die in battle. These sentiments are skillfully stated in "Ha férfi vagy, légy férfi" (if you are a man, then be one)—a poetic declaration of principles in which didacticism does not detract from poetic value.

A sense of responsibility to his wife and family did not interfere with Petőfi's commitment to his people; if anything, it contributed to the commitment. Júlia shared his sentiments and supported her husband, and he considered her his partner in his work. "Feleségem és kardom" (my wife and my sword) must be read in conjunction with "Ha férfi vagy, légy férfi," for it balances the picture. His wife, an equal partner, will tie the sword on her husband's waist and send them off together, if necessary. Her heroism is to be admired no less than bravery on the battlefield.

In the early years, Petőfi's patriotic poetry had some nostalgic moments. By 1846, however, he had moved beyond the glorification of the past to the criticism of the present and suggestions for reforms. He called on poets to be active in bringing about reforms, and he urged his readers to take pride in Hungarian traditions. In "Magyar vagyok" (I am a Hungarian), he stated his unequivocal loyalty; "Erdélyben" (in Transylvania) shows the dedication to this eastern region of Hungary that had preserved Hungarian traditions and language in the trying years of the Turkish wars and the Austrian Partition—a dedication echoed by Hungarian poets today.

"Nemzeti dal"

The events of March 15, which were to transform not only Petőfi's life but also the history of his country, seemed to crown with success the efforts of the reformers. Petőfi's "Nemzeti dal" (national ode) inspired the demonstrators, and the Twelve Points made clear to everyone the goals they were espousing. The spirited call to arms in the refrain—"By the God of the Magyars,/ We swear/ We swear that captives/ We'll no longer be!"—became the rallying cry of the nation. In the poem, nostalgia for the past is united with faith in the future, and the urgency and immediacy of the situation are emphasized in the words that virtually leap at the listener: "Up Magyar, the country calls!/ Here's the time, now or never!/ Shall we be free or captives ever?/ This the question you must answer!" In contrast to the direct address here, the refrain is in a collective mode. A dialogue is thus established, with the poet calling on his audience to respond and prompting their response through the oath phrased in the refrain.

In the six stanzas of this poem, Petőfi chides his countrymen for enduring servitude. It is time for the sword to replace the chain, he urges, so that the Hungarian name will again be great and future generations will bless them. The language and the images are as direct as the tone, and throughout, the poet emphasizes the need for heroic action regardless of the consequences. Understandably, the poem had great impact. If Petőfi had made only this contribution to the independence movement, he would have been remembered, but he did much more.

The Revolution that had begun peacefully, and seemed, at first, to accomplish its goals through legal reform, escalated into war when Hungarian territory was invaded, first by the Croatian armies of Jellačić, who had Imperial support, and later by Austrian forces, as the Chancery consolidated around the new king, Franz Joseph. National minorities within the country were urged by the Austrian government to attack the Hungarians, and some did. Others, notably the German towns, remained neutral or espoused the Hungarian cause. As the war became an open struggle between the Hungarian Ministry and the Habsburgs, Hungarian leader Lajos Kossuth was able to force a final break with Austria, and the Habsburgs were formally deprived of their position as monarchs of Hungary. Petőfi became increasingly involved in both the political and the military events, seeing a break with Austria and the establishment of a republic as the only means of achieving social reform. Of the nearly 150 short lyrics he wrote in 1848 and 1849, almost all deal with the political and military turmoil in Hungary. Some are antimonarchist or anti-Habsburg, some chide the nationalities for turning on the land that gave them shelter earlier, and an increasing number glorify national virtues and ancient constitutional rights that had long been ignored by the monarchs.

War poems

Petőfi was not sanguine, however, and hopeful poems such as "1848" alternate with ones that express bitter disappointment, such as "Európa csendes, ujra csendes" ("Europe is quiet, is quiet again"). He saw that Europe had given up its democratic ideals, and no hope of support was left. However, he did not speak of Hungary's cause as a hopeless if glorious one. Even the combined forces of Austria and Russia were no match for his poetic belief in victory, expressed in "Bizony mondom, hogy gyoz most a magyar" ("truly I say, now the Hungarians will win").

Though they constitute a relatively small percentage of his poetic work, Petőfi's war poems deserve attention. For the most part, they are spirited, upbeat marches or a lively mixture of narrative and lyric moods, emphasizing the dedication and heroism of the soldiers. They do not glorify war for its own sake, but rather emphasize the patriotic reason for the combat. "Bordal" (wine song) returns to a traditional genre to urge all men to defend their homeland, "draining blood and life" from anyone who seeks to destroy it just as they "empty the glass of wine."

Petőfi's confidence in the ultimate triumph of his cause, if not on the battlefield or in the treaty rooms then at least in the judgment of history, can be sensed in one of the last battle songs he wrote, "Csatában" (in battle). This poem is also notable for the personal involvement of the poet. He begins the poem by re-creating a battle in vivid natural images and giving it a cosmic frame:

> Wrath on the earth,
> Wrath in the sky!
> The red of spilt blood and
> The red rays of the sun!
> The setting sun glows
> In such a wild purple!
> Forward, soldiers,
> Forward, Magyars!

Through such images and a wonderfully effective onomatopoeia, the whole universe seems to become involved in the strife. The poet's own involvement, symbolic of the involvement of the nation, is signaled in the change in the refrain from "Forward" to "Follow me."

Shortly after composing this poem, Petőfi died on the battlefield of Segesvár. Within weeks, the Hungarian Resistance was also over, but Petőfi lives on in legend and in his poetry.

Legacy

Petőfi's short poetic career established him as a poet of the first rank. The variety of themes and styles he handled with success is amazing; even the less powerful lyrics of his early years have enriched Hungarian literature and music, many of them having been set to music and passing into the modern "folk-song" repertory. His early fame and his fame abroad rested on both his republican sentiments and his romantic early death. Early translations into German were followed by English versions based on the German. His popularity grew with the worldwide interest in the Hungarian Revolution of 1848 and its brutal suppression; it also waned as political realities changed. The Petőfi behind the legend was neglected even in Hungary for a long time; abroad, he is still mostly known as a revolutionary hero, not as a poet. Translations, prepared with enthusiasm but lack of knowledge or skill, seldom do him justice. In Hungary, the most talented of his contemporaries recognized his talents independent of his political views. Today, there is general agreement about his position as a central figure in Hungarian literature and in the development of the Hungarian lyric. His republican, nationalistic, and patriotic ideas are also recognized; they are an essential part of the poet who spoke from the heart of his generation, who spoke for his people, and who spoke for the masses and indeed to give all classes of society a voice. He was truly a poet of national consciousness.

Other major works

LONG FICTION: *A hóhér kötele*, 1846 (novella; *The Hangman's Rope*, 1973).

SHORT FICTION: "A szökevények," 1845; "A fakó leány s a pej legény," 1847; "A nagyapa," 1847.

PLAYS: *Tigris és hiéna*, pb. 1847; *Coriolanus*, pb. 1848 (translation of William Shakespeare's play).

NONFICTION: "Úti jegyzetek," 1845; "Úti levelek Kerényi Frigyeshez," 1847; *Lapok Petőfi Sándor naplójából*, 1848; *Petőfi Sándor összes prózai muvei és levelezése*, 1960; *Petőfi Sándor by Himself*, 1973; *Rebel or Revolutionary? Sándor Petőfi as Revealed by His Diary, Letters, Notes, Pamphlets, and Poems*, 1974.

MISCELLANEOUS: *Works of Sándor Petőfi*, 1973.

BIBLIOGRAPHY

Basa, Enikő Molnár, ed. *Hungarian Literature*. New York: Griffon House, 1993. This overview of Hungarian literature helps place Petőfi in context.

———. *Sándor Petőfi*. Boston: Twayne, 1980. An introductory biography and critical study of selected works by Petőfi. Includes bibliographic references.

Ewen, Frederick. *A Half-Century of Greatness: The Creative Imagination of Europe, 1848-1884*. New York: New York University Press, 2007. Contains a chapter on Petőfi, examining his role as a soldier and discussing his work.

Illyés, Gyula. *Petőfi*. Translated by G. F. Cushing. 1973. Reprint. Budapest: Kortárs Kiadó, 2002. An exhaustive biography and critical examination of the life and works of Petőfi.

Szirtes, George. Foreword to *John the Valiant*, by Sándor Petőfi. Translated by John Ridland. London: Hesperus Press, 2004. Noted translator Szirtes provides background and some literary analysis for this bilingual translation of *János Vitéz*.

Enikő Molnár Basa (including original translations)

PIERRE REVERDY

Born: Narbonne, France; September 13, 1889
Died: Solesmes, France; June 17, 1960

PRINCIPAL POETRY
Poèmes en prose, 1915 (*Prose Poems*, 2007)
La Lucarne ovale, 1916
Quelques poèmes, 1916
Les Ardoises du toit, 1918 (*Roof Slates*, 1981)
Les Jockeys camouflés, 1918
La Guitare endormie, 1919
Cœur de chêne, 1921
Étoiles peintes, 1921
Cravates de chanvre, 1922
Grande Nature, 1925
La Balle au bond, 1928
Sources du vent, 1929
Pierres blanches, 1930
Ferraille, 1937
Plein verre, 1940
Plupart du temps, 1945 (collected volume, 1913-1922)
Le Chant des morts, 1948
Main d'œuvre: Poèmes, 1913-1949, 1949
Pierre Reverdy: Selected Poems, 1969
Roof Slates, and Other Poems of Pierre Reverdy, 1981
Selected Poems, 1991

OTHER LITERARY FORMS

Pierre Reverdy (ruh-VEHR-dee) worked extensively in other forms besides poetry. He wrote two novels and many stories and published collections of prose poems. Most of these are in a Surrealist vein, mixing experimentation in language with personal and unconscious reflection. As an editor of an avant-garde review, Reverdy also contributed important theoretical statements on cubism and avant-garde literary practice. Later in his career, he published several volumes of reminiscences, including sensitive reevaluations of the work of his near contemporaries, including Guillaume Apollinaire.

ACHIEVEMENTS

Pierre Reverdy is one of the most central and influential writers in the tradition of twentieth century avant-garde poetry. Already well established in terms of both his

Pierre Reverdy

work and his theoretical stance by the mid-1910's, Reverdy exerted considerable influence over the Dada and Surrealist movements, with which he was both officially and informally affiliated.

Reverdy's firm conviction was in a nonmimetic, nontraditional form of artistic expression. The art he championed and practiced would create a reality of its own rather than mirror a preexisting reality. In this way, the language of poetry would be cut loose from restraining conventions of meter, syntax, and punctuation in order to be able to explore the emotion generated by the poetic image.

In connection with the avant-garde artists of cubism, Dada, and Surrealism, Reverdy's formulations helped to break down the traditional models of artistic creation that then held firm sway in France. Reverdy's firm conviction was that artistic creation precedes aesthetic theory. All the concrete means at an artist's disposal constitute his aesthetic formation.

Along with Apollinaire, his slightly older contemporary, Reverdy became a central figure and example for a whole generation of French poets generally grouped under the Surrealist heading. His having been translated into English by a range of American poets from Kenneth Rexroth to John Ashbery shows the importance of his work to the modern American tradition as well.

Biography

Pierre Reverdy was born on September 13, 1889, in Narbonne, France, a city in the Languedoc region. The son and grandson of sculptors and artisans in wood carving, he grew up with this practical skill in addition to his formal studies. The Languedoc region at the turn of the century was an especially volatile region, witnessing the last major peasant uprising in modern French history.

After completing his schooling in Narbonne and nearby Toulouse, Reverdy moved to Paris in 1910, where he lived on and off for the rest of his life. Although exempted from military service, he volunteered at the outbreak of World War I, saw combat service, and was discharged in 1916. By profession a typesetter, Reverdy also worked as the director of the review *Nord-Sud*, which he founded in 1917.

From 1910 to 1926, Reverdy worked in close contact with almost all the important artists of his time. He had especially close relationships with Pablo Picasso and Juan Gris, both of whom contributed illustrations to collections of his verse. As the editor of an influential review, he had close contact with and strong influence on the writers who were to form the Dada and Surrealist movements. Already an avant-garde poet and theorist of some prominence by the late 1910's, Reverdy was often invoked along with Apollinaire as one of the precursors of Surrealism. He collaborated with the early Surrealist efforts and continued his loose affiliation even after a formal break in 1926.

That year saw Reverdy's conversion to a mystic Catholicism. From then until his death in 1960, his life became more detached from the quotidian, and he spent much of his time at the Abbey of Solesmes, where he died.

Analysis

In an early statement on cubism, Pierre Reverdy declaimed that a new epoch was beginning, one in which "one creates works that, by detaching themselves from life, enter back into it because they have an existence of their own." In addition to attacking mimetic standards of reproduction, or representation of reality, he also called for a renunciation of punctuation and a freeing of syntax in the writing of poetry. Rather than being something fixed according to rules, for Reverdy, syntax was "a medium of literary creation." Changing the rules of literary expression carried with it a change in ideas of representation. For Reverdy, the poetic image was solely responsible to the discovery of emotional truth.

From 1915 to 1922, Reverdy produced many volumes of poetry. The avant-garde called for an overturning of literary conventions, and Reverdy contributed with his own explosion of creative activity. In addition to editing the influential review *Nord-Sud*, he used his experience as an engraver and typesetter to publish books, including his own. The list of artists who contributed the illustrations to these volumes of poetry by Reverdy reads like a Who's Who of the art world of the time: Gris, Picasso, André Derain, Henri Matisse, Georges Braque, among others. Reverdy's work, along with that of Apollinaire, was cited as the guiding force for Surrealism by André Breton in his

Manifestes du surréalisme (1962; *Manifestoes of Surrealism*, 1969).

Reverdy's early work achieves an extreme detachment from mimetic standards and literary conventions that allows for the images to stand forth as though seen shockingly for the first time. The last two lines from "Sur le Talus" (on the talus), published in 1918, show this extreme detachment: "L'eau monte comme une poussière/ Le silence ferme la nuit" (The water rises like dust/ Silence shuts the night). There can be no question here of establishing a realistic context for these images. Rather, one is cast back on the weight of emotion that they carry and that must thus guide their interpretation. Reflections off water may appear to rise in various settings, though perhaps particularly at twilight. The dust points to a particular kind of aridity that may be primarily an emotional state. The sudden transition from an (implied) twilight to an abrupt nightfall undercuts any kind of conventional emotional presentation. The quick cut is a measure perhaps of the individual's lack of control over external phenomena and, by extension, inner feelings as well.

"CARREFOUR"

Much of Reverdy's early work is based on just such an imagistic depiction of interior states, with a strong element of detachment from reality and a certain resulting confusion or overlapping. The force of emotion is clearly there, but to pin it down to a particular situation or persona proves difficult because any such certainty is constantly being undercut by the quick transitions between images. The complete suppression of punctuation as well as a certain freedom of syntax as one moves from line to line are clearly tools that Reverdy developed to increase the level of logical disjunction in his poetry. At times, however, this disjunction in the logical progression of word and image gives way to a resolution. The short poem "Carrefour" (crossroad) sets up a surreal image sequence:

> De l'air
> De la lumière
> Un rayon sur le bord du verre
> Ma main déçue n'attrape rien
>
> Air
> Light
> A ray on the edge of the glass
> My disappointed hand holds nothing

Here the elements are invoked, and then two images, one of an inanimate object and one the hand of the speaker. From this atmosphere of mystery and disjunction, the poem's conclusion moves to a fairly well-defined emotional statement:

> Enfin tout seul j'aurai vécu
> Jusqu'au dernier matin
> Sans qu'un mot m'indiquât quel fut le bon chemin

> After all I will have lived all alone
> Until the last morning
> Without a single word that might have shown me
> which was the right way

Here, as in many of Reverdy's poems, the emotion evoked is a kind of diffused sadness. The solitary individual is probably meant to stand for an aspect of the human condition, alone in a confrontation with an unknown destiny.

It was Reverdy's fate to see actual military duty during World War I, and it may well be that the magnitude of human tragedy he witnessed at the front lines served to mute the youthful enthusiasm that pervades his earliest works. It may also be the case that Reverdy, while espousing radical measures in literary practice, still was caught in the kind of bittersweet ethos that characterizes fin de siècle writers generally.

"Guerre"

Whatever the case may be, there is no question that Reverdy wrote some of the most affecting war poems in the French language. One of the most direct is titled simply "Guerre" (war). Running through a series of disjointed, if coherent, images, Reverdy toward the end of the poem approaches direct statement, when the speaker says:

> Et la figure attristée
> Visage des visages
> La mort passe sur le chemin
>
> And the saddened figure
> Visage of visages
> Death passes along the road

Close to a medieval allegorizing of death, this figure also incorporates a fascination with the effect of the gaze. One's face is revealing of one's emotion because of the way one looks—the distillation of the phenomenon into a general characteristic is a strong term to describe death. If this image is strong, the poem's ending is more forceful still:

> Mais quel autre poids que celui de ton corps
> as-tu jeté dans la balance
> Tout froid dans le fossé
> Il dort sans plus rêver
>
> But what other weight than that of your body
> have you thrown in the balance
> All cold in the ditch
> He sleeps no longer to dream

Philosophers have questioned whether the idea of death is properly an idea, since strictly speaking, it has no content. Caught between viewing another's death from the outside and facing one's own death, which one can never know, death is a supreme mystery of human existence. Reverdy in these lines seems to cross the line between the exterior, objective view of another's death and the unknowable, subjective experience of the individual. This is what he means by the emotion communicated through the poetic image.

Despite a continued tendency toward the surreal image in Reverdy's work, these poems in *Sources du vent* (sources of the wind) also represent the first major collection of poems after Reverdy's conversion to a mystic Catholicism in 1926. Increasingly, his poetry of the postconversion period tends toward an introjection of the conflicts raised through the poetic image. While a tone of lingering sadness had always been present from the earliest work, in these poems, the atmosphere of sadness and loss moves to the center of the poet's concerns. Unlike the conservative Christian poets Charles-Pierre Péguy and Paul Claudel, the content of the poems is never directly religious. Rather, a mood of quietism seems to become more prominent in the collections of poems after the conversion. A concurrent falling off in the level of production also takes place. After 1930, Reverdy publishes only two more individual collections of verse, along with two collected volumes and works in other forms. After 1949, for the last twelve years of his life, the heretofore prolific Reverdy apparently ceased to write altogether.

"MÉMOIRE"

The poem "Mémoire" (memory) from *Pierres blanches* (white stones), shows this mood of increasing resignation in the face of worldly events. The poem invokes a "she," someone who has left or is going to leave, but then, in apparent reference to the title, says there will still be someone:

> Quand nous serons partis là-bas derrière
> Il y aura encore ici quelqu'un
> Pour nous attendre
> Et nous entendre
>
> When we will have gone over there behind
> There will still be someone
> To wait for us
> And to understand us

The positive mood of these lines, however, is undercut by the poem's ending: "Un seul ami/ L'ombre que nous avons laissée sous l'arbre et qui s'ennuie" ("A single friend/ The shadow we have left beneath a tree and who's getting bored"). The impersonality tending toward a universal statement that was present in Reverdy's early work here seems to work toward an effacement of the individual personality. If memory can be imaged as a bored shadow left beneath a tree, the significance of the individual seems tenuous at best. The emotion generated through the poetic image here seems to be one of sadness and extreme resignation.

The interpretation of a poet's work through biography must always be a hazy enterprise, all the more so in a poet such as Reverdy, whose life directly enters into his work not at all. In a general sense, then, the course of his poetic life and production might be said to mirror the course of French literary life generally. The enthusiasm of the avant-garde literary and artistic movements in Europe generally in the early years of the twentieth century saw a reaction in the post-World War I years toward an art that questioned societal assumptions. Dada and Surrealism can be seen in terms of this large movement, and Reverdy's work as an example. The coherence of the Surrealist movement in turn breaks down in the late 1920's and early 1930's with the split coming over what political allegiance the Surrealist artists should take, according to its leaders. Reverdy's personal religious convictions cause him to cease active involvement with the movement altogether. It is a measure of his status as a strong precursor to the movement that he is not attacked directly by the more politically motivated leaders of Surrealism.

"Main-Morte"

With the extreme politicization of the Surrealist movement in the late 1930's, even some of the most dedicated younger adherents to Surrealism cut their formal ties with the movement. René Char is an example. The young Yves Bonnefoy is an example of a poet with early leanings toward Surrealism who in the late 1940's moved more in the direction of a poetry expressive of essential philosophical and human truths. It might be possible, in like manner, to trace Reverdy's increasing distance from Surrealism as a movement to some kind of similar feelings that have been more openly expressed by his younger contemporaries. His collection *Plein Verre* (full glass) does indeed move more toward the mode of longer, contemplative poems, still in the atmosphere of sadness and resignation to life. The end of "Main-Morte" (dead-hand) shows this well:

> Entre l'aveu confus et le lien du mystère
> Les mots silencieux qui tendent leur filet
> Dans tous les coins de cette chambre noire
> Où ton ombre ni moi n'aurons jamais dormi
>
> Between the confused vow and the tie of mystery
> The silent words which offer their net
> In every corner of this black room
> Where your shadow nor I will have ever slept

Even the highly suggestive early lyrics do not contain quite the level of hovering mystery and intricate emotional states offered in these lines. One may well wonder if the "you" invoked here even refers to a person or whether it might be a quasi-human interior presence such as that invoked in the later poems of Wallace Stevens (such as "Final Soliloquy of the Interior Paramour"). The weight of the images in the direction of silence lends to this whole utterance an aura of high seriousness.

"Enfin"

The last poem in *Plein Verre*, titled "Enfin" (at last), also ends with a statement hinting at a highly serious attitude. The speaker states:

> À travers la poitrine nue
> Là
> Ma clarière
> Avec tout ce qui descend du ciel
> Devenir un autre
> À ras de terre
>
> By means of the naked breast
> There
> My clearing
> Along with all that descends from the sky
> To become an other
> At earth level

More and more in the later poems, a level of ethical statement seems to emerge. Whereas the early poems introduce strange and startling images in an apparently almost random fashion, the images here seem to be coordinated by an overall hierarchy of values, personal and religious. The naked breast at the beginning of this passage thus could refer to the lone individual, perhaps alone with his or her conscience. This is in contrast to something which descends from the sky, an almost unavoidably religious image. The wish "To become an other/ At earth level" might then be interpreted as the fervent desire of an extremely devoted individual to attain a higher level of piety here on earth.

Le Chant des morts

The extended sequence, *Le Chant des morts* (the song of the dead), composed in 1944-1948 and published in 1948 as part of the collected volume *Main d'œuvre* (work made by hand), presents an extended meditation on the emotional inner scene of war-devastated France. In this sequence, as in his earlier poems on World War I that drew on his direct experience of the horrors of war, Reverdy uses a diction stripped bare of rhetoric, preferring instead the direct, poignant images of death and suffering. Death in these poems is both inescapable and horrible, or as he calls it: "la mort entêtée/ La mort vorace" ("stubborn death/ Voracious death"). As a strong countermovement to the implacable march of death, there is also a tenacious clinging to life. As the poet says: "C'est la faim/ C'est l'ardeur de vivre qui dirigent/ La peur de perdre" ("It is hunger/ It is the ardor to live that guide/ The fear of losing"). The poet of the inner conscience in these poems confronts the essential subject of his deepest meditations: the conscious adoption of his authentic attitude toward death.

The ultimate renunciation of poetry that characterizes the last years of Reverdy's life is preceded by an exploration of the subject most suited to representing death (remembering Sigmund Freud)—that is, silence.

"Et Maintenant"

The poem that Reverdy seems to have chosen to come at the end of his collected poems, titled "Et Maintenant" (and now), ends with a poignant image of silence: "Tous les fils dénoués au delà des saisons reprennent leur tour et leur ton sur le fond sombre du silence" ("All the unknotted threads beyond the seasons regain their trace and their tone against the somber background of silence"). Reverdy here seems to hint at what lies beyond poetic expression in several senses. His entire ethos of poetic creation has been consistently based on an act of communication with the reader. Thus, the threads he refers to here could well represent the threads of intention and emotion that his readers follow in his poetry to achieve an experience of that emotion themselves, or to discover an analogous emotional experience in their own memory or personal background. He might also be hinting at those threads of intention and emotion that led beyond the limitations of individual life in a reunification with a divine creator. In the former interpretation, the background of silence would be that silence which precedes the poetic utterance or act of communication, as well as the silence after the act of communication or once the poet has ceased to write. In the religious interpretation, the background of silence would be that nothingness or nonbeing out of which the divine creation takes place and which, in turn, has the capability of incorporating silence or nonbeing into self, a religious attitude of a return to the creator even in the face of one's own personal death.

Legacy

Reverdy is a complex and fascinating figure in the history of French poetry in the first half of the twentieth century. He was a committed avant-garde artist in the years directly preceding, during, and following World War I; his outpouring of poetry and aesthetic statements made him one of the most significant precursors to the movements of Dada and Surrealism. Though his formal affiliation with the Surrealist movement was of brief duration, his example of using the poetic image to communicate emotion is central to everything for which Surrealism stood. The extreme respect shown to his work by other poets and artists confirms his importance as a creative innovator. Reverdy, in turn, paid respectful homage to his poet and artist contemporaries a stance that shows his ongoing intellectual commitment to the importance of art and literature in human terms, despite his personal isolation and quietism toward the end of his life. The poems from the end of his career that bear the weight of a continued meditation on death are a moving commentary on that from which language emerges and into which it returns: silence.

OTHER MAJOR WORKS
LONG FICTION: *Le Voleur de Talan*, 1917; *La Peau de l'homme*, 1926.
SHORT FICTION: *Risques et périls*, 1930.
NONFICTION: *Self Defence*, 1919; *Le Gant de crin*, 1927; *Le Livre de mon bord*, 1948; *Cette émotion appellée poésie: Écrits sur la poésie, 1932-1960*, 1975; *Nord-Sud, Self Defence, et autres écrits sur l'art et la poésie*, 1975; *Note éternelle du présent*, 1975.

BIBLIOGRAPHY
Greene, Robert W. *The Poetic Theory of Pierre Reverdy*. 1967. Reprint. San Bernardino, Calif.: Borgo Press, 1990. An analysis of Reverdy's work in poetic theory.
Pap, Jennifer. "Transforming the Horizon: Reverdy's World War I." *Modern Language Review* 101, no. 4 (October, 2006): 966-978. Pap examines the theme of war in Reverdy's works, noting that although he favored an art that followed its own aims, he did treat the war in his poetry.
Rizzuto, Anthony. *Style and Theme in Reverdy's "Les Ardoises du toit."* Tuscaloosa: University of Alabama Press, 1971. Rizzuto's critical study of one of Reverdy's poetic works. Includes bibliographic references.
Rothwell, Andrew. *Textual Spaces: The Poetry of Pierre Reverdy*. Atlanta: Rodopi, 1989. A critical analysis of Reverdy's works. Includes bibliographic references.
Schroeder, Jean. *Pierre Reverdy*. Boston: Twayne, 1981. An introductory biography and critical study of selected works by Reverdy. Includes an index and bibliographic references.
Sweet, David LeHardy. *Savage Sight/Constructed Noise: Poetic Adaptations of Painterly Techniques in the French and American Avant-gardes*. Chapel Hill: Department of Romance Languages, University of North Carolina, 2003. The poetry of experimental poets Reverdy, Guillaume Apollinaire, André Breton, Frank O'Hara, and John Ashbery is examined for the poets' use of painterly techniques.

Peter Baker

ISAAC ROSENBERG

Born: Bristol, England; November 25, 1890
Died: Near Arras, France; April 1, 1918

PRINCIPAL POETRY
Night and Day, 1912
Youth, 1915
Moses, 1916 (includes verse drama)
Poems, 1922 (Gordon Bottomley, editor)
The Collected Poems, 1949

OTHER LITERARY FORMS

Isaac Rosenberg's *Moses* combines poetry with verse drama. Rosenberg's prose, letters, and drawings can be found in two collections of his works, one edited by Gordon Bottomley and Denys Harding and published in 1937 and the other edited by Ian Parsons and published in 1979.

ACHIEVEMENTS

Isaac Rosenberg was one of a group of young poets, including Rupert Brooke, Edward Thomas, and Wilfred Owen, whose lives were tragically cut short by World War I. Rosenberg's early poems were slight; it is as a war poet that his reputation was established, largely through the efforts of his mentor, Gordon Bottomley. What makes him unusual among British poets in general and war poets in particular is his Jewish perspective. That aspect coupled with his working-class background sets his poetry apart from the Georgian tones of Thomas or Brooke, or the upper-class tones of Siegfried Sassoon or Robert Graves.

BIOGRAPHY

Isaac Rosenberg was the son of Barnett Rosenberg and Hacha Davidov. His father was a Lithuanian Jew whose impoverished family had emigrated from Russia to Bristol, England, shortly before Rosenberg's birth. Soon after, they moved to the East End of London, which was then the center of the Jewish immigrant community, a community that existed as a tightly knit group until the 1960's and from which emerged such Jewish writers as the dramatists Bernard Kops and Arnold Wesker.

His father opened his own butcher shop; when that failed, he became an itinerant peddler. The family lived in constant poverty, but it was cohesive, and Isaac Rosenberg grew up in a religious atmosphere. After an elementary school education, Rosenberg showed some artistic promise, and in 1907, he began attending evening classes at

Birkbeck College, an affiliated college of the University of London, set up especially to help poor students. In 1908, he won the Mason Prize for his nude studies as well as several other awards. To earn a living, he became apprenticed to an engraver.

A few people noticed Rosenberg's talent and sponsored him at the Slade, London's most prestigious art school, which he entered in 1911. There he was influenced by such British artists as the Pre-Raphaelites, particularly Dante Gabriel Rossetti, and also by William Blake and the modernist Roger Fry. While continuing to study at the Slade, he struck out as an artist, setting up a studio in 1912 in Hampstead Road. He had also been writing poetry and sent some of it to Laurence Binyon, an established Georgian poet who worked at the British Museum, and some to the *English Review*. He received encouragement from both the poet and the journal, and he decided to publish these poems at his own expense in a twenty-four-page pamphlet.

The next year, he met Edward Marsh, editor of *Georgian Poetry* and an influential literary figure in London. Marsh purchased some of his paintings and encouraged him to go on writing, introducing him to other poets such as the modernists T. E. Hulme and Ezra Pound. Rosenberg was still undecided as to whether he was better as a painter or as a poet.

At this point, Rosenberg's health deteriorated, and he sailed to South Africa to stay with one of his sisters. He remained there during 1914, returning to England in March, 1915. Marsh bought three more of his paintings, and Rosenberg published another volume of verse, again at his own expense. However, with the war on, the literary and artistic scene in London had broken up, and there were no immediate prospects or contacts for him. In the light of this, he decided, reluctantly, to enlist, though feeling no particular patriotism.

He was not in good health, rather underweight and undersized. Nevertheless, he was accepted by the army, joining the "Bantams" of the 12th Suffolk Regiment, later transferring to the King's Own Royal Lancasters. After initial training, he was dispatched to the Somme battle area of northern France in June, 1916. During this time, he wrote a play, *Moses*, and then several other dramatic pieces based loosely on Jewish mythology.

He continued to write poetry, now influenced by his experience of war. By 1916, there were few illusions left about the nature of modern warfare. Rosenberg was able to embrace what he saw and sought some positive response to it. Apart from ten days of leave in September, 1917, and a few short spells in the hospital, he served continuously on or just behind the front lines until his death. He was killed shortly before the end of the war while riding dispatches at night. His body was never recovered. His war poems were first collected and published in 1922 by Gordon Bottomley.

Analysis

Such is the lateness in poetic development in Isaac Rosenberg's short life that the majority of his output could be termed "early." His earliest dated poem is from 1905, but the so-called trench poems, on which his reputation solely depends, did not begin until 1916, when he enlisted and was posted to France. Thus the earlier poems span eleven years, with the best gathered into the 1912 and 1915 collections. The total number of poems gathered by his editors, including all the unpublished ones, is 154, of which only 10 percent represent the war poems.

Even though he did have friendships with several Imagist poets—Imagism being the first flowering of modern poetry—his early poetry, unlike his painting, seems typically Georgian. This movement, spanning the first fifteen years of the twentieth century, is best typified as Romantic in a suburban, restrained way, with the emphasis on nature as recreation and pretty images, being nostalgic in tone and with harmonious versification. Some critics have seen the influence of the Pre-Raphaelite painter-poet Dante Gabriel Rossetti, though the most obvious echoing is that of John Keats, another London city poet, whose poetry is full of woods, light, and shade and heightened sensory perceptions, with nature as an escape for the trapped urban spirit.

"Night and Day"

The long opening poem of the 1912 collection is titled "Night and Day" and apostrophizes the stars as he walks out of the city into the woods. The poet feels himself "set aside," seeking symbolic meaning in nature. Keats's "Sleep and Poetry" forms an obvious comparison. Echoes also sound of E. M. Forster's character Leonard Bast in his novel *Howards End* (1910). Other poems in the volume talk of "Desire" with an interesting religious reference; others show sympathy for the common people, a sympathy Rosenberg was to demonstrate later in his war poems.

Youth

Youth, the 1915 volume, shows in some of its lyrics somewhat more focus and control, but the emotions stay at a very generalized level. "God Made Blind" is more like a poem by Thomas Hardy, England's most senior poet at the time. "The Dead Heroes" shows an entirely conventional view of patriotism at this stage.

"On Receiving News of the War"

The uncollected "On Receiving News of the War," written from Cape Town, South Africa, shows a much less conventional and more genuine response. He writes, "God's blood is shed/ He mourns from His lone place/ His children dead." There is no heroism here, only divine pity. In 1915, he sent some of these poems to Lascelles Abercrombie, one of the most popular of the Georgians, whom Rosenberg considered "our best living poet." Abercrombie found the poems to possess a "vivid and original impulse," though he noted that Rosenberg had not yet found his true voice.

MOSES

Rosenberg was also attracted to dramatic verse. In 1916, he had published *Moses*, which consisted of a small number of poems added to a fragment of what was presumably intended to be a larger dramatic work on the Israelite leader Moses. He took considerable license with the biblical story, placing Moses at the moment he was still a prince of Egypt, but just beginning to find his identity as a Hebrew. The speech rhythms and dramatic ideas show much more poetic talent than anything done before, but there is still too much verbiage to be truly dramatic.

Some of the other poems in the volume are much bolder in their conceptual range than anything before. "God" makes a defiant Promethean statement. "Chagrin" uses the image of Absalom hanging by his hair, linking this to Christ hanging on the cross, quite a new sort of poem. "Marching" is the first soldier poem, with taut strong rhythms. The language is much richer and more imagistic. In the volume as a whole, there is for the first time some awareness of modernism, as there had been for some time in his painting.

THE LILITH THEME

While enlisted, Rosenberg also experimented with another Jewish myth, that of Lilith, mixing it strangely with unicorn myths and even a "Rape of the Sabine Women" theme. In his unpublished papers, there were a number of versions of this, titled variously "The Unicorn" or "The Amulet." As he works through various drafts, the blank verse becomes more dramatic, but his own imagination is revealed as mythic rather than dramatic, and there is no overall conceptual grasp of dramatic ideas or structure. Most of the verse consists of soliloquies or long monologues. Yet when it is considered that most of it was done under the most appalling physical conditions, it shows considerable commitment on the poet's part.

TRENCH POEMS

Once under the pressure of fighting in France, Rosenberg's poetic talents crystallized quickly. Flowery sentiments and unfocused images, typical also of Keats's early style, were, as with Keats himself, left behind, and a genuine unsentimental human sympathy was revealed. "The Dying Soldier" sets the tone: it is lyrical, almost balladic, but it focuses on the pathos of the actual death, not the stark horrors of the overall scene. "In War" shows a great advance in poetic technique: The controlled stanza form displays a control of tone and emotion, taking the reader from an almost anaesthetized calm to a sudden panic of realizing it was his brother they were burying. This movement from something "out there" to "right here" becomes typical of these war poems.

Several themes and poetic ideas are revealed. One is the "titan." "Girl to a Soldier on Leave" uses this image for the infantry soldier: Romantic love cannot really be sustained in the face of trench experience. Some new mode of tragedy is being forged. In "Soldier: Twentieth Century," Rosenberg makes a political comment for the first time. The modern soldier is a "great new Titan." In the past, soldiers were fodder to keep tyrants in power. Now it is time that they wake up from sleeping "like Circe's swine" and rebel.

The second theme is a Jewish one: the burning of Solomon's Temple. "Destruction of Jerusalem by the Babylonian Hordes" is too anachronistic to be fully effective. The theme is reworked in "The Burning of the Temple." The poet asks if Solomon is angry at the burning of his glorious temple, to which the answer is, apparently not. If "God" is read for "Solomon" and the human body for the "Temple," then a powerful statement emerges: God's anger can be only ambiguously discerned.

The third theme is humorous. "The Immortals" is mock heroic, leading the reader to believe the soldier is fighting a heroic battle. In fact, he is fighting lice, which are immortal. Similarly, "Louse Hunting" depicts the real enemy in its "supreme littleness." In fact, Rosenberg has very little conception of the "enemy." For example, "Break of Day in the Trenches" shows a poet who strikes no poses, makes no gestures, and retains all his sensitivities after two years of continuous warfare. Others were driven insane. It is a gentle, sad, slightly ironic poem that shows Rosenberg as a human being rather than as a soldier. In fact, death on the battlefields is described as "murder," hardly a military perception.

The poem is an address to a rat, which like lice, were all too common in the trenches. However, the rat is not treated as vermin here. Rosenberg apostrophizes it for making no distinction between friend and foe, crossing indiscriminately between the two sides. The rat is "sardonic"; it "inwardly grins" as it sees fine young men from both sides being killed randomly and haphazardly, "sprawled in the bowels of the earth."

"Dead Man's Dump"

Among the best war poems ever written are two by Rosenberg, "Returning We Hear the Larks," with its sense of precarious joy still possible for the human spirit, and "Dead Man's Dump." This poem is about the quintessential war dilemma: seeing individuals, living and worthy of life, even if on the point of dying, as against seeing the mass of impersonal lifeless corpses that are fit only for throwing into the ground and burying. Rosenberg seems to be on some sort of burial fatigue, jolting along in a mule-drawn cart somewhere in no-man's-land. All around "The air is loud with death," and corpses of friend and foe alike lie scattered around. Sometimes the cart jolts over them, crushing their bones. They approach a dying man who must have heard them coming, as he tried to cry aloud. However, by the time the cart gets to him, he is dead, and "our wheels grazed his dead face."

The poet writes as a human being: There is pity but no sentimentality. Rosenberg's visual imagination is most clearly seen in his images of the corpses, their former strength and spirit seen against their present contorted lifelessness, especially in relationship to the earth, which is sensed as a living entity, to whose embrace the living return in a haphazard, random way. His imagination is also engaged in motion and motionlessness. Verbs are particularly vivid: "lurched," "sprawled," "crunched," "huddled," "go crying," and "breaking," "crying," "torturing," "break," "broke," "quivering," "rushing" in the climactic ending. These verbs are so violent they push away the poet's natural inclination to pity: "The drowning soul was sunk too deep/ For human tenderness." He writes of a soldier whose "brains splattered on/A stretcher-bearer's face."

This is a much more sustained poem than many of the other war poems. It is in free verse, divided into irregular stanzas, twelve in all, with occasional rhymes and half-rhymes. It is modern in its versification, unlike that of fellow war poets Brooke, Owen, and Sassoon, who tried, not always successfully, to adapt forms of the gentle, restrained Georgian versification to the horrendous scenes and emotions they were describing. Rosenberg's images and rhythmic structures create drama and movement much more fluidly, and the climax of the poem is as powerful as anything else in World War I poetry. Clearly, Rosenberg could have become a great poet had he lived. The very control of the poem, written in conditions of chaos and horror, suggests the triumph of the human spirit.

OTHER MAJOR WORKS

MISCELLANEOUS: *The Collected Works of Isaac Rosenberg: Poetry, Prose, Letters, and Some Drawings*, 1937 (Gordon Bottomley and Denys Harding, editors); *The Collected Works of Isaac Rosenberg: Poetry, Prose, Letters, Paintings, and Drawings*, 1979 (Ian Parsons, editor); *The Poems and Plays of Isaac Rosenberg*, 2004 (Vivien Noakes, editor); *Poetry Out of My Head and Heart: Unpublished Letters and Poem Versions*, 2007.

BIBLIOGRAPHY

Bloom, Harold, ed. *Poets of WWI: Wilfred Owen and Isaac Rosenberg*. Broomall, Pa.: Chelsea House, 2002. A collection of essays about the war poets Wilfred Owen and Rosenberg. Contains a biography of Rosenberg and five essays on his works.

Cohen, Joseph. *Journey to the Trenches: The Life of Isaac Rosenberg, 1890-1918*. London: Robson, 1975. Three biographies of Rosenberg were published in 1975, their combined effect being to bring him to public notice as a significant war poet. Cohen's account is the most sympathetic to his Jewish roots and background.

Desmond, Graham. *The Truth of War: Owen, Blunden, Rosenberg*. Manchester, England: Carcanet Press, 1984. A thoughtful approach to three contrasting World War I poets. A good bibliography with good commentaries on all of Rosenberg's trench poems.

Giddings, Robert. *The War Poets: The Lives and Writings of the 1914-18 War Poets*. London: Bloomsbury, 1988. A popular biographical approach, enacting Rosenberg's life and experience in the context of his contemporaries.

Liddiard, Jean. *Isaac Rosenberg: The Half-Used Life*. London: Gollancz, 1975. The second of the 1975 biographies, and probably the most straightforward one. A good approach to the poems.

Maccoby, Deborah. *God Made Blind: Isaac Rosenberg, His Life and Poetry*. Chicago: Science Reviews, 1999. This biography and critical analysis examines how Rosenberg's Jewish faith played a role in his life and writings.

Quinn, Patrick, ed. *British Poets of the Great War: Brooke, Rosenberg, Thomas—A Documentary Volume*. Detroit: Gale Group, 2000. Looks at Rupert Brooke, Edward Thomas, and Rosenberg and compares and contrasts their work.

Roberts, David. *Essential Poetry of the First World War in Context*. Burgess Hill, England: Saxon, 1996. Several critical books have tried to bring a historicist approach to Rosenberg and the other war poets, trying to reconstruct the overall social and political context out of which the poetry was generated. Roberts deals more with the poetic material than some others. Full bibliography.

Wilson, Jean Moorcroft. *Isaac Rosenberg, Poet and Painter: A Biography*. London: Cecil Woolf, 1975. The third of the 1975 biographies, this time tracing the growth of Rosenberg's artistic ideas and the interplay between poetry and painting.

_____. *Isaac Rosenberg: The Making of a Great War Poet—A New Life*. Evanston, Ill.: Northwestern University Press, 2009. This biography of the war poet, whose brief life produced some memorable poems, expands on Wilson's earlier work.

David Barratt

SIEGFRIED SASSOON

Born: Brenchley, Kent, England; September 8, 1886
Died: Heytesbury, England; September 1, 1967
Also known as: Saul Kain; Pinchbeck Lyre; Sigmund Sashun

PRINCIPAL POETRY
The Daffodil Murderer, 1913
The Old Huntsman, and Other Poems, 1917
Counter-Attack, and Other Poems, 1918
War Poems, 1919
Picture Show, 1920
Recreations, 1923
Selected Poems, 1925
Satirical Poems, 1926
The Heart's Journey, 1927
Poems of Pinchbeck Lyre, 1931
The Road to Ruin, 1933
Vigils, 1935
Poems Newly Selected, 1916-1935, 1940
Rhymed Ruminations, 1940
Collected Poems, 1947
Common Chords, 1950
Emblems of Experience, 1951
The Tasking, 1954
Sequences, 1956
Lenten Illuminations and Sight Sufficient, 1958
The Path to Peace, 1960
Collected Poems, 1908-1956, 1961
An Octave, 1966

OTHER LITERARY FORMS

Siegfried Sassoon (suh-SEWN) is nearly as well known for his prose works as for his poetry. From 1926 to 1945, he spent most of his time working on the two trilogies that form the bulk of his work in prose. The first of these was the three-volume fictionalized autobiography published in 1937 as *The Memoirs of George Sherston*. It begins in *Memoirs of a Fox-Hunting Man* (1928), by recounting the life of a well-to-do young country squire in Georgian England up to his first experiences as an officer in World War I. The second volume, *Memoirs of an Infantry Officer* (1930), and the third,

Sherston's Progress (1936), describe the young man's war experiences. In the later trilogy, Sassoon discarded the thinly disguised fiction of the Sherston novels and wrote direct autobiography, with a nostalgic look back at his pleasant pastoral life in prewar England in *The Old Century and Seven More Years* (1938) and *The Weald of Youth* (1942). In *Siegfried's Journey, 1916-1920* (1945), Sassoon looks again at his own experiences during and immediately following the war. These autobiographical works are invaluable to the student of Sassoon's poetry because of the context they provide, particularly for the war poems.

Two other significant prose works should be mentioned. The first is Sassoon's *Lecture on Poetry*, delivered at the University of Bristol on March 16, 1939, in which Sassoon delineated what he considered to be the elements of good poetry. The second work is Sassoon's critical biography of the poet George Meredith, titled simply *Meredith* (1948), which also suggests some of Sassoon's views on poetry.

Achievements

According to Bernard Bergonzi, Siegfried Sassoon was the only soldier-poet to be widely read during the war itself. This gave Sassoon a unique opportunity to influence other war poets, which he did. Though his war poetry has been criticized for being mere description, for appealing to only the senses and not the imagination, and for being uncontrolled emotion without artistic restraint, there can be no doubt than Sassoon's poetry represented a complete break with the war poetry of the past in tone, technique, and subject matter. With uncompromising realism and scathing satire, Sassoon portrayed the sufferings of the front-line soldier and the incompetency of the staff for the express purposes of convincing his readers to protest continuation of the war. His *Counter-Attack, and Other Poems* was nearly suppressed because of poems such as "The General," which broke the prohibition against criticizing those in charge of the war effort.

Unquestionably, Sassoon's realistic subject matter and diction influenced other poets, most notably his friend Wilfred Owen, whose poetry was posthumously published by Sassoon in 1920; but Sassoon failed to influence later poetry because, as John Johnston notes, his war poetry was all negative—he provided no constructive replacement for the myths he had destroyed. Nor did Sassoon influence poetry in the 1930's because, according to Michael Thorpe, he was still a prisoner of war, and through his autobiographies he retreated from the political struggle of W. H. Auden and Stephen Spender and others into his own earlier years.

When in the 1950's Sassoon finally did have something positive to offer, no one was willing to listen. He was no longer well known or critically acknowledged. Certainly his future reputation will rest on the war poems; but in his religious poems of the 1950's, Sassoon did achieve a style of simple expression, compact brevity, and concrete imagery with a universally appealing theme, and this should be noted as a remarkable though largely unrecognized achievement.

Biography

Siegfried Lorraine Sassoon was born in the Kentish weald in 1886, the second of three sons of Alfred Ezra Sassoon and Theresa Georgina Thornycroft. His father was descended from a long line of wealthy Jewish merchants and bankers who, after wandering through Spain, Persia, and India, had come to settle in England. The family was proud of its orthodoxy, and Siegfried's father was the first to marry outside the faith. Siegfried's mother, in contrast, was an artist, the close relative of three well-known sculptors, and a member of the landed gentry. The marriage was a failure, and Alfred Sassoon left when Siegfried was five, leaving the younger Sassoon to be reared by his mother as an Anglican.

Siegfried had no formal schooling as a child, though from the ages of nine to fourteen he learned from private tutors and a German governess. In 1902, he attended Marlborough, and in 1905, he entered Clare College, Cambridge. Sassoon's temperament was not disciplined enough for scholarly pursuits; he began by reading law, switched to history, and ultimately left Cambridge without a degree. He returned to Kent, where, on an inherited income of five hundred pounds a year, he was able to devote his energies to foxhunting, racing, and writing poetry. Sassoon loved the pastoral beauty of the Kentish downs and attempted to portray it in a number of dreamy, sentimental lyrics.

Between the ages of nineteen and twenty-six, Sassoon had nine volumes of poetry privately published, before he enjoyed a mild success with *The Daffodil Murderer* in 1913. The poem was chiefly intended as a parody of John Masefield's *The Everlasting Mercy*, but Sassoon's poem had a strong human appeal of its own. By this time, Sassoon had been befriended by Edward Marsh, the editor of *Georgian Poetry*. Marsh encouraged Sassoon's literary endeavors and persuaded him to come to London in May, 1914, where Sassoon began to move in the literary world and to meet such notable authors as Rupert Brooke. Sassoon, however, felt unhappy and lacked a sense of purpose, and when he enlisted in the army on August 3, 1914 (two days before England entered the war), it was to escape a sterile existence.

Sassoon's early life had been extremely sheltered, even pampered, and it was a very immature twenty-eight-year-old who went to war, totally unprepared for what he would find. After convalescence from injuries received in a fall during cavalry training, he accepted a commission and went through training as an infantry officer. Thus, he did not arrive in France until November, 1915, where he became transport officer for the First Battalion of the Royal Welch Fusiliers. Here he met and befriended the poet Robert Graves. In *Goodbye to All That* (1929), Graves describes his first meeting with Sassoon and relates how, when he showed Sassoon his first book of poems, *Over the Brazier* (1916), Sassoon, whose early war poems were idealistic, had frowned and said that war should not be written about in such a realistic way. Graves, who had been in France six months, remarked that Sassoon had not yet been in the trenches.

Graves already knew what Sassoon would soon discover, indeed what all the British troops in France were coming to feel: growing disillusionment at the frustration and the staggering casualties of trench warfare. There were 420,000 British casualties in the Somme offensive beginning on July 1, 1916—an offensive that gained virtually nothing. The Somme was Sassoon's most bitter experience in the trenches; after it, he would never write the old kind of poetry again.

In spite of his pacifist leanings, Sassoon distinguished himself in the war. Called "Mad Jack" by his troops, Sassoon was awarded the Military Cross and recommended for the Distinguished Service Order for his exploits in battle: After a raid at Mametz, he took it upon himself to bring back the wounded; in the Somme in early July, he singlehandedly occupied a whole section of an enemy trench, after which he was found in the trench, alone, reading a book of poetry. Ill with gastric fever in late July, he was sent home for three months, where he worked on poems to be included in *The Old Huntsman, and Other Poems*.

While in England, Sassoon met Lady Ottoline Morrell and her liberal husband, Philip, at whose home he spoke with such pacifists as Bertrand Russell, listened to open criticism of the war, and heard of Germany's peace overtures and the impure motives of members of parliament who wanted the war to continue.

Sassoon returned to active service in France in February, 1917, but in April, he was wounded in the Battle of Arras and sent home again. Haunted by nightmares of violence and by what the pacifists were saying, Sassoon resolved to protest the war on a grand scale. In July, in a remarkable move, risking public disgrace and military court-martial, Sassoon refused to return to active duty and wrote a formal declaration of protest to his commanding officer, which was reproduced in the press and which Russell arranged to have mentioned in the House of Commons. In his letter, Sassoon charged that the war was being deliberately prolonged by the politicians for ignoble purposes, even though there was a chance for a negotiated settlement with Germany, thus leading the men at the front line to be slaughtered needlessly. Sassoon hoped to be court-martialed, so that his protest would have propaganda value. To his dismay, however, the official reaction was largely to minimize the letter. In a moment of despair, Sassoon flung his Military Cross into the Mersey River and vowed to continue his protest.

At that point, Graves stepped in. Graves agreed with Sassoon's letter, but considered the gesture futile and feared for Sassoon's personal welfare. Graves arranged to have Sassoon appear before a medical board, and chiefly on Graves's testimony, Sassoon was found to be suffering from shell shock. The incident was closed, and Sassoon was sent to Craiglockhart hospital in Edinburgh, where physician W. H. R. Rivers became his counselor and friend, and where in August he met the brilliant young poet Wilfred Owen. Owen knew and idolized Sassoon as the author of *The Old Huntsman, and Other Poems* (which had appeared in May), and Sassoon's encouragement and insistence on realism had greatly influenced him. At Craiglockhart, during the autumn of 1917,

Sassoon composed many of the poems of *Counter-Attack, and Other Poems*, which was published the following year.

Owen returned to active duty in November, and Sassoon, feeling that he was betraying his troops at the front by staying away in comfort, returned to duty a few weeks later. He went first to Ireland, then to Egypt, where he became a captain, then back to France in May. On July 15, 1918, Sassoon, returning from an attack on a German machine gun, was wounded in the head by one of his own sentries. He was sent to a London hospital, where he spent the rest of the war.

After the war, Sassoon retreated from the active life, becoming more and more contemplative (he had always been introspective and solitary) until he acquired a reputation as a virtual hermit. Immediately after the war, he joined the Labor Party and became editor of the literary pages of the *Daily Herald*, where he published satirical pieces with a socialist point of view. His satire of the 1920's, however, was uneasy and awkward, stemming from the fact that the issues of the day were not as clear-cut as the right and wrong about the war had been. Besides, he was not really sure of himself, feeling a need to explore his past life and find some meaning in it. Still, as the 1930's grew darker, Sassoon wrote poems warning of the horror of chemical and biological warfare. No one seemed to want to listen, however, and Sassoon, disillusioned, forsook "political" poetry completely. In part, the autobiographies that he worked on in those years were a rejection of the modern world and an idealization of the past. In part, too, they were an effort to look inside himself, and that same urge characterizes most of his later poetry, which is concerned with his personal spiritual struggle and development.

Thus, the incidents of Sassoon's later life were nearly all spiritual. Only a few isolated events are of interest: In 1933, he finally married; he had a son, George, but Sassoon kept his personal relationships private, never mentioning them in his poetry. During World War II, Sassoon's home was requisitioned for evacuees, and later, fifteen hundred American troops were quartered on his large estate. After the war, Sassoon remained very solitary and appears to have cultivated his image as the "hermit of Heytesbury." When his volumes of poetry appeared in the 1950's, they were largely ignored by critics and public alike. The fiery war poet had outlived his reputation, but he had reached a great personal plateau: On August 14, 1957, Sassoon was received into the Catholic Church at Downside Abbey. His last poems, appearing in a privately published collection, *An Octave*, on his eightieth birthday (a year before his death), display a serene and quiet faith.

Analysis

In 1939, Siegfried Sassoon delineated his views on poetry in a lecture given at Bristol College. While what he said was not profound or revolutionary, it did indicate the kind of poetry Sassoon liked and tried to write, at least at that time. First, Sassoon said, poetry should stem from inspiration, but that inspiration needs to be tempered by control and discipline—by art. Second, the best poetry is simple and direct—Sassoon disliked the tendency toward complexity initiated by T. S. Eliot and Ezra Pound. Third, Sassoon held the Romantic view that poetry should express true feeling and speak the language of the heart. Fourth, poetry should contain strong visual imagery, the best of which is drawn from nature. Finally, the subject matter of the best poetry is not political (again, he was reacting against the avowedly political poetry of Auden and his associates), but rather personal, and this examination of self led Sassoon to write spiritual poetry.

A review of Sassoon's poetry will reveal, however, that even in his best poems he did not always follow all these precepts, and that in his worst poems he seldom followed any. Sassoon's worst poems are most certainly his earliest ones. Sassoon's prewar lyric verses are lush and wordy, in weak imitation of Algernon Charles Swinburne and the Pre-Raphaelites, but full of anachronisms and redundancies. Some, such as "Haunted" and "Goblin Revel," are purely escapist; Lewis Thorpe suggests that Sassoon was looking for escape from his own too-comfortable world. The best thing about these early poems is their interest in nature—an interest that Sassoon never lost and that provided him with concrete images in later pieces. The best poems that Sassoon wrote before the war, *The Daffodil Murderer* and "The Old Huntsman," abandon the poetic diction for a colloquial style, and "The Old Huntsman" reveals a strong kinship with nature.

THE WAR POETRY

Sassoon's early, idealistic war poetry is characterized by an abstract diction and generalized imagery. He was writing in the "happy warrior" style after the manner of Rupert Brooke's famous sonnet sequence and was even able to write of his brother's death early in the war as a "victory" and his ghost's head as "laureled." Perhaps the best example of these early poems is "Absolution," written before Sassoon had actually experienced the war. Sassoon romanticizes war, speaking of the glorious sacrifice of young comrades in arms who go off to battle as "the happy legion," asserting that "fighting for our freedom, we are free." The poem is full of such abstractions, but no concrete images. Its language is often archaic ("Time's but a golden wind"), and it is the sort of thing that Sassoon soon put behind him.

Edward Marsh, after reading some of Sassoon's earlier poetry, had told him to write with his eye directly on the object. As Sassoon began to experience the horrors of trench warfare, he did exactly that. His poems became increasingly concrete, visual, and realistic, his language became increasingly colloquial, and his tone became more and more bitter as the war went on. Early in 1916, he wrote "Golgotha," "The Redeemer," and "A Working Party," in which he tried to present realistically the sufferings of the common soldier. Such realistic depiction of the front lines characterized one of two main types of war poetry that Sassoon was to write in the next few years. The best example of sheer naturalistic description is "Counter-Attack," the title poem of Sassoon's most popular and most scathing volume of poetry. "Counter-Attack" begins with a description of the troops, who, having taken an enemy trench, begin to deepen it with shovels. They uncover a pile of dead bodies and rotting body parts—"naked sodden buttocks, mats of hair,/ Bulged, clotted heads."

"REPRESSION OF WAR EXPERIENCE"

The horror of this description is without parallel, but where Sassoon really excels is in his realistic portrayal of the psychological effects of the war. Perhaps his best poem in this vein is "Repression of War Experience," from *Counter-Attack, and Other Poems*. The poem, in the form of an interior monologue, explores a mind verging on hysteria, trying to distract itself and maintain control while even the simplest, most serene events—a moth fluttering too close to a candle flame—bring nightmarish thoughts of violence into the persona's mind. In the garden, he hears ghosts, and as he sits in the silence, he can hear only the guns. In the end, his control breaks down; he wants to rush out "and screech at them to stop—I'm going crazy;/ I'm going stark, staring mad because of the guns."

"THEY"

Sassoon was not merely presenting realistic details; he was being deliberately didactic, trying to use his poetry to incite a public outcry against the war. When home on leave, he had been appalled by the jingoistic ignorance and complacency on the home front. Sassoon's second main type of war poetry made a satirical attack on these civilians, on those who conducted the war, and on the irresponsible press that spread the lying propaganda. Justly the most famous of these poems is "They" (*The Old Huntsman, and Other Poems*), in which Sassoon demolishes the cherished civilian notion that the war was divinely ordained and that the British were fighting on God's side. Sassoon presents a pompous bishop declaring that, since the "boys" will have fought "Anti-Christ," none will return "the same" as he was. The irony of this statement is made clear when the "boys" return quite changed: blind, legless, and syphilitic. The bishop can only remark, "The ways of God are strange." "They" caused a great outcry in England by ruthlessly attacking the Church for forsaking the moral leadership it should have provided.

"They" also illustrates Sassoon's favorite technique in satire: concentration of his ironic force in the last line of the poem. This kind of "knock-out punch" may be seen most vividly in the poem "The One-Legged Man" (*The Old Huntsman, and Other Poems*), which describes a soldier, discharged from the war, watching the natural beauty of the world in autumn and considering the bright, comfortable years ahead. The poem ends with the man's crushingly ironic thought, "Thank God they had to amputate!"

Certainly there are flaws in Sassoon's war poetry. Some of the verses are nothing more than bitter invectives designed merely to attack a part of his audience, such as

"Glory of Women," "Blighters," and "Fight to the Finish." Even the best poems often lack the discipline and order that Sassoon himself later advanced as one main criterion of poetry. Further, Sassoon almost never got beyond his feelings about immediate experiences to form theoretical or profound notions about the broader aspects of the war. Sassoon himself realized this lack in 1920, when he brought out his slain friend Wilfred Owen's war poetry, which converted war experiences into something having universal meaning.

"The Dug Out"

The war poetry, however, has a number of virtues as well. It uses simple, direct, and clear expression that comes, as Sassoon advocated, from the heart. Further, it uses vivid pictures to express the inexpressible horror of the trenches. "The Dug Out" (*Picture Show*) is an example of Sassoon's war poetry at its best. In its eight lines, Sassoon draws a clear picture of a youth sleeping in an awkward and unnatural position. The simple, colloquial language focuses on the emotional state of the speaker, and much is suggested by what is left unsaid. The speaker's nerves are such that he can no longer bear the sight of the young sleeper because, as he cries in the final lines, "You are too young to fall asleep for ever;/ And when you sleep you remind me of the dead." Arthur Lane compares such poems, in which the ironic effect is achieved through the dramatic situation more than through imagery, to those in the *Satires of Circumstance* (1914) of Sassoon's idol, Thomas Hardy, suggesting an influence at work.

"Everyone Sang"

Perhaps the culmination of Sassoon's attempt to transcend his war experience is the much-admired lyric "Everyone Sang" (*Picture Show*). It is a joyous lyric expressing a mood of relief and exultation, through the imagery of song and of singing birds. Sassoon seems to have been expressing his own relief at having survived: "horror/ Drifted away." Lane calls these lines "pure poetry" of "visionary power," comparing them to poems of William Wordsworth and William Blake. He might have also mentioned Henry Vaughan, Sassoon's other idol, whose path toward poetry of a very personal spirituality Sassoon was soon to follow.

"Lines Written in Anticipation . . ."

Unquestionably, it is for his war poetry that Sassoon is chiefly admired. Still, he lived for nearly fifty years after the armistice, and what he wrote in that time cannot be disregarded. He first flirted with socialism after the war; "Everyone Sang" may be intended to laud the coming utopian society. Then he attempted satiric poetry during the 1920's, which must be regarded as a failure. His targets varied from the upper classes to political corruption and newspapers, but the poetry is not from the heart; the satire is too loud and not really convincing. Michael Thorpe points out the wordiness of Sassoon's style in these satires, together with the length of his sentences. One blatant example is "Lines Written in Anticipation of a London Paper Attaining a Guaranteed Circulation of Ten Million Daily." Even the title is verbose, but note the wordy redundancy of the lines:

> Were it not wiser, were it not more candid,
> More courteous, more consistent with good sense,
> If I were to include all, all who are banded
> Together in achievement so immense?

RELIGIOUS SEARCHING AND SPIRITUALITY

Though he soon abandoned the satiric mode, Sassoon did maintain what Joseph Cohen calls the role of prophet that he had assumed in the war years, by continually warning, through *The Road to Ruin* and *Rhymed Ruminations*, of the coming disaster of World War II. His total despair for the modern world is expressed in "Litany of the Lost" (1945), wherein, with the ominous line "Deliver us from ourselves," Sassoon bid farewell to the poetry of social commentary. By now he was more interested in his spiritual quest.

Next to his war poems, Sassoon's poems of religious searching are his most effective. The quest begins with "The Traveller to His Soul" (1933), in which Sassoon asks, as the "problem which concerns me most," the question "Have I got a soul?" He spends over twenty years trying to answer the question. His work, beginning with *The Heart's Journey* and *Vigils*, is concerned with exploration of self and uncertainty about the self's place in the universe, with increasing questioning about what lies behind creation. With *Rhymed Ruminations*, Sassoon ends the 1930's on a note of uneasiness and uncertainty.

SEQUENCES

The questions are answered in the three volumes *Common Chords*, *Emblems of Experience*, and *The Tasking*, which were combined to make the book *Sequences*. In the poem "Redemption" (*Common Chords*), Sassoon yearns for a vision of the eternal, which he recognizes as existing beyond his senses. Sassoon's lines recall Vaughan's mystical visions when he asks for "O but one ray/ from that all-hallowing and eternal day." In *The Tasking*, Sassoon reached what Thorpe calls a spiritual certainty, and his best poems in that volume succeed more clearly than the war poems in satisfying Sassoon's own poetic criteria as expressed in 1939. In "Another Spring," Sassoon speaks in simple, direct, and compact language about feelings of the heart—an old man's emotions on witnessing what may be his last spring. The natural imagery is concrete and visual as well as auditory, concentrating on "some crinkled primrose leaves" and "a noise of nesting rooks." Though the final three lines of the poem add a hint of didacticism, the poem succeeds by leaving much unsaid about the eternal rebirth of nature and its implications for the old man and the force behind the regenerative cycle of nature. It is a fine poem, like many in *The Tasking*, with a simple, packed style that makes these poems better as art, though doomed to be less familiar than the war poems.

OTHER MAJOR WORKS

LONG FICTION: *The Memoirs of George Sherston*, 1937 (includes *Memoirs of a Fox-Hunting Man*, 1928; *Memoirs of an Infantry Officer*, 1930; and *Sherston's Progress*, 1936).

NONFICTION: *The Old Century and Seven More Years*, 1938; *Lecture on Poetry*, 1939; *The Weald of Youth*, 1942; *Siegfried's Journey, 1916-1920*, 1945; *Meredith*, 1948; *Siegfried Sassoon Diaries, 1920-1922*, 1981; *Siegfried Sassoon Diaries, 1915-1918*, 1983; *Siegfried Sassoon Diaries, 1923-1925*, 1985.

EDITED TEXT: *Poems by Wilfred Owen*, 1920.

BIBLIOGRAPHY

Bloom, Harold, ed. *Poets of World War I: Rupert Brooke and Siegfried Sassoon*. Philadelphia: Chelsea House, 2003. Contains numerous essays on Sassoon, covering topics such as realism, satire, and spirituality in his poetry.

Caesar, Adrian. *Taking It Like a Man: Suffering, Sexuality, and the War Poets: Brooke, Sassoon, Owen, Graves*. New York: Manchester University Press, 1993. Caesar explores how four British poets reconciled their ideologies inherited from Christianity, imperialism, and Romanticism with their experiences of World War I.

Campbell, Patrick. *Siegfried Sassoon: A Study of the War Poetry*. Jefferson, N.C.: McFarland, 1999. Through primary documents and research, Campbell provides critical analyses of Sassoon's war poetry. Includes bibliographical references and an index.

Egremont, Max. *Siegfried Sassoon: A Life*. New York: Farrar, Straus and Giroux, 2005. This biography of Sassoon examines his life, including his relationship with Stephan Tennant, its breakup, and his subsequent marriage.

Fussell, Paul. *The Great War and Modern Memory*. 1975. Reprint. New York: Oxford University Press, 2000. This classic study of the literature arising from the experience of fighting in World War I pays special attention to Sassoon's fiction, autobiography, and poetry. Provides a useful context for Sassoon's work in comparison to other writers of the period.

Hipp, Daniel. *The Poetry of Shell Shock: Wartime Trauma and Healing in Wilfred Owen, Ivor Gurney, and Siegfried Sassoon*. Jefferson, N.C.: McFarland, 2005. Contains chapters examining the lives and works of three war poets: Sassoon, Wilfred Owen, and Ivory Gurney.

Lane, Arthur E. *An Adequate Response: The War Poetry of Wilfred Owen and Siegfried Sassoon*. Detroit: Wayne State University Press, 1972. Lane highlights the use of satire and parody as he analyzes Sassoon's war verse. Contends that Sassoon and others, when faced with the horrors of trench warfare, were charged with creating a new mode of expression since the traditional modes proved inadequate.

Moeyes, Paul. *Siegfried Sassoon: Scorched Glory—A Critical Study*. New York: St. Martin's Press, 1997. Moeyes draws on Sassoon's edited diaries and letters to explore Sassoon's assertion that his poetry was his real autobiography. Includes bibliography and an index.

Wilson, Jean Moorcroft. *Siegfried Sassoon: The Journey from the Trenches—A Biography, 1918-1967*. London: Duckworth, 2003. Describes the later years of Sassoon's life, looking at his life after the war.

———. *Siegfried Sassoon: The Making of a War Poet—A Biography*. New York: Routledge, 1999. Details Sassoon's early life, covering the years from his birth through 1918, and in doing so, closely examines his struggle to come to terms with being gay.

Jay Ruud

ALAN SEEGER

Born: New York, New York; June 22, 1888
Died: Belloy-en-Santerre, France; July 4, 1916

PRINCIPAL POETRY
Poems, 1916

OTHER LITERARY FORMS

Known primarily for his poetry, Alan Seeger also wrote occasional journalism. A wartime diary, which includes a series of insightful letters to his mother and his friends, was published as *Letters and Diary of Alan Seeger*, 1917.

ACHIEVEMENTS

During his life, Alan Seeger won no major awards for his poetry. However, his death in the early stages of World War I brought his poetry to an enormous audience. His death seemed to demonstrate his commitment to the values he espoused in his poems, such as honor, sacrifice, and valor. The poems and the example of his short life earned him recognition in the early 1920's from the French government, which erected a monument honoring him and other American volunteers who served in the French Foreign Legion prior to the United States' entering World War I. Several sections of Seeger's memorial poem, "Ode in Memory of the American Volunteers Fallen for France," which was completed two months before Seeger's death in combat, are engraved on the memorial.

BIOGRAPHY

Born in 1888, Alan Seeger spent most of his early years in New York City. From 1900 to 1902, he lived with his family in Mexico, where his father had business interests; for much of the next eight years, Seeger lived in Mexico off and on, acquiring what he called a fair command of Spanish and a deep appreciation for Mexican culture.

In 1906, Seeger matriculated at Harvard University, where he studied literature and served as editor of the *Harvard Monthly*. After graduating in 1910, Seeger moved back to New York, to the then-quiet neighborhood of Greenwich Village, where he tried to make ends meet with poetry, occasional journalism, and a short-term job as a library clerk. In a letter he wrote to a potential employer in New York in 1910, Seeger wrote that he knew from boyhood that he wanted to be a poet and seriously considered no other profession. In the same letter, he noted that he had been offered a job with good potential for advancement in a publishing firm but was not going to take the position.

By 1912, Seeger had begun to realize that New York did not offer a productive environment for his attempts to write and grow as a poet. In the middle of 1912, Seeger left New York for Paris, joining a small colony of American expatriates, most of whom were artists or writers. At that time, Paris was a world center for the arts; French culture seemed particularly attractive and nonjudgmental to those who wanted to pursue new directions in music, poetry, sculpture, and painting. Although by nature a conservative poet whose models were John Keats, Lord Byron, Arthur Rimbaud, and Alfred, Lord Tennyson, Seeger also found Paris a congenial place in which to write. In "Paris," Seeger delights that:

> looking out over the domes and towers
> That chime the fleeting quarters and the hours,
> While the bright clouds banked eastward back of them
> Blush in the sunset, pink as hawthorn flowers,
>
> You cannot fail to think, as I have done,
> Some of life's ends attained, so you be one
> Who measures life's attainment by the hours
> That Joy has rescued from oblivion.

By July, 1914, Seeger had assembled a collection of poems and was actively seeking a publisher. However, this volume—or any other collection of his poems—was not published in his lifetime.

In August, 1914, the start of World War I, Seeger volunteered to serve in the French Foreign Legion. In letters, Seeger observed that he did so not out of dislike for Germany—in fact, he counted himself an admirer of German culture—but out of love for France. Like many other expatriate Americans in Paris in 1914, Seeger enlisted because he wanted to protect France and its culture in the war. In addition, Seeger joined the legion because he saw warfare as a heroic enterprise and anticipated that the war would change the course of Western civilization and because he felt he owed it to his friends, especially those who did not have the freedom to choose.

Seeger saw his share of combat and hardship during the first two years of the war, which gave a thorough fatalism to many of his best poems. Service in the field damaged Seeger's respiratory system, and in 1916, he was hospitalized for acute bronchitis. While convalescing, Seeger wrote his most famous poem, "I Have a Rendezvous with Death." In early July, 1916, in the early phases of the Battle of the Somme, Seeger and his detachment were ordered to Belloy-en-Santerre, a small town near Amiens. Contemporary reports indicate that the French forces were expected to capture fortified German positions by means of a bayonet charge across open fields. In the early stages of the attack, on July 4, 1916, Seeger was hit by machine-gun fire and died while trying to dress his wound.

Analysis

Although he wrote an enormous number of poems from his boyhood to his death in 1916, Alan Seeger remains known primarily as a poet of the early years of World War I. In at least one study of the literature of that war, Seeger and other early poets (including Rupert Brooke and Julian Grenfell) are contrasted with the more cynical and purportedly more truthful poets of 1916-1918, such as Siegfried Sassoon and Wilfred Owen. The point is sometimes made that the earlier poets, Seeger among them, offered an immature, view of the war that was highly idealized and, hence, thoroughly false. In the words of one critic, Adam Zagajewski, the experiences of the war "thrust writers in the direction of an outraged realism." Anything that was not either outraged or realistic was contemptible.

In Seeger's case, such an argument is unfair because his most noteworthy poems clearly detail the human costs of war. These were costs that he, like most other combatants, knew well. In fact, what the poems champion is not warfare and what they glorify is not violence; instead, what the best of Seeger's poems celebrate is human courage, devotion, and honor.

"Ode in Memory of the American Volunteers Fallen for France"

Apart from "I Have a Rendezvous with Death," Seeger's most famous poem is "Ode in Memory of the American Volunteers Fallen for France," which was written for public reading in Paris on Memorial Day, a date in the United States set aside to honor those who died in service to their country. At the time the poem was written, early 1916, the United States was neutral and isolationist, and President Woodrow Wilson was lauded for keeping the country out of what was perceived to be a European war.

Seeger's task, at that historical moment, was not to represent the horrors of war as he surely knew them, but rather to convince his audience that a scant handful of Americans who died in the French Foreign Legion were more truly American than those who wanted to stay out of the war. To the poet, the legionnaires connected directly with those who died in the American Civil War and the American Revolutionary War; their deaths answered those who questioned the American devotion to freedom:

> If there be any here
> Who wonder if her manhood be decreased,
> Relaxed its sinews and its blood less red
> Than that at Shiloh and Antietam shed.

For a Francophile like Seeger, American isolationism was repugnant, little better than cowardice; therefore, he referred to several Civil War battles to demonstrate his contention that those expatriates who fought for a foreign nation were truer to the American ideal than those who wanted to keep the United States out of the war. The volunteers, in other words, were fighting not just for France but for freedom itself. They fought against the enemies who

> in that hour that most imperiled her,
> Menaced her liberty who foremost raised
> Europe's bright flag of freedom, some there were
> Who, not unmindful of the antique debt,
> Came back the generous path of Lafayette.

As a public poem to honor the fallen, to move a neutral nation, and to celebrate sacrifice, "Ode in Memory of the American Volunteers Fallen for France" could hardly be expected to be anything other than laudatory. Seeger's death, within six months of the poem's dedication, made Seeger himself one of the fallen American volunteers.

"I Have a Rendezvous with Death"

Seeger's view of the war, at least as it is expressed in his poems (as opposed to his letters or his diary) is certainly idealized, but it is hardly immature. "I Have a Rendezvous with Death," perhaps Seeger's finest poem, was completed in early 1916 while he was hospitalized in Biarritz and Paris, recovering from acute bronchitis. He had served almost two years, and the letters he wrote at the time reveal he had already experienced his share of violence. In this poem, the speaker describes the changing seasons of the year, and although he points out the expected beauties of spring in France, he also observes the likelihood that he will die sometime in the new year.

Throughout the poem, there is an extended interweaving of clear contrasts between living—which is represented beautifully and sensuously, with "rustling shade" and "apple-blossoms" that scent the air—and dying—which is always shown in the poem as short, quick, and ugly, as in "On some scarred slope of battered hill." Toward the end of the poem, the speaker opines that he could choose one escape from the likelihood of death, and that is to remain laying in bed:

> God knows 'twere better to be deep
> Pillowed in silk and scented down,
> Where Love throbs out in blissful sleep,
> Pulse nigh to pulse, and breath to breath,
> Where hushed awakenings are dear . . .

However, he rejects this option: He has given his "pledged word" and must keep his promises, no matter the result.

Like the speaker in the poem, the poet himself was lying in bed—albeit a hospital bed—and all too aware that as the year progressed the chances of his dying in battle would increase. Within three months of completing the poem, Seeger was killed in battle on a scarred slope in northern France.

Other major work

NONFICTION: *Letters and Diary of Alan Seeger*, 1917.

BIBILIOGRAPHY

Archer, William. Introduction to *Poems by Alan Seeger*, edited by William Archer. 1917. Reprint. Charleston, S.C.: BiblioBazaar, 2008. The introduction to Seeger's posthumously published collection provides literary criticism and a biography. Archer calls the poet a "very rare spirit" and praises his decision to fight in the war, seeing it as a determination to live life to the fullest. This early introduction enhances readers' understanding of its early reception.

Cross, Tim. *The Lost Voices of World War I: An International Anthology of Writers, Poets and Playwrights*. Iowa City: University of Iowa Press, 1989. Places Seeger's work in context, showcasing his poem "I Have a Rendezvous with Death" as one of the finest examples of early war poetry.

Poë, Simon. "Among the First to Fall." *New Statesman* 134, no. 4746 (2005): 40-42. Summarizes the often-repeated critical maxim that the early war poets, like Seeger, were flawed by an idealized, romantic view of the conflict, and therefore, their poetry is flawed.

Saunders, Max. "Friendship and Enmity in First World War Literature." *Literature and History* 17, no. 1 (2008): 62-77. A brief essay that uses psychological criticism to uncover a series of themes in World War I literature. One such theme, with particular importance in light of Seeger's love of France, is how the war complicated the issue of national identity.

Seeger, Alan. *Alan Seeger: The Complete Works*. Edited by Amanda Harlech. Paris: Edition 7L, 2001. Draws together Seeger's poems, his diary, and letters, and contains photographs of the locations described in the works.

Winn, James Anderson. *The Poetry of War*. New York: Cambridge University Press, 2008. In this wide-ranging discussion of war and poetry, Winn provides some analysis of Seeger's poetry, using his diary and the poetry itself. He looks in particular at the concept of shame as evidenced in Seeger's poetry.

Zagajewski, Adam. "The Shabby and the Sublime." *The New Republic* 220 (April 5, 1999): 32-37. Argues that the horrors of World War I forced a radical redefinition in poetic diction used to represent extreme experiences; the prewar taste for elevated diction and heroic sentiments (of the kind Seeger expresses) would come to be seen as propaganda later in the war and well into the 1930's.

Michael R. Meyers

LOUIS SIMPSON

Born: Kingston, Jamaica; March 27, 1923

PRINCIPAL POETRY
The Arrivistes: Poems, 1940-1949, 1949
Good News of Death, and Other Poems, 1955
A Dream of Governors, 1959
At the End of the Open Road, 1963
Selected Poems, 1965
Adventures of the Letter I, 1971
Searching for the Ox, 1976
Caviare at the Funeral, 1980
The Best Hour of the Night, 1983
People Live Here: Selected Poems, 1949-1983, 1983
Collected Poems, 1988
In the Room We Share, 1990
Jamaica Poems, 1993
There You Are, 1995
The Owner of the House: New Collected Poems, 1940-2001, 2003
Struggling Times, 2009

OTHER LITERARY FORMS

Louis Simpson's contributions to criticism and literary analysis include *The New Poets of England and America* (1957; edited with Donald Hall and Robert Pack) and *James Hogg: A Critical Study* (1962). These two studies pointed the direction poetry, especially Simpson's own, was to take in subsequent years. Simpson wrote several other works of literary criticism in following years, including *Three on the Tower: The Lives and Works of Ezra Pound, T. S. Eliot, and William Carlos Williams* in 1975. Another volume of criticism, *A Revolution in Taste: Studies of Dylan Thomas, Allen Ginsberg, Sylvia Plath, and Robert Lowell*, appeared in 1978. This work was followed by two other volumes, *A Company of Poets* (1981) and *The Character of the Poet* (1986), which expanded and defined Simpson's literary tastes, principles, and objectives. Prolific into the 1990's, Simpson published more literary studies in *Ships Going into the Blue: Essays and Notes on Poetry* in 1994.

Simpson's only novel, *Riverside Drive* (1962), won critical respect but convinced him that his talent was better suited to poetry, although his reputation as a literary critic brought him much respect in later years. *North of Jamaica* (1972) is a prose account of his childhood in Jamaica, his wartime experiences, and his teaching career at Columbia

University and the University of California, Berkeley. This autobiography introduces the reader to Simpson's ideas on poetry as he saw it being practiced and as he thought it should be written. The book shows how much of Simpson's poetry derives from his own life and how seamlessly the two are joined. The autobiographical account is continued in *The King My Father's Wreck* (1995).

Achievements

Louis Simpson's literary career has generated enough commentary to rank him among the major poets of the second half of the twentieth century. His war poems have been called the best to come out of World War II, and his literary criticism has gained him additional respect. His poetic reputation was barely established when he was awarded the Prix de Rome in 1957, and this award was followed in 1964 by a Pulitzer Prize for his collection of poems *At the End of the Open Road*. He also received the Edna St. Vincent Millay Award (1960), a Silver Medal from the Commonwealth Club of California (1965) for *Selected Poems*, Guggenheim Fellowships (1962, 1970), and an Academy Award in Literature (1976) from the American Academy and Institute of Arts and Letters. His *Modern Poets of France: A Bilingual Anthology* garnered the Harold Morton Landon Translation Award in 1998. Perhaps much of the respect he has earned as a critic stems from his not aligning himself with any literary school or movement. In 2004, he was a finalist for the Griffen prize.

Biography

Louis Simpson's life is especially important because of its relation to his poetic development. He was born Louis Aston Marantz Simpson in Kingston, Jamaica, on March 27, 1923. His father was a lawyer of Scottish descent, his mother a Jewish immigrant from southern Russia. His parents had met when Rosalind de Marantz went to Kingston from New York City to appear in a film. A brother had been born first, then Louis. Following the breakup of the marriage in 1930, Rosalind went to Toronto. Louis was sent with his brother to Munro College, a private school about eighty miles from Kingston. Louis was to remain at Munro College until he was seventeen years old. His father remarried, and another child was born. When Louis was near graduation, his father died, leaving most of his estate to his new family. Louis and his brother were made to leave their parental home immediately. On his own, Louis returned to school, where he excelled in literary studies and developed two goals: to be a writer and to leave Jamaica. At sixteen, he was already writing and publishing poetry and prose. This principle would guide him in writing about all the "real wars" he was to wage back in the United States.

In New York, Simpson entered Columbia University, where he studied under Mark Van Doren. In 1943, he joined the U.S. Army and was sent to Texas. Military life turned him into a dog soldier with little respect for officers. The Army also enabled him to see Texas, Louisiana, and Missouri. He took part in the Normandy invasion, fought at

Bastogne, and visited London and Paris, leaving the service in 1947. By war's end, he had gained United States citizenship, won the Bronze Star with cluster, twice earned the Purple Heart, and grown cynical. He was married to Jeanne Rogers (1949-1953) and to Dorothy Roochvarg (1955-1979). He received a B.S. (1948), an M.A. (1950), and a Ph.D. (1959) from Columbia University. He taught at the University of California, Berkeley, from 1959 to 1967, and the State University of New York at Stony Brook from 1967 to 1993. Making his permanent residence in Setauket, New York, he has traveled extensively, to Australia and Europe. After his retirement, Simpson continued to write literary essays and poetry and to translate French poetry.

Analysis

Louis Simpson's development as a poet encompasses virtually the entire second half of the twentieth century. At a time when the Academic poets warred with the Beat poets, Simpson marched to his own poetic rhythms. He passed through the waters of the Deep Image without being caught in its currents. Wordsworthian influences have been noted in his poetry, and Simpson gives important attention to Walt Whitman in both his poetry and prose, but Whitman's influence is perhaps more psychological and theoretical than overt. Using forms and devices that were necessary to express his poetic vision and to speak in a voice that was his own, Simpson has stood apart from literary traditions and popular trends, finding a unique voice and vantage point to illuminate a common humanity.

The Arrivistes

Simpson's first volume, *The Arrivistes*, includes poems of mixed forms and subjects. A sestina, a ballad, and a versified dialogue are found among lyrics on war, love, and death. In the book's mixture of classical and modern materials, one finds Simpson's major interests—the city, love, war, and art—all explored with irony and wit. His images have sharpness and emotive force: for example, "the sun was drawn bleeding across the hills" ("Jamaica"). Simpson's interest in the wanderer is evident in "The Warrior's Return" (the warrior being Odysseus) and in "Lazarus Convalescent," in which the biblical Lazarus faintly suggests the poet coming from the "hell" of war to speak to the living. Succinct to the point of aphoristic, many lines cut through literary self-consciousness. "Room and Board" creates a somber city scene; set in France, it expresses genuine feelings through vivid imagery.

Good News of Death, and Other Poems

In *Good News of Death, and Other Poems*, Simpson continues to show interest in romantic love, war, death, the loss of hope, and the ironic contrast between classical and modern values. Here the rhythms are less regular, and the rhymes have loosened. Simpson's characteristic irony and wit are well represented, along with a sensitivity to the seasons, a softening of war's disillusionment, and a corresponding emphasis on lyrical love tinged by a sense of loss or mild sorrow. "The Man Who Married Magdalene" demonstrates the confident handling of voice, tone, and manner that is found increasingly in the poems: "But when he woke and woke alone/ He wept and would deny/ The loose behavior of the bone/ And the immodest thigh." In "Memories of a Lost War," Simpson has discovered a way to shape experience into a form that releases sharp meaning: "The scene jags like a strip of celluloid,/ A mortar fires,/ Cinzano falls, Michelin is destroyed,/ The man of tires." Simpson's gift for juxtaposition has given him a way to mix disparate bits of information into a vivid, moving collage.

Literary portraiture, another of Simpson's strengths, often combines with his interest in objective reality. In "American Preludes," America's past comes under scrutiny, and "West," in open stanza and irregular line, shows a growing interest in modern America. The social commentary in many of the poems hints at a growing interest in the direction American society is taking and an interest in the lives of those who inhabit the land. He finds that boredom is widespread and that many people have founded their lives on values that are false or fragile. "Good News of Death," a pastoral, returns to the bucolic past in rhyme and regular lines to express the idea that the classical past is reborn in the birth of Christ. The "good news" is that Christ offers salvation to humankind.

A Dream of Governors

A Dream of Governors is Simpson's first collection to be divided into sections, each titled, reflecting the poet's concern with the arrangement of the poems. In the first group, poems are cast mainly in regular lines and rhymed stanzas, and there is a mixture of classical and modern. The classical lovers in "The Green Shepherd" remain unaffected by the great westward thrust of empire, while the "dragon rises crackling in the air" over the Western Hemisphere. The dragon as symbol of ensuing devastation of the land appears again in the title poem, "A Dream of Governors," the dream being "The City," which the Knight rescues from the dragon, only to become king and grow "old/ and ludicrous and fat." The poem ends as the dragon rises again. Demoniac characters and gloomy overtones are to be found in other poems in this collection as well. "To the Western World" concludes grimly: "And grave by grave we civilize the ground." "The country that Columbus thought he found . . . looks unreal," the poet muses in "Landscape with Barns." "Only death looks real." Even America's vaunted freedom "is the basilisk," and the poet's reaction to the Land of Opportunity is to realize that "the melancholy of the possible/ Unmeasures me" ("Orpheus in America").

The idyllic past, only a fantasy, sends the poet to the Old World, where he finds a graveyard. The poetry is becoming more autobiographical as the lines and stanzas continue to open. The poet's voice sounds more like natural speech: "But I am American, and bargain . . . where the junk of culture/ Lies in the dust" ("An American in the Thieves' Market"). In "The Runner," which occupies roughly a third of the entire volume, war is seen through the eyes of a soldier whose journey takes the reader through war as Simpson saw it himself. Following it, "The Bird" injects a fairy-tale quality into the grim aspect of war. Simpson's interest in the surreal may have suggested the vision of a young German soldier who is sent to work in a concentration camp, all the while singing the refrain, "I wish I were a bird." The rhymed quatrains with their three-stress lines create an otherworldly atmosphere. There are Russian tanks, and there is "a little bird . . . flitting"—the transformed soldier. The same stanzaic pattern is used in one of Simpson's most celebrated war poems, "Carentan, O Carentan," which reads somewhat like a ballad and focuses on the poignancy of death in war with ironic overtones.

The love poems in the final section continue the mixture of pastoral and classical with modern characters and scenes rendered in regular rhymed stanzas. The volume ends with "Tom Pringle," a poem spoken in the voice of a young man who "will watch the comets' flight . . . And wonder what they mean." Tom Pringle could watch the comets' flight, but Simpson had to return to America.

AT THE END OF THE OPEN ROAD

At the End of the Open Road looks squarely at modern America and its recent past. The voice is often conversational, classical allusions have been dropped, and the lines and stanzas are unrhymed and irregular. Simpson's penchant for focusing on the objects of his world and its people is clearly evident. The mood is serious, and the irony is restrained. "In California" begins with the poet speaking in his own voice—"Here I am"—but by the end, the "I" has become "we." He has joined those who travel the open road and come to the western gate, where they must "turn round the wagons." He discovers that "there's no way out" ("In the Suburbs"). The suburbs trap the body and spirit, and the seeking continues: "I tread the burning pavement. . . . I seek the word. The word is not forthcoming" ("There Is").

Turning to his own past, the poet remembers his grandmother's house, where "there was always chicken soup/ And talk of the old country" ("A Story About Chicken Soup"). He has learned "not to walk in the painted sunshine/ . . . But to live in the tragic world forever." Simpson employs again the narrative form to reveal his vision of the world, blending the open form with a voice closer to his own, as in "Moving the Walls," in which a modern voyager, collecting gewgaws, misses the deeper mystery of the world. The men who sought the golden fleece sought the grand and beautiful mysteries. Looking around, the poet doubts that he sees "any at sea."

Many of the poems reflect the poet's journey from Europe to Japan as if in search of fulfillment, a deeper perception. Searching is thematic and culminates thus: "I am going into the night to find a world of my own" ("Love, My Machine"). Simpson has found that Whitman's open road "goes to the used-car lot"; in "Walt Whitman at Bear Mountain," the angel from "In California" appears again, dancing "like Italy, imagining red," still ambiguous. The search is for a way out of a spiritual cul-de-sac. In the final poem,

"Lines Written near San Francisco," the American dream turns out to be "cheap housing in the valleys// Where lives are mean and wretched."

Selected Poems

A dozen new pieces in *Selected Poems* revive thoughts of impending disaster, rendered in striking imagery. In "The Union Barge on Staten Island," the poet sees a threat in nature itself: "Under your feet, the wood seems deeply alive./ It's the running sea you feel." The animals "felt the same currents," and ominous clouds drift "over the Wilderness, over the still farms." The poet discovers in "Things" that "machines are the animals of the Americans." Nevertheless, he finally feels a kinship with those whom he has been observing from a distance: "Who lives in these dark houses?/ I am suddenly aware/ I might live here myself" ("After Midnight").

Adventures in the Letter I

The eye turned inward becomes the basis of *Adventures in the Letter I*, in which Simpson looks beyond contemporary America and finds the Russia his mother used to describe. The poems are often autobiographical, freed of rhymed stanzas and regular lines. The lines do not invariably begin with capital letters. Simpson wants his poetic language to look more like the speech it is becoming. "Adam Yankev" creates a portrait of the artist looking at himself, realizing that, though his head is "full of ancient life," he sees "houses,/ streets, bridges, traffic, crowds," people whose "faces are strangely familiar." No longer alienated by what he sees, the poet finds that "things want to be understood."

Though still somewhat disengaged from the world, the poet feels a kinship. In "The Photographer," a still life gives ideas "a connection." Simply to look is to find meaning, a kinship. In a longer poem telling of a man having an affair that ends in the grim reality of paying alimony and child support, the poet's sympathy is evident in the final vision of the man's life: "Maybe/ he talks to his pillow, and it whispers,/ moving red hair" ("Vandergast and the Girl"). Kinship is also evident in the poet's speaking as the ghost of a dead man: "And I, who used to lie with the moon,/ am here in a peat-bog" ("On a Disappearance of the Moon"). In "An American Peasant," the poet shares the peasant's trust in "silence" and distrust of "ideas."

Some of the poems read like letters to the reader: "My whole life coming to this place,/ and understanding it better" ("Port Jefferson"). In the poet's ancestral past lies the meaning he has been seeking. In "A Friend of the Family," the technology that deadens the spirit of America spreads to Asia while the speaker envisions nights in Russia, where a "space-rocket rises" and is called "Progress." The poet realizes that Anton Chekhov "was just a man," that the world is peopled by Vanya and Ivanov, that "people live here... you'd be amazed." As Simpson says in "Sacred Objects," people find their "sacred objects" by living in the moment and for the moment.

SEARCHING FOR THE OX

Searching for the Ox opens with Simpson reminiscing about his boyhood on the shore of Kingston harbor and tracing his life to the present. The wanderer's life has been poetically circular. To advance is to come back to the starting place, though one continues to change, to discover. In many of the poems, the poet's life unfolds without a sense of kinship or connection with the objects and people that earlier had taught him where the mystery lies and perhaps how to engage with it. "Words are realities," he reminds the reader. "They have the power/ to make us feel and see" ("The Springs of Gadara"), as do people, places, things. Mechanical lives and repetitious rounds continue as though waiting for some meaning to break the cycle; when they are transformed into a poetic vision, their meaning becomes felt, implicit.

The poet's sense of pointless repetition and continued disengagement threads through places, times, and the lives of the people remembered or envisioned. "Cliff Road" ends at "a fence on a cliff,/ looking at the lights on the opposite shore." The way through and beyond this impasse lies in the word. Baruch always wanted to study the Torah ("Baruch"). Like the old man, the poet says, "We have been devoted to words." With this faith in the word and its redemptive power goes a continuing attachment to the real world just beyond the senses. Abstractions lead away from the objects that give meaning. In "Searching for the Ox," the speaker says, "I find my awareness/ of the world . . . has increased." The search ends in the discovery: "There is only earth."

The final section includes more snapshots of the world the poet is journeying through, a trip that shifts back to his ancestral past and forward to the present. At the same time, the poet looks outward and inward. Changed by what he sees, he changes it, the part humankind imposes on the world, the "Machine." By recognizing the monotonous, mechanical nature of a shelling machine, for example, he has changed it. Recognition by "a total stranger" of the thing that makes human life mechanical gives character, even life, to both.

CAVIARE AT THE FUNERAL

In *Caviare at the Funeral*, Simpson continues seeing kinship between the inner and outer worlds, and he finds a connection between the past and present. The opening poem, "Working Late," weaves memories of the poet's father with images from nature that suggest the poet's mother. The moon "has come all the way from Russia," as the mother had done, a sojourner like her son. Still, the son feels a kinship with his father, whose light shines in the study—it "now shines as late in mine." Shards from the everyday world resonate in his memory as the portraits of individuals unfold around and through them. As the artist's sensibility gives them meaningful shape, a world of meaning is created. Poetry gives the poet what he seeks: meaning from the inert objects that claim his attention.

The poet remains the outsider, observing events and individuals and occasionally commenting on them, though he often lets a description of a scene make the comment. In "Little Colored Flags," the poet envisions the bland typicalness of small-town life; the sea is tucked away "behind the last house at the end of the street," all but unnoticed, suggesting that those who do not see the world around them become prisoners of their own limited vision. The poet paints scenes in which people sense the futility of life, having surrendered to the mechanical motions of a technological world. "Unfinished Life" provides a telling symbol: "A hubcap went rolling in circles, ringing as it settled." The sound is not the music of the spheres, nor the sirens's call. It is the shrill voice of trapped spirits.

Simpson reiterates his faith in the redemptive power of words in "Profession of Faith" and again in "Why Do You Write About Russia?" The soul of poetry is the "voice." That voice deserves to be heard, for it expresses the poet's "love," his "infinite wonder." Only it, the poet suggests, offers a way out of the "dream" everyone lives. The quest is for "a life in which there are depths/ beyond happiness." A kinship with the past, geographical and ancestral, is nurtured by sound, "such as you hear/ in a sea breaking along a shore." The sounds of nature, of the past, and of people form a universal bond.

In the final section of the volume, Simpson's trip to Australia is presented in poetic snapshots and a prose piece. The theme of the outsider persists in "Out of Season": "when I am away from home/ . . . it is as though there were another self/. . . waiting to find me alone." Persisting too is the faith that there may be a reason for being "in one place rather than another."

THE BEST HOUR OF THE NIGHT

The series of poems in *The Best Hour of the Night* reflects an ongoing interest in the scenes and characters that Simpson encountered in Russia and the United States. The forms remain free, and the dramatic narrative continues to weave commentary and image out of ordinary things and people. "Quiet Desperation" portrays another individual trapped in the monotony of modern life. All his searching can accomplish is a "feeling of pressure" that leads to a vague idea of the depths, the wonder and mystery, beyond the surface world, but they evade him. "The Previous Tenant" offers a similar portrait, that of a man in yet another suburb whose illicit affair has destroyed his marriage. The speaker approves of the affair, for in "such ordinary things" the vigor, if not the beauty, of life can be seen. Modern life still exacts a heavy price: One's spirit is buried "under the linoleum," ingested by the things the culture has disgorged, "brown material/ grained like wood, with imitation knotholes" ("In Otto's Basement").

PEOPLE LIVE HERE

The poems in *People Live Here* are grouped without attention to chronology, Simpson points out. He ends with a prose reflection on his early life, up to World War II, and his artistic credo: "I don't write for myself. . . . I write poems in order to express feelings I have had since I was a child . . . to express the drama, the terror and beauty of life." The close affinity between Simpson's poetry and prose reflections is evident in the final section of *People Live Here* and *In the Room We Share*. Fully a third of this latter volume is given over to journal entries describing a trip to visit his mother in Italy. In both his poetry and his prose, Simpson continues to record the world. The poetry, because it is more compressed and focused than the prose, becomes a window through which the reader sees what the poet sees. The elements synthesize; poetry is achieved.

IN THE ROOM WE SHARE

Simpson has always been keenly aware of nature's presence—the trees, the sea, the wind. These elements surround many of his experiences, like ministering spirits. The poems in *In the Room We Share* show him returning again and again to his past, to his search beyond happiness, to the drama of life and the scenes and characters that generate it. In "Words," the poet is reading his poems to a group of students, talking to them as through a glass, seen but not heard. Memories of his own youth return to the room he is sharing with the young people, who wonder what he might have to say that might have meaning to them. He tells them how he began to write: When his senses were stirred by an image of "gray eyes, long golden hair," he found the genesis of poetry, "a vision of beauty." Are the youths listening to him? Probably not.

Simpson recapitulates familiar subjects: his war experiences, life in New York City and the suburbs, experiences in Germany, France, Italy, Jamaica, Russia, and various sites in the United States. The poet is the transcontinental observer, giving life to what he sees, voice to nature and people, and meaning to everything, though he is always the outsider, the other person in the room "we" share. Considering the lives of his neighbors ("Neighbors"), the poet remains attuned to sights and sounds, "as though a world were building/ its likeness through the ear."

Simpson's circular journey has taken him from gloomy predictions of disaster and a sense of alienation to an enfolding vision. In sound, the sea, and the word, Simpson sees kinship. The walls of his world form concentric circles from the poet outward, enclosing himself, his neighborhood, city, country, and the whole world, but these walls dissolve in the poem. Form both encloses and releases. The poem is a glass that alternates as a mirror and a transparent pane. Simpson's poetic has constructed a room shared by all those who read him, but without walls. The past and present are interwoven, and a kinship is achieved in the shared vision. By speaking in his own voice and in the language of the "common man," Simpson has made his poetry an experience that synthesizes thinking and feeling into a common humanity. In the end, he comes back to himself, the end of the open road, and finds a world of things and individuals in a room constructed out of his memory—seeing through the used-car lot, beyond the empty dreams, like an angel in the gate.

ESSAYS AND TRANSLATIONS

Simpson's interest in both literary theory and French poetry is manifest in his later essays and translations. His essay, "'The Man Freed from the Order of Time': Poetic Theory in Wordsworth and Proust" (1990), for example, is a study of the poetic theory of the British poet William Wordsworth and the French novelist Marcel Proust. Simpson sees in the work of these two writers the expression of a power of mind that transcends time and place, making their theories of literary creation as relevant in the present as when they were written. Simpson has also continued to be interested in the work of Whitman, addressing the nature of Whitman's sexuality in *Leaves of Grass* (1855) in an essay published in 1994. In an interview given after his retirement from teaching, Simpson reveals a familiarity with literary history and contemporary poetry that gives his views both substance and authority.

Despite this prolific output, all the while keeping up with his own poetry, Simpson devoted much of his literary effort in the 1990's to translating French poets. These translations represent considerable effort and scholarship on Simpson's part as well as a desire to bring French poetry to the English reader. He translated some poems by Stéphane Mallarmé when he found the available translations beneath the quality that he thought he himself could achieve. In his introduction to those poems, he also explained Mallarmé's influence on major poets writing in English. He followed this publication with a translation of seven poems by Robert Desnos, giving a brief biography of the poet in the introduction. When Simpson published his translations of two poems by Jules Laforgue in 1996, he again explained in an introduction the poet's importance to English literature and the freshness of Laforgue's subjects—the experience of adolescence, for example. This time, Simpson included the original poems alongside his translation. He repeated this practice in his next translations, two poems by Charles Baudelaire, two by Léon-Paul Fargue, and four by Marceline Desbordes-Valmore. In all of these translations, Simpson's aim seems to be to keep French poetry fresh in the American mind, and one may imagine, indulge his own literary tastes at the same time.

Simpson's crowning achievement in this kind of writing, however, was his translation of François Villon's *The Legacy* and *The Testament* in a bilingual edition with a brief introduction and notes. His versions of these two famous poems are marked by simplicity of language and stylistic informality. Simpson sought to make the poems as close to the original as English allowed without sacrificing the music of poetry and losing the special quality of Villon's language and imagery. Since his own poetry excels in these qualities and his other translations had given him much experience in translating French poetry, one can only assume that he succeeded with Villon.

THE OWNER OF THE HOUSE

The Owner of the House: New Collected Poems, 1940-2001, like the 1988 volume *Collected Poems*, brings together Simpson's poetic output over the years. However, "collected" does not mean complete, and the poems in this volume are a mixture of poems selected from earlier volumes and new poems. *The Owner of the House* omits some eighty of the poems included in *Collected Poems*, such as "Lines Written Near San Francisco," "Encounter on the 7:07," and "Peter." Added are a number of poems from *In the Room We Share* and *There You Are*, but none from *Jamaica Poems*, although that volume was published after the first collection appeared. Simpson also includes forty-two new poems, some of which had appeared in literary magazines, particularly *American Poetry Review* and *Hudson Review*.

Poems drawn from earlier volumes include those poems that have become widely anthologized, thus making Simpson's name known to a wider public. Among these poems are the war poems "Carentan, O Carentan" and "Memories of a Lost War," the memorable but rare long poem "The Runner," and poems remembering his childhood, such as "My Father in the Night Commanding No." From *In the Room We Share*, only eight poems have been selected, including the Chekhov poem "Another Boring Story," and others harking back to the war, the very fine "Numbers and Dust" and the Holocaust-themed "Sea of Grass."

There You Are is better represented, with some twenty-two poems. These are all written in the conversational, free-verse style Simpson adopted earlier. It is a style that has served many poets as they have written well into old age. It allows for memories to run easily into everyday happenings and thoughts on literary topics and authors, one enlightening the other and giving significance. However, Simpson questions the depth of such significance in "After a Light Snowfall." He quotes, without attribution, some lines from the poet Constantine P. Cavafy about wasting time. These words of accusation haunt him. How can Cavafy have written so personally to him? Of course, he has not, but these words are the inner accusations many people have to face as their career ends and they reach old age. Simpson is unable to rebut these accusations, but at the same time, he is simply unable to keep from writing and seeking meaning for any given moment of life.

Another memorable poem from *There You Are* is "A Clearing," which is the last poem in *The Owner of the House*. Simpson recalls his Australian teaching experience, as he does in other poems. One evening, he is invited to a particularly energetic and loud party. Feeling, as he often did, like an outsider, he walks into the bush, mindful of all its dangers. Inside, the house is unpleasant and raucous; outside, the bush is dangerous. In a clearing, he looks up at the night sky: "I had ceased to exist," he writes. He has a sense of being able to see eternity, with nothing between himself and his vision. It is a moment of epiphany, and another poet might have claimed it as a moment of spiritual enlightenment. Simpson, as materialist and cynical as he has become, cannot claim that, but he realizes there is significance beyond himself.

The title of the volume comes from one of the new poems, which are placed first. In "The Owner of the House," the sense is of a house of death and haunting through untimely death. Definitely, the house does not belong to the poet but to its previous owner. Also gone is his parents' home, which the poet revisits in "The Listeners" to find it in the hands of squatters. Likewise, none of the other houses mentioned in these new poems belongs to the poet. He is one of the "Homeless Men." "A Wandering Life" suggests wandering also means not belonging. However, despite taking "A Farewell to His Muse," the reader senses that Simpson will go on writing: It is his one way of belonging.

OTHER MAJOR WORKS

LONG FICTION: *Riverside Drive*, 1962.

NONFICTION: *James Hogg: A Critical Study*, 1962; *North of Jamaica*, 1972; *Three on the Tower: The Lives and Works of Ezra Pound, T. S. Eliot, and William Carlos Williams*, 1975; *A Revolution in Taste: Studies of Dylan Thomas, Allen Ginsberg, Sylvia Plath, and Robert Lowell*, 1978; *A Company of Poets*, 1981; *The Character of the Poet*, 1986; *Ships Going into the Blue: Essays and Notes on Poetry*, 1994; *The King My Father's Wreck*, 1995 (autobiography).

EDITED TEXTS: *The New Poets of England and America*, 1957 (with Donald Hall and Robert Pack); *An Introduction to Poetry*, 1967.

TRANSLATIONS: *Modern Poets of France: A Bilingual Anthology*, 1997; *"The Legacy" and "The Testament,"* 2000 (of François Villon).

MISCELLANEOUS: *Selected Prose*, 1989.

BIBLIOGRAPHY

Beaver, Harold. "Foot Soldier for Life." *Parnassus* 21, nos. 1/2 (1996): 138-145. Beaver takes an overview of Simpson's poetic career, picking up on the promise of his early war poems and asking to what extent this has been fulfilled.

Lazer, Hank. "Louis Simpson and Walt Whitman: Destroying the Teacher." *Walt Whitman Quarterly Review* 1 (December, 1983): 1-21. Lazer believes that Simpson's poetic development since 1963 has been shaped by Simpson's "dialogue" with Whitman.

_____, ed. *On Louis Simpson: Depths Beyond Happiness*. Ann Arbor: University of Michigan Press, 1988. Simpson himself said that one "should definitely have" this book. Lazer's introduction surveys the criticism of Simpson's work. The book itself offers shorter reviews and longer essays.

Makuck, Peter. "The Simpson House: Sixty-one Years in Construction." Review of *The Owner of the House*. *Hudson Review* 57, no. 2 (Summer, 2004): 335-344. Makuck sympathetically reviews the work, using the theme of the title poem to create an overview of Simpson's main directions.

Mason, David. "Louis Simpson's Singular Charm." *Hudson Review* 48, no. 3 (Autumn, 1995): 499-507. Mason examines Simpson's literary theories and ideas as they are revealed in his poetry, criticism, and memoirs, particularly his latest publications.

Moran, Ronald. *Louis Simpson.* New York: Twayne, 1972. A book-length study of Simpson's literary career. Opens with a brief biography and then examines the first five collections of poems and Simpson's novel *Riverside Drive.* Moran discusses the critical response to each of the publications and places many of the poems in the larger context of Simpson's thought, emphasizing the development of the "emotive imagination" in his poetry.

Roberson, William H. *Louis Simpson: A Reference Guide.* Boston: G. K. Hall, 1980. Hank Lazer describes this work as "an invaluable book for anyone interested in Louis Simpson's writing and in critical reactions to that body of writing." Begins with a survey of Simpson's poetic career and critical reputation. Part 1 lists writings by Simpson, and part 2 lists writings about him.

Simpson, Louis. "Louis Simpson: An Interview." Interview by Ronald Moran. *Five Points* 1, no. 1 (Fall, 1996): 45-63. Moran's questions lead Simpson through a wide range of subjects, including his views on other poets, such as Sylvia Plath, themes in his own poetry, some favorites of his own poems, and contemporary poetry.

Stitt, Peter. "Louis Simpson: In Search of the American Self." In *The World's Hieroglyphic Beauty: Five American Poets.* Athens: University of Georgia Press, 1985. Stitt follows Simpson's development through "three distinct phases" and traces the unifying sensibility in the poetry, looking closely at a number of the poems along the way. One of the longer essays on Simpson, this is one of the most illuminating as well.

Vaughan, David K. *Words to Measure a War: Nine American Poets of World War II.* Jefferson, N.C.: McFarland, 2009. Vaughan looks at war poets, contrasting those who became famous before and during World War II, with those who became known as poets after the war, including Simpson.

Bernard E. Morris
Updated by David Barratt

EDWARD THOMAS

Born: London, England; March 3, 1878
Died: Arras, France; April 9, 1917

PRINCIPAL POETRY
Six Poems, 1916
Poems, 1917
Last Poems, 1918
Collected Poems, 1920, 1928
The Poetry of Edward Thomas, 1978

OTHER LITERARY FORMS

Although Edward Thomas is remembered today as a poet, throughout his working life, he supported himself and his family by writing various sorts of prose. He always considered himself to be a writer, and the lasting tragedy of his life was that he never seemed able, until the outbreak of World War I, to buy enough time to devote himself to the art of writing as he obviously wished to do. Ironically, the war in which he died also provided him with the structured, organized environment and the freedom from financial anxiety that enabled him to produce the work which has secured his reputation.

His entire prose opus runs to nearly forty volumes, most of which were published during his lifetime. The titles cover a variety of subjects. It is also possible to see what a remarkable volume of work he produced in the years 1911 to 1912, a productivity that culminated, after nine published works, in a breakdown in 1912. Although the prose work of Thomas is often dismissed as being unimportant, it is obvious from merely reading the titles where his main interests lay. Themes of nature and of the British countryside predominate, together with literary criticism.

In fact, Thomas was a remarkably perceptive literary critic. He was among the first reviewers to appreciate the work of Robert Frost, and he also recognized Ezra Pound's achievement in *Personae* (1909), which he reviewed in its first year of publication. When he began to write, he was heavily influenced by Walter Pater's code of aesthetics, his love of rhetoric, and his formality. He was later to have to work hard to rid his prose of those features, which he recognized as being alien to his own poetic voice.

ACHIEVEMENTS

In his poetry, Edward Thomas succeeded in realizing two ambitions, which another poet of nature set out as his aims more than a century earlier. In the preface to the *Lyrical Ballads* (1798), William Wordsworth stated that his intent in writing poetry was "to exalt and transfigure the natural and the common" and also to redefine the status of the poet so that he would become "a man speaking to men." Wordsworth's poetry received both acclaim and abuse when it first appeared and formed an expectation of poetry that continued until the end of the nineteenth century. By that time, the aesthetic movement had come to the fore, and poetry was well on its way, at the outbreak of World War I, toward suffocating itself with overblown rhetoric.

Thomas is not generally regarded as a war poet, being discussed more often in conjunction with Thomas Hardy and Walter de la Mare than with Wilfred Owen, Siegfried Sassoon, and Isaac Rosenberg. By combining his acute perceptions of both nature and political events, however, Thomas produced poetry in which evocations of place and detailed descriptions of nature become a metaphor for humanity's spiritual state. F. R. Leavis, writing in *New Bearings in English Poetry* (1932) made this observation: "He was exquisitely sincere and sensitive, and he succeeded in expressing in poetry a representative modern sensibility. It was an achievement of a very rare order, and he has not yet had the recognition he deserves." Thomas's poetry has become widely known, and he has become almost an establishment figure in the literature of the early twentieth century. It is a measure of his achievement that in returning to his slender *Collected Poems*, it is always possible to be stimulated and surprised by his work.

Biography

Edward Philip Thomas was born in London, the eldest of six boys. Both of his parents were Welsh, and Thomas always had an affinity with the principality, spending much time there during his childhood, although the landscapes of his poetry are predominantly those of the south of England. Thomas's father was a stern, unyielding man who had risen by his own efforts to a social position far above that which might be expected from his poor background. Having succeeded in elevating himself, he was naturally very ambitious for his eldest son, and Thomas received an excellent education, attending St. Paul's School, Hammersmith (as a contemporary of G. K. Chesterton and E. C. Bentley, among others), and going on from there to Jesus College, Oxford.

Shortly before going to Oxford, Thomas met Helen Noble; it was one of the momentous events in his life. Both he and Noble had very advanced ideas for their time; they were already lovers while Thomas was still an undergraduate. They discussed their future lives together and how they would bring up their children in accordance with Richard Jeffries's theories of freedom and the open-air life. Noble herself said, "We hated the thought of a legal contract. We felt our love was all the bond there ought to be, and that if that failed it was immoral to be bound together. We wanted our union to be free and spontaneous." In the spring of 1899, Noble discovered that she was pregnant and was rather appalled to discover that Edward himself, as well as her friends in the bohemian community in which she lived, thought that they should be married. Noble's family were shocked to learn of her pregnancy, insisting on a hurried marriage and refusing to help the young couple in any way. Thomas's family was more sympathetic, allowing

Noble to live with them and helping Thomas while he worked toward his degree.

Once he graduated, the need to earn money to support his family became pressing, and determined not to become submerged in the drudgery of an office job, Thomas solicited work from publishers. Until the time that he joined the Artists' Rifles, Thomas supported himself and his family by writing. They were always poor, and he often reproached himself bitterly because he had no regular source of income.

Writing became a chore to him, something to be done merely for the sake of the money. In 1912, he suffered a breakdown brought on by overwork. At about that time, also, he met Frost and formed a close friendship with the American poet. Thomas was among the first to appreciate Frost's poetry, and Frost encouraged Thomas to try his hand at writing poetry himself; Thomas gradually gained confidence in his ability to say what he wanted in poetry. When he was killed by a bombshell in the spring of 1917, what might have become a considerable voice in English poetry was tragically silenced.

Analysis

Perhaps the most notable feature of Edward Thomas's poetry, which strikes the reader immediately, is its characteristic quietness of tone and its unassertive, gentle quality. He is primarily a poet of the country, but through his descriptions of the English landscape, impressionistic and minutely observed, he also attempts to delineate some of the features of his own inner landscape.

As may be seen from the titles of the many books of prose that he wrote before beginning to write poetry at the behest of Frost, he was always deeply interested in nature and the land. Many of the fleeting observations in his poetry are drawn from his notebooks, in which he recorded such things as the first appearance of a spring blossom and the first sightings of various species of birds. In his prose, as opposed to the notebooks, his style was highly rhetorical, so that the keen observations that make his poetry so effective are lost in a plethora of adjectival excess. In one of his reviews, he wrote that "The important thing is not that a thing should be small, but that it should be intense and capable of unconsciously symbolic significance." In his poetry, by the acuity of his observation and the spareness and tautness of his language, he certainly achieves remarkable—if low-key—intensity. He also achieves, in his best work, an unforced symbolic resonance.

"As the Team's Head-Brass"

"As the Team's Head-Brass" is one of Thomas's most impressive achievements; at first reading, it may appear to be only an account of a rural dialogue between the poet and a man plowing a field. It begins with a reference to the plowman, and to some lovers who are seen disappearing into the wood behind the field being plowed. The lovers are not directly relevant to the substance of the poem, but they are an important detail. The poem begins and ends with a reference to them, and although they are in no sense representative of a Lawrentian "life-force," their presence in the poem does suggest the triumph of life and love over death and destruction. The very mention of the lovers reinforces the image of the plow horses "narrowing a yellow square of charlock"—that is, destroying the (living) weeds, that better life may grow.

"If we could see all all might seem good" says the plowman, and this seems to be Thomas's contention in this poem. The writing throughout is highly controlled, the structure of the poem reinforced with alliteration and internal rhyme—seeming to owe something to Gerard Manley Hopkins and ultimately even to the Welsh *cynghanedd* form, with the use of "fallen/fallow/plough/narrowing/yellow/charlock" all in four lines, and then later in the same opening section, "word/weather/war/scraping/share/screwed/furrow." Leavis observes that "we become aware of the inner life which the sensory impressions are notation for." This is particularly true of "As the Team's Head-Brass." The closing lines bring the whole poem together most succinctly—the lovers, forgotten since the opening lines, emerge from the wood; the horses begin to plow a new furrow; "for the last time I watched" says Thomas, and the reader must pause here to ask whether he means "for the last time on this particular occasion" or "for the last time ever." All the conversation in the poem has been about war, and in the last two lines come the words "crumble/topple/stumble," which, although used ostensibly with reference to the horses and the soil, may equally be taken to refer back to the fallen tree on which the poet is sitting, the plowman's workmate who has been killed in the war, the changing state of society, and the relentless passage of time.

"ADLESTROP"

"As the Team's Head-Brass" is not typical of Thomas's work, however, for it is longer and much more detailed and elaborate than most of his poems. More typical of his work are poems such as "Tall Nettles" and "Adlestrop," which evoke the moment without attempting to do more than capture the unique quality of one particular place or one particular moment in time. "Adlestrop" is a poem much anthologized and much appreciated by those who love the English countryside. It has been described as the most famous of modern "place" poems, and yet it also seems to conjure up an almost sexual tension (perhaps by the use of the words "lonely fair"?) of a kind that is often implicit in such hot summer days. This is a sense of the poem that the contemporary poet Dannie Abse has obviously found, for he has written a poem titled "Not Adlestrop," in which the unspecified lady actually makes an appearance in a train going in the opposite direction. Abse's poem is something of a literary joke, but it does pinpoint an element of unresolved sexual tension in several of Thomas's poems. "Some Eyes Condemn," "Celandine," and "The Unknown" all seem to be worlds away in mood from "And You, Helen," a poem written for his wife.

"No One So Much as You"

The poignant "No One So Much as You," a kind of apologia for an imperfectly reciprocated love, was written for Mary Elizabeth Thomas, the poet's mother, although it has often been mistaken for a love poem to his wife. In either case it would seem that familiarity did not necessarily increase Thomas's love for his family—in fact, it was obvious, both from his despairing reaction to the news of his wife's second pregnancy and from his well-documented impatience with domestic life—that distance and mystery were important elements of attraction for him. Perhaps fortunately for all concerned, Thomas's dissatisfactions and unfulfilled longings seem to have made up only a very small part of his nature. Having come to poetry late, he wastes little time in cataloging regrets for what he might have been and concentrates mainly on what he was able to do best—that is, to capture his own impressions of English rural life and country landscapes and combine them in poetry with various insights into his own personality.

Affinity for country life

It would not be possible to offer a succinct analysis of Thomas's poetry without referring to his deeply felt patriotism. In *Edward Thomas: A Poet for His Country* (1978), Jan Marsh describes an incident that occurred soon after Thomas enlisted in the British army, although he was in fact over the usual age limit for enlistment. A friend asked the poet what he thought he was fighting for; Thomas bent down and picked up a pinch of earth and, letting it crumble through his fingers, answered, "Literally, for this."

This is the predominant impression that the reader carries away from an encounter with Thomas's poetry, for here is a sensitive, educated man who, despite his cultivation, is deeply attuned to the land. This affinity is particularly clear in the country people who inhabit Thomas's poetry, for they are always portrayed as being part of a long and noble tradition of rural life. Thomas does not romanticize his vision: He portrays the cruelties of nature as well as its beauties. A recurring image in his poetry is that of the gamekeeper's board, hung with trophies in an attempt to discourage other predators. Perhaps because he makes an honest attempt to describe the reality of country life without attempting to gloss over or soften its less attractive aspects, he succeeds superbly. Since his life, when his poetry was scarcely known, Thomas's work has become steadily more popular, so that he has become known as one of England's finest nature poets.

Other major works

NONFICTION: *The Woodland Life*, 1897; *Horae Solitariae*, 1902; *Oxford*, 1903; *Rose Acre Papers*, 1904; *Beautiful Wales*, 1905; *The Heart of England*, 1906; *Richard Jeffries*, 1909; *The South Country*, 1909; *Feminine Influence on the Poets*, 1910; *Rest and Unrest*, 1910; *Rose Acre Papers*, 1910; *Windsor Castle*, 1910; *Celtic Stories*, 1911; *The Isle of Wight*, 1911; *Light and Twilight*, 1911; *Maurice Maeterlinck*, 1911; *The Tenth Muse*, 1911; *Algernon Charles Swinburne*, 1912; *George Borrow: The Man and*

His Books, 1912; *Lafcadio Hearn*, 1912; *Norse Tales*, 1912; *The Country*, 1913; *The Happy-Go-Lucky Morgans*, 1913; *The Icknield Way*, 1913; *Walter Pater*, 1913; *In Pursuit of Spring*, 1914; *The Life of the Duke of Marlborough*, 1915; *A Literary Pilgrim in England*, 1917; *Cloud Castle, and Other Papers*, 1922; *Chosen Essays*, 1926; *Essays of Today and Yesterday*, 1926; *The Last Sheaf*, 1928; *The Childhood of Edward Thomas*, 1938; *The Prose of Edward Thomas*, 1948 (Roland Gant, editor); *Letters from Edward Thomas to Gordon Bottomley*, 1968; *Letters to America, 1914-1917*, 1978.

CHILDREN'S LITERATURE: *Four-and-Twenty-Blackbirds*, 1915.

BIBLIOGRAPHY

Cuthbertson, Guy, and Lucy Newlyn, eds. *Branch-Lines: Edward Thomas and Contemporary Poetry*. Chester Springs, Pa.: Dufour Editions, 2007. Contains essays on Thomas and poems by him and the poets he influenced.

Emeny, Richard, comp. *Edward Thomas, 1878-1917: Towards a Complete Checklist of His Publications*. Edited by Jeff Cooper. Blackburn, Lancashire, England: White Sheep Press, 2004. A bibliography of Thomas's numerous publications, from the poetry to the many prose writings.

Farjeon, Eleanor. *Edward Thomas: The Last Four Years*. Rev. ed. Foreword by P. J. Kavanagh. Edited by Anne Harvey. Stroud, Gloucestershire, England: Sutton, 2007. A double memoir that uses Thomas's letters and Farjeon's diaries to provide a candid account of their developing friendship. Offers a unique account of Thomas's development as a poet, including his meeting Robert Frost, whose encouragement led to Thomas's first poems. Thomas's letters describe his family, his friendships with other writers, and provides a detailed account of his experiences in World War I.

Frost, Robert, and Edward Thomas. *Elected Friends: Robert Frost and Edward Thomas to One Another*. Edited by Matthew Spencer. New York: Handsel Books, 2003. Contains the letters and poems that Frost and Thomas wrote to each other. Frost's influence helped Thomas develop as a poet.

Kirkham, Michael. *The Imagination of Edward Thomas*. New York: Cambridge University Press, 1986. Kirkham ignores chronology as he explores Thomas's imagination by identifying the characteristic style that is evidenced in his poetry. Augmented with a solid bibliography and an index.

Motion, Andrew. *The Poetry of Edward Thomas*. 1980. Reprint. London: Hogarth, 1991. Motion approaches Thomas's poetry as drawing from the Georgian tradition while anticipating the arrival of the modernists in content and in form. Motion examines the subtle style of Thomas and introduces him as an evolutionary poet.

Smith, Stan. *Edward Thomas*. London: Faber & Faber, 1986. Thomas is considered in this book as the "quintessential English poet," whose devotion to the rural countryside is reflected in his poetry. Presents several critical approaches. Helpful selected bibliography.

Thomas, R. George. *Edward Thomas: A Portrait*. 1985. Reprint. Oxford, England: Clarendon Press, 1987. This book provides rare insight into the life and work of Thomas by making use of letters, memoirs, and personal papers. Biographical in nature, and supported by an excellent bibliography, the book gives a solid foundation for the study of his prose and poetry.

Wiśniewski, Jacek. *Edward Thomas: A Mirror of England*. Newcastle upon Tyne, England: Cambridge Scholars, 2009. Critical analysis of the works of Thomas, whom the author finds to be representative of England.

Vivien Stableford

BRUCE WEIGL

Born: Lorain, Ohio; January 27, 1949

PRINCIPAL POETRY
Executioner, 1976
A Sack Full of Old Quarrels, 1976
A Romance, 1979
The Monkey Wars, 1985
Song of Napalm, 1988
What Saves Us, 1992
Lies, Grace, and Redemption, 1995 (Harry Humes, editor)
Not on the Map, 1996 (with Kevin Bowen; John Deane, editor)
Sweet Lorain, 1996
After the Others, 1999
Archeology of the Circle: New and Selected Poems, 1999
The Unraveling Strangeness: Poems, 2002
Declension in the Village of Chung Luong: New Poems, 2006

OTHER LITERARY FORMS

Although Bruce Weigl (WI-gehl) has published primarily poetry, he also translated poetry from the Vietnamese—*Poems from Captured Documents* (1994; with Thanh Nguyen) and *Mountain River: Vietnamese Poetry from the Wars, 1945-1995* (1998; with Nguyen Ba Chung and Kevin Bowen)—and Romanian, Liliana Ursu's *Angel Riding a Beast* (1998; with the author). Weigl's translations make available poems that are not readily accessible to the common reader. Weigl has spoken of how pervasive poetry is in Southeast Asia; reading the Vietnamese perspective provides a fuller picture of the impact of the war. In addition, Weigl has written several volumes of criticism, including *The Giver of Morning: On Dave Smith* (1982), *The Imagination as Glory: The Poetry of James Dickey* (1984; with T. R. Hummer), and *Charles Simic: Essays on the Poetry* (1996), as well as a memoir, *The Circle of Hahn: A Memoir* (2000).

ACHIEVEMENTS

Published internationally, Bruce Weigl's poetry has been translated into Vietnamese, Czech, Dutch, German, Spanish, Chinese, Slovenian, Bulgarian, and Romanian. He has received many national awards, including a Paterson Poetry Prize, two Pushcart Prizes, a Cleveland Arts Prize, and the Poet's Prize from the Academy of American Poets, as well as fellowships from the Bread Loaf Writers' Conference, the Yaddo Foundation, and the National Endowment for the Arts. In 1988, he was nominated for a Pulitzer Prize for *Song of Napalm*. He served as a poetry panel chair for the National Book Award in 2003 and won the Lannan Literary Award for Poetry in 2006 and the Ohioana Book Award for Poetry in 2007. His poems have appeared in *The Nation*, *American Poetry Review*, *Ploughshares*, *The New Yorker*, and *Paris Review*, as well as many other magazines and journals.

Biography

Bruce Weigl was born in Lorain, Ohio, on January 27, 1949, to Albert Louis Weigl and Zora Grasa Weigl. Weigl served in the U.S. Army in Vietnam from 1967 until 1970, earning the Bronze Star. He earned a B.A. in English from Oberlin College in 1974 and an M.A. from the University of New Hampshire in 1975. In 1979, he received a Ph.D. from the University of Utah, where he was mentored by poet Dave Smith. He has two children (a son and a daughter) with his wife, artist Jean Kondo.

Weigl has had an extensive teaching career. He was an instructor at Lorain County Community College from 1975 to 1976 and assistant professor of English at the University of Arkansas, Little Rock. At Old Dominion University in Norfolk, Virginia, he was assistant professor of English and director of the associated writing program. He then taught in the writing program at Pennsylvania State University for fourteen years and in the M.F.A. in writing program at Vermont College. In 2000, he became a visiting distinguished professor at Lorain County Community College.

Analysis

In the poetry of Bruce Weigl, two themes emerge, seemingly at cross purposes. First is the horror of war, especially its effect on the psyches of young men who were ill prepared for what would come. The second is the primacy of love that at once underscores that horror and attempts to atone for it. The love poems undercut the rules of the society that would control the course of love, as war situations do.

Weigl describes the impetus for his work by saying that a writer must come to terms with his or her background, as it is the major source of the writer's subject matter. Weigl grew up in and around industry, amid steel mills and the working class. Weigel was born in industrial and agricultural Middle America, and his working-class background informs his poetry and shapes the way he perceives the Vietnam War. The speaker of these poems is often a young, fairly naïve man who gets caught up in an unpopular cause and who must find a way to transcend the limitations of mere survival. The poet, therefore, finds himself trying to bring his imaginative sensibilities to a hostile environment in an attempt to transform it and make it livable, with as little cost to his psyche as he can manage. Weigl's poetry clearly demonstrates the care that the poet takes to render a full account of the situations in which he finds himself and to do so with a high degree of craft. The artistic development of his style does not take a backseat to his important message, however.

Influence of the Vietnam War

Except for the American Civil War, no war in American history has been as controversial or as divisive as the Vietnam War. Soldiers did not come home to the welcoming crowds that filled World War II newsreels. Called "baby killers" and generally reviled, soldiers had few official support systems to help them return to a society that disowned them. Sometimes, families themselves embodied national divisions, with members for and against the war living under the same roof. Thus, Weigl's poetry reflects a common reality of personal and familial rupture.

Poems speaking about familial life stateside seem to present a conclusion to the struggle to relate. In some poems, when Weigl speaks with great tenderness about his wife and child, about chance encounters in a supermarket, or about memories of work, a pervasive sadness still informs the poems. However, an emotional salvation occurs for the poet when he is able to ground himself in those relationships that are stronger than his nightmares about the war. "The Happiness of Others," the poet says in the poem of that name, "is not like the music I hear/ after sex/ with my wife of the decades." He refers to her as "my wife my rope my bread." His wife is the rope that holds him firmly tethered to the present, the bread that nourishes his existence. Without her, the horrible trauma of his war memories could overtake his soul. Although his private world is forever marked by his war experiences, it is beauty (found in his familial attachments, the natural world, and language itself) that provides the safe haven necessary to access those memories without being overwhelmed by them. The great body of work results from the poet's willingness to go into a darkened landscape and emerge wholly creative.

Weigl's poetry serves to give voice to thousands of soldiers who saw action in the Vietnam War during the late 1960's and early 1970's. If Tim O'Brien may be considered the prose writer of the horror, trauma, and regret of the Vietnam War, Weigl could be rightly called the poet. War casts a deep shadow over Weigl's writings, and the disillusionment generated from his experiences in Vietnam seep into even his more hopeful lines. Although he is often considered a Vietnam War poet by literary critics, Weigl's extensive use of irony and craft with blank verse elevate his poetry beyond such a label. While the sincerity of these poems provides a forum of discourse so that these experiences may benefit from national attention, their high literary quality merits the esteem in which they are held as literature.

"Song of Napalm"

"Song of Napalm," from *The Monkey Wars*, begins with a bucolic description of horses that the speaker and his wife watch. The initial description of the poet and his wife lifts them beyond the concerns of this world into a holy realm. However, this domestic scene foreshadows a frightening darkness that the poet experiences: "Trees scraped their voices in the wind, branches/ Crisscrossed the sky like barbed wire/ But you said they were only branches."

The speaker pauses as if to catch his breath and take stock of himself, believing that the "old curses" have gone. However, visions from his war experiences intrude once again:

> Still I close my eyes and see the girl
> Running from her village, napalm
> Stuck to her dress like jelly,
> Her hands reaching for the no one
> Who waits in waves of heat before her.

These lines evoke the famous photograph of a young Vietnamese girl burned by napalm, running naked along a road toward the camera that immortalized her. The poet is alienated from both the domestic tranquility that his wife represents and the haunting visions that his memory brings; however, he forces a door to open between these two worlds.

The girl runs with wings of escape beating inside her, using a freedom that she does not possess. In fact, she is able to run only a few feet before her burns and wounds bring her down, as she dies in a fetal position: "Nothing/ Can change that, she is burned behind my eyes." The poet is forced to accept the world as something that his words alone cannot change. Not even the redemptive, healing love of his wife fades this vision. A persistent theme in Weigl's other poems is the poet's struggle to find solace in the love of family and friends to dispel the power that his war experience exerts.

"On the Anniversary of Her Grace"

In "On the Anniversary of Her Grace," from *Song of Napalm*, the poet evokes his power to show how the war scarred his ability to love. The opening description of weather conditions foreshadows the desperate state of the poet's mind. Images of darkness, floods, and destruction presage the devastation that the war wreaks on the poet's spirit. Although the poet dreams of his beloved, these dreams are restive in spite of his recalling a kiss, because "Inside me the war had eaten a hole./ I could not touch anyone." The war robs the poet of his openness to love, central to his self-image.

Often the use of repetition induces a meditative, trancelike state. The poet uses that device, repeating "I could . . . I could," until finally he says, "I could not." The effect mesmerizes. Images of the war erode his sensibilities, ensuring that the poet cannot accept the forgiveness and healing which the woman offers. He fears his "body would catch fire," recalling the image of the napalm-burned children, joining them in their unwilling sacrifice.

Intense feelings of love remind the poet that he is a stranger in two worlds, with one foot planted firmly in each. Even when the poet is not ostensibly narrating his experiences of the war, even when the love poem focuses on the beloved, the war intrudes as if he cannot manage two disparate worlds.

"First Letter to Calumpang"

In "First Letter to Calumpang," from *Sweet Lorain*, the poet expresses love to his wife by using images that reflect the war: "There is a blood from touching, and a fire;/ I've had them in my mouth." The poet's use of blood echoes both the blood rush of sexual excitement and the blood certainly present in war. Fire carries the dual connotation of sexual desire and the fire of war and napalm. With these images that are at once tender and fierce, the war is never far away.

Archeology of the Circle

The poems in *Archeology of the Circle* represent both new works and selections from Weigl's previous volumes. In them, he continues to struggle with his feelings of love for others as well as self-acceptance. The war has taken its toll. In "Anniversary of Myself," the poet says:

> The fingers of my gloves had holes.
> I don't know what I was doing.
> There had been a war
> and my people
> had grown disenchanted.

Disillusionment comes from the poet's growing awareness of his numbness to his inner being, the core of himself, the part of himself that nurtures love relationships.

Consequently, the poet comes to relive the advice that he was given during the war, in "Our Independence Day," saying, "Let it go, boy,// let the green/ untangle from your body." These poems represent a letting go that empowers the speaker. These are not poems of surrender to a greater power; instead, the poet releases these poems into the community of discourse wherein they can become change agents in the lives of other men and women who know war.

The Unraveling Strangeness

Weigl's common themes of guilt, regret, and loss receive a more nuanced and sedate treatment in *The Unraveling Strangeness* than in some of his previous collections. There is a haunting weight to the lines that belies the mixture of nostalgia and regret that characterizes many of the poems here. Weigl's rearview gaze provides ample fodder for introspection and the comingling of past events with the present in poems such as "Oh, Atonement," "I Waited for the Spirit Soldiers" (both initially published in *American Poetry Review*), and the lengthy "Incident at Eagle's Peak," all of which showcase the regret that constantly looking back to the past often engenders.

However, Weigl asserts an obligation in the midst of memory in "Nixon." Referring to the fallen soldiers of the Vietnam War, the speaker remarks, ". . . Anymore/ the anniversaries of the deaths/ are so many/ that there is little time/ for anything else." Weigl reminds his reader that the act of remembering can be its own sacred duty. Having little time for anything besides observing the death of fallen comrades implies surviving carries with it an obligation to those who did not live. In this way, the specter of war again haunts many of the lines in this collection, unifying them around a common desire for healing.

Many of the poems in this volume, like the others, speak of a longing for redemption that the speaker seems skeptical of ever obtaining. In "For A, At Fourteen," the speaker observes that, "We need at last a life without the grief/ we've brought into the house. A life that would/ allow us both our tenderness, our pain released." Here, the house serves as a metaphor for a common place of interaction between human beings. However, the grief that all human beings carry with them seems to keep both the adult speaker and the teenage subject from the desired communion. The poet suggests a similar longing for wholeness in "Baby Crying, 3 A.M.," in which he writes, ". . . Our eyes/ won't close as easily, our nights arranged/ around the hungry cry that comes in waves." Here, a baby's hungry cry becomes a symbol of the desperate longing for completion that Weigl offers as a universal characteristic of the human condition.

As in previous collections, Weigl does seem to find respite and solace within the natural world. Poems such as "My Autumn Leaves" and "Incident at Eagle's Peak" depict natural beauty as a salve for the human spirit. Weigl often uses natural objects and landscapes as metaphors for the emotional states of his speakers in ways that help these characters access and interpret traumatic events. The predominance of natural imagery unites his body of work and links Weigl to great American poets such as Emily Dickinson and Robert Frost.

DECLENSION IN THE VILLAGE OF CHUNG LUONG

Declension in the Village of Chung Luong contains many of the same stylistic patterns as *The Unraveling Strangeness* and earlier volumes. Both books are divided into three sections, which mirror one another thematically. Both rely on blank verse and terse line breaks to convey irony and emotion. The language in these volumes is stripped down and sparse, as if cognizant of the inability of language to convey emotional associations with any certainty (or suspicious of its ability to convey anything at all). Instead, Weigl conjures up phrases, glimpses of meaning floating by, as if waiting for his reader to seize the words, arrest their dissipation, and extract some level of meaning from them. Although some view Weigl as a confessional poet (in the sense of one who writes of their own experiences using a first-person speaker), this volume applies its themes of regret, trauma, and loss to the experiences of modern life more generally than his previous collections, especially in its discussion of war.

Declension in the Village of Chung Luong provides a window into the trauma of modern life through its discussion of the modern American military engagements of the early twenty-first century. "Home of the Brave" (originally published in the *American*

Poetry Review) discusses the aftermath of the terrorist attacks on the World Trade Center on September 11, 2001, lamenting that, "so much was taken from them, and a hole/ had been torn into their world,/ that one man hung a thousand flags from his house." "Portal" (first published in *Irish Pages*) shifts that window onto the effects of war on the children inside the countries against which America retaliated, who, "sleep the sleep of weary warriors/ beaten down and left for nothing in their lonely deaths/ that come so slowly you would wish/ your own heart empty of blood." War functions as an important site for individual reflection in these poems, but unlike in earlier collections, Weigl evokes the conflicts in Iraq and Afghanistan instead of his personal experience in Vietnam. As a result, the emotions stirred up by these poems are intimately familiar to a new generation of readers whose lives may not have been directly touched by the Vietnam War.

However, it would be overly simplistic to assert that all of Weigl's poetry is of war. Weigl shifts between deeply introspective musings on his own subjective experiences to more general observations of the current state of American society. For example, Weigl's "Elegy for Biggie Smalls" could apply to many superstars transfixed within the modern media's incessant spotlight. Weigl's lines, "no one stays at the edge too long there's no song/ that can keep you or defeat you no one to beseech you/ to step back from the edge when you're Big," aptly capture the power and freedom of fame, while simultaneously proffering a cautionary observation of the inevitable loneliness of the human condition. In fact, these lines illustrate one of the primary attractions of this modern poet, who deftly holds up his own feelings of regret and loss to events within the popular society more generally, suggesting that his own experiences, although unique and personal, mirror those of an entire culture.

Other major works

nonfiction: *The Giver of Morning: On Dave Smith*, 1982; *The Imagination as Glory: The Poetry of James Dickey*, 1984 (with T. R. Hummer); *Charles Simic: Essays on the Poetry*, 1996; *The Circle of Hahn: A Memoir*, 2000.

translations: *Poems from Captured Documents*, 1994 (with Thanh Nguyen); *Angel Riding a Beast*, 1998 (of Liliana Ursu; with the author); *Mountain River: Vietnamese Poetry from the Wars, 1945-1995*, 1998 (with Nguyen Ba Chung and Kevin Bowen).

edited text: *Writing Between the Lines: An Anthology on War and Its Social Consequences*, 1997 (with Kevin Bowen).

Bibliography

Beidler, Philip. *Re-writing America: Vietnam Authors in Their Generation*. Athens: University of Georgia Press, 1991. Beidler notes the development of Weigl's career as a direct emergence from the evolution of his mythic consciousness as a result of the war. The book presents an examination of *A Romance* and *The Monkey Wars* within the tradition of a visionary quest.

Christopher, Renny. *The Viet Nam War: The American War*. Amherst: University of Massachusetts Press, 1995. This book discusses how Weigl's poetry moves beyond reportage into a realm of introspection, an internal dialogue in the context of external events. Uses "Him, on the Bicycle" to illustrate Weigl's use of perceived and experienced distance from self and other as an attempt to bridge cultures.

Gotera, Vincente F. "Bringing Vietnam Home: Bruce Weigl's *The Monkey Wars*." In *Search and Clear*, edited by William J. Searle. Bowling Green, Ohio: Bowling Green State University Popular Press, 1988. The author notes how Weigl never allows the reader to dismiss the inextricable link to American violence and pathos. War is an exaggeration of common forms of violence. Weigl's work breaks apart the myth that the United States regained national innocence by admitting that its involvement in Vietnam was a mistake.

Humes, Harry. "Death, Beauty, and Redemption." *Southern Review* 36, no. 4 (Autumn, 2000): 870-873. Offers an excellent close reading of *After the Others* and explicates common themes found in Weigl's poetry according to the poet's own life. His discussion of the search for meaning and redemption amidst the trauma of war are especially cogent.

Jason, Philip K. *Acts and Shadows: The Vietnam War in American Culture*. Lanham, Md.: Rowman and Littlefield, 2000. Presents an examination of *Song of Napalm*. The author questions the source of love and cruelty and notes that the poems speak of the poet's awareness of violence deep within all people. A further examination of those images that confront, then upset, reader expectations.

Keplinger, David. "On Bruce Weigl: Finding a Shape for the Litany of Terror." *War, Literature, and the Arts* 12, no. 2 (Fall/Winter, 2000): 141-158. Written by a former student of Weigl's, this article explains why Weigl is more than a mere poet of the Vietnam War. The author examines Weigl's poetic style and influences in the first part of this piece; the second contains an interview between the former student and poet.

Parini, Jay, ed. *American Writers: A Collection of Literary Biographies—David Budbill to Bruce Weigl*. Supplement 19. Farmington Hills, Mich.: Thomson Gale, 2010. Contains an entry on Weigl.

Rielly, Edward J. "Bruce Weigl: Out of the Landscape of His Past." *Journal of American Culture* 16, no. 3 (1993): 47-52. Explains the function of memory in Weigl's body of work by exploring the ways past experiences are "superimposed" on the present. He illustrates war's influence over poems that do not deal explicitly with that experience.

Weigl, Bruce. "Poetry Grabbed Me by the Throat." Interview by Eric James Schroeder. In *Vietnam: We've All Been There*, edited by Schroeder. Westport, Conn.: Praeger,

1992. Weigl emphatically rejects the notion that writing was a form of therapy for him. He suggests, paradoxically, that the war both ruined his life and made him a writer. He speaks of his emergence as a poet and his affinity to Wilfred Owen's work. Weigl states that writing is the greatest act of affirmation life can accomplish.

Martha Modena Vertreace-Doody
Updated by Ryan D. Stryffeler

CHECKLIST FOR EXPLICATING A POEM

I. The Initial Readings

A. Before reading the poem, the reader should:
1. Notice its form and length.
2. Consider the title, determining, if possible, whether it might function as an allusion, symbol, or poetic image.
3. Notice the date of composition or publication, and identify the general era of the poet.

B. The poem should be read intuitively and emotionally and be allowed to "happen" as much as possible.

C. In order to establish the rhythmic flow, the poem should be reread. A note should be made as to where the irregular spots (if any) are located.

II. Explicating the Poem

A. *Dramatic situation.* Studying the poem line by line helps the reader discover the dramatic situation. All elements of the dramatic situation are interrelated and should be viewed as reflecting and affecting one another. The dramatic situation serves a particular function in the poem, adding realism, surrealism, or absurdity; drawing attention to certain parts of the poem; and changing to reinforce other aspects of the poem. All points should be considered. The following questions are particularly helpful to ask in determining dramatic situation:
1. What, if any, is the narrative action in the poem?
2. How many personae appear in the poem? What part do they take in the action?
3. What is the relationship between characters?
4. What is the setting (time and location) of the poem?

B. *Point of view.* An understanding of the poem's point of view is a major step toward comprehending the poet's intended meaning. The reader should ask:
1. Who is the speaker? Is he or she addressing someone else or the reader?
2. Is the narrator able to understand or see everything happening to him or her, or does the reader know things that the narrator does not?
3. Is the narrator reliable?
4. Do point of view and dramatic situation seem consistent? If not, the inconsistencies may provide clues to the poem's meaning.

C. *Images and metaphors.* Images and metaphors are often the most intricately crafted vehicles of the poem for relaying the poet's message. Realizing that the images and metaphors work in harmony with the dramatic situation and point of view will help the reader to see the poem as a whole, rather than as disassociated elements.
   1. The reader should identify the concrete images (that is, those that are formed from objects that can be touched, smelled, seen, felt, or tasted). Is the image projected by the poet consistent with the physical object?
   2. If the image is abstract, or so different from natural imagery that it cannot be associated with a real object, then what are the properties of the image?
   3. To what extent is the reader asked to form his or her own images?
   4. Is any image repeated in the poem? If so, how has it been changed? Is there a controlling image?
   5. Are any images compared to each other? Do they reinforce one another?
   6. Is there any difference between the way the reader perceives the image and the way the narrator sees it?
   7. What seems to be the narrator's or persona's attitude toward the image?

D. *Words.* Every substantial word in a poem may have more than one intended meaning, as used by the author. Because of this, the reader should look up many of these words in the dictionary and:
   1. Note all definitions that have the slightest connection with the poem.
   2. Note any changes in syntactical patterns in the poem.
   3. In particular, note those words that could possibly function as symbols or allusions, and refer to any appropriate sources for further information.

E. *Meter, rhyme, structure, and tone.* In scanning the poem, all elements of prosody should be noted by the reader. These elements are often used by a poet to manipulate the reader's emotions, and therefore they should be examined closely to arrive at the poet's specific intention.
   1. Does the basic meter follow a traditional pattern such as those found in nursery rhymes or folk songs?
   2. Are there any variations in the base meter? Such changes or substitutions are important thematically and should be identified.
   3. Are the rhyme schemes traditional or innovative, and what might their form mean to the poem?
   4. What devices has the poet used to create sound patterns (such as assonance and alliteration)?
   5. Is the stanza form a traditional or innovative one?
   6. If the poem is composed of verse paragraphs rather than stanzas, how do they affect the progression of the poem?

7. After examining the above elements, is the resultant tone of the poem casual or formal, pleasant, harsh, emotional, authoritative?

F. *Historical context*. The reader should attempt to place the poem into historical context, checking on events at the time of composition. Archaic language, expressions, images, or symbols should also be looked up.

G. *Themes and motifs*. By seeing the poem as a composite of emotion, intellect, craftsmanship, and tradition, the reader should be able to determine the themes and motifs (smaller recurring ideas) presented in the work. He or she should ask the following questions to help pinpoint these main ideas:
1. Is the poet trying to advocate social, moral, or religious change?
2. Does the poet seem sure of his or her position?
3. Does the poem appeal primarily to the emotions, to the intellect, or to both?
4. Is the poem relying on any particular devices for effect (such as imagery, allusion, paradox, hyperbole, or irony)?

BIBLIOGRAPHY

General Reference Sources

Biographical sources

Dictionary of Literary Biography. 254 vols. Detroit: Gale Research, 1978-   .

International Who's Who in Poetry and Poets' Encyclopaedia. Cambridge, England: International Biographical Centre, 1993.

Seymour-Smith, Martin, and Andrew C. Kimmens, eds. *World Authors, 1900-1950*. Wilson Authors Series. 4 vols. New York: H. W. Wilson, 1996.

Thompson, Clifford, ed. *World Authors, 1990-1995*. Wilson Authors Series. New York: H. W. Wilson, 1999.

Wakeman, John, ed. *World Authors, 1950-1970*. New York: H. W. Wilson, 1975.

_____. *World Authors, 1970-1975*. Wilson Authors Series. New York: H. W. Wilson, 1991.

Willhardt, Mark, and Alan Michael Parker, eds. *Who's Who in Twentieth Century World Poetry*. New York: Routledge, 2000.

Criticism

Brooks, Cleanth, and Robert Penn Warren. *Understanding Poetry*. 4th ed. Reprint. Fort Worth, Tex.: Heinle & Heinle, 2003.

Contemporary Literary Criticism. Detroit: Gale Research, 1973-   .

Day, Gary. *Literary Criticism: A New History*. Edinburgh, Scotland: Edinburgh University Press, 2008.

Habib, M. A. R. *A History of Literary Criticism: From Plato to the Present*. Malden, Mass.: Wiley-Blackwell, 2005.

Jason, Philip K., ed. *Masterplots II: Poetry Series, Revised Edition*. 8 vols. Pasadena, Calif.: Salem Press, 2002.

Lodge, David, and Nigel Wood. *Modern Criticism and Theory*. 3d ed. New York: Longman, 2008.

Magill, Frank N., ed. *Magill's Bibliography of Literary Criticism*. 4 vols. Englewood Cliffs, N.J.: Salem Press, 1979.

MLA International Bibliography. New York: Modern Language Association of America, 1922-   .

Vedder, Polly, ed. *World Literature Criticism Supplement: A Selection of Major Authors from Gale's Literary Criticism Series*. 2 vols. Detroit: Gale Research, 1997.

Young, Robyn V., ed. *Poetry Criticism: Excerpts from Criticism of the Works of the Most Significant and Widely Studied Poets of World Literature*. 29 vols. Detroit: Gale Research, 1991.

POETRY DICTIONARIES AND HANDBOOKS

Carey, Gary, and Mary Ellen Snodgrass. *A Multicultural Dictionary of Literary Terms*. Jefferson, N.C.: McFarland, 1999.

Deutsch, Babette. *Poetry Handbook: A Dictionary of Terms*. 4th ed. New York: Funk & Wagnalls, 1974.

Drury, John. *The Poetry Dictionary*. Cincinnati, Ohio: Story Press, 1995.

Kinzie, Mary. *A Poet's Guide to Poetry*. Chicago: University of Chicago Press, 1999.

Lennard, John. *The Poetry Handbook: A Guide to Reading Poetry for Pleasure and Practical Criticism*. New York: Oxford University Press, 1996.

Matterson, Stephen, and Darryl Jones. *Studying Poetry*. New York: Oxford University Press, 2000.

Packard, William. *The Poet's Dictionary: A Handbook of Prosody and Poetic Devices*. New York: Harper & Row, 1989.

Preminger, Alex, et al., eds. *The New Princeton Encyclopedia of Poetry and Poetics*. 3d rev. ed. Princeton, N.J.: Princeton University Press, 1993.

Shipley, Joseph Twadell, ed. *Dictionary of World Literary Terms, Forms, Technique, Criticism*. Rev. ed. Boston: George Allen and Unwin, 1979.

INDEXES OF PRIMARY WORKS

Frankovich, Nicholas, ed. *The Columbia Granger's Index to Poetry in Anthologies*. 11th ed. New York: Columbia University Press, 1997.

_____. *The Columbia Granger's Index to Poetry in Collected and Selected Works*. New York: Columbia University Press, 1997.

Hazen, Edith P., ed. *Columbia Granger's Index to Poetry*. 10th ed. New York: Columbia University Press, 1994.

Hoffman, Herbert H., and Rita Ludwig Hoffman, comps. *International Index to Recorded Poetry*. New York: H. W. Wilson, 1983.

Kline, Victoria. *Last Lines: An Index to the Last Lines of Poetry*. 2 vols. Vol. 1, *Last Line Index, Title Index*; Vol. 2, *Author Index, Keyword Index*. New York: Facts On File, 1991.

Marcan, Peter. *Poetry Themes: A Bibliographical Index to Subject Anthologies and Related Criticisms in the English Language, 1875-1975*. Hamden, Conn.: Linnet Books, 1977.

Poem Finder. Great Neck, N.Y.: Roth, 2000.

POETICS, POETIC FORMS, AND GENRES

Attridge, Derek. *Poetic Rhythm: An Introduction*. New York: Cambridge University Press, 1995.

Brogan, T. V. F. *Verseform: A Comparative Bibliography*. Baltimore: Johns Hopkins University Press, 1989.

Fussell, Paul. *Poetic Meter and Poetic Form*. Rev. ed. New York: McGraw-Hill, 1979.
Hollander, John. *Rhyme's Reason*. 3d ed. New Haven, Conn.: Yale University Press, 2001.
Padgett, Ron, ed. *The Teachers and Writers Handbook of Poetic Forms*. 2d ed. New York: Teachers & Writers Collaborative, 2000.
Pinsky, Robert. *The Sounds of Poetry: A Brief Guide*. New York: Farrar, Straus and Giroux, 1998.
Preminger, Alex, and T. V. F. Brogan, eds. *New Princeton Encyclopedia of Poetry and Poetics*. 3d ed. Princeton, N.J.: Princeton University Press, 1993.
Turco, Lewis. *The New Book of Forms: A Handbook of Poetics*. Hanover, N.H.: University Press of New England, 1986.
Williams, Miller. *Patterns of Poetry: An Encyclopedia of Forms*. Baton Rouge: Louisiana State University Press, 1986.

WAR POETS

Baird, Jay W. *Hitler's War Poets: Literature and Politics in the Third Reich*. New York: Cambridge University Press, 2008.
Boland, Eavan, ed. and trans. *After Every War: Twentieth-Century Women Poets*. Princeton, N.J.: Princeton University Press, 2004.
Quinn, Patrick, ed. *British Poets of the Great War: Brooke, Rosenberg, Thomas: A Documentary Volume*. Dictionary of Literary Biography 216. Detroit: Gale Group, 2000.
Reilly, Catherine W. *English Poetry of the Second World War: A Biobibliography*. Boston: G. K. Hall, 1986.

GUIDE TO ONLINE RESOURCES

Web Sites

The following sites were visited by the editors of Salem Press in 2010. Because URLs frequently change, the accuracy of these addresses cannot be guaranteed; however, long-standing sites, such as those of colleges and universities, national organizations, and government agencies, generally maintain links when their sites are moved.

Academy of American Poets
http://www.poets.org
    The mission of the Academy of American Poets is to "support American poets at all stages of their careers and to foster the appreciation of contemporary poetry." The academy's comprehensive Web site features information on poetic schools and movements; a Poetic Forms Database; an Online Poetry Classroom, with educator and teaching resources; an index of poets and poems; essays and interviews; general Web resources; links for further study; and more.

Contemporary British Writers
http://www.contemporarywriters.com/authors
    Created by the British Council, this site offers profiles of living writers of the United Kingdom, the Republic of Ireland, and the Commonwealth. Information includes biographies, bibliographies, critical reviews, and news about literary prizes. Photographs are also featured. Users can search the site by author, genre, nationality, gender, publisher, book title, date of publication, and prize name and date.

LiteraryHistory.com
http://www.literaryhistory.com
    This site is an excellent source of academic, scholarly, and critical literature about eighteenth, nineteenth, and twentieth century American and English writers. It provides individual pages for twentieth century literature and alphabetical lists of authors that link to articles, reviews, overviews, excerpts of works, teaching guides, podcasts, and other materials.

Literary Resources on the Net
http://andromeda.rutgers.edu/~jlynch/Lit
    Jack Lynch of Rutgers University maintains this extensive collection of links to Web sites that are useful to researchers, including numerous sites about American and English literature. This collection is a good place to begin online research about poetry, as it

links to other sites with broad ranges of literary topics. The site is organized chronologically, with separate pages about twentieth century British and Irish literature. It also has separate pages providing links to Web sites about American literature and to women's literature and feminism.

LitWeb
http://litweb.net
    LitWeb provides biographies of hundreds of world authors throughout history that can be accessed through an alphabetical listing. The pages about each writer contain a list of his or her works, suggestions for further reading, and illustrations. The site also offers information about past and present winners of major literary prizes.

The Modern Word: Authors of the Libyrinth
http://www.themodernword.com/authors.html
    The Modern Word site, although somewhat haphazard in its organization, provides a great deal of critical information about writers. The "Authors of the Libyrinth" page is very useful, linking author names to essays about them and other resources. The section of the page headed "The Scriptorium" presents "an index of pages featuring writers who have pushed the edges of their medium, combining literary talent with a sense of experimentation to produce some remarkable works of modern literature."

Outline of American Literature
http://www.america.gov/publications/books/outline-of-american-literature.html
    This page of the America.gov site provides access to an electronic version of the ten-chapter volume *Outline of American Literature*, a historical overview of poetry and prose from colonial times to the present published by the Bureau of International Information Programs of the U.S. Department of State.

Poetry Foundation
http://www.poetryfoundation.org
    The Poetry Foundation, publisher of *Poetry* magazine, is an independent literary organization. Its Web site offers links to essays; news; events; online poetry resources, such as blogs, organizations, publications, and references and research; a glossary of literary terms; and a Learning Lab that includes poem guides and essays on poetics.

Poet's Corner
http://theotherpages.org/poems
    The Poet's Corner, one of the oldest text resources on the Web, provides access to about seven thousand works of poetry by several hundred different poets from around the world. Indexes are arranged and searchable by title, name of poet, or subject. The

site also offers its own resources, including "Faces of the Poets"—a gallery of portraits—and "Lives of the Poets"—a growing collection of biographies.

Representative Poetry Online
http://rpo.library.utoronto.ca

This award-winning resource site, maintained by Ian Lancashire of the Department of English at the University of Toronto in Canada, has several thousand English-language poems by hundreds of poets. The collection is searchable by poet's name, title of work, first line of a poem, and keyword. The site also includes a time line, a glossary, essays, an extensive bibliography, and countless links organized by country and by subject.

Voice of the Shuttle
http://vos.ucsb.edu

One of the most complete and authoritative places for online information about literature, Voice of the Shuttle is maintained by professors and students in the English Department at the University of California, Santa Barbara. The site provides countless links to electronic books, academic journals, literary association Web sites, sites created by university professors, and many other resources.

Voices from the Gaps
http://voices.cla.umn.edu/

Voices from the Gaps is a site of the English Department at the University of Minnesota, dedicated to providing resources on the study of women artists of color, including writers. The site features a comprehensive index searchable by name, and it provides biographical information on each writer or artist and other resources for further study.

ELECTRONIC DATABASES

Electronic databases usually do not have their own URLs. Instead, public, college, and university libraries subscribe to these databases, provide links to them on their Web sites, and make them available to library card holders or other specified patrons. Readers can visit library Web sites or ask reference librarians to check on availability.

Canadian Literary Centre

Produced by EBSCO, the Canadian Literary Centre database contains full-text content from ECW Press, a Toronto-based publisher, including the titles in the publisher's Canadian fiction studies, Canadian biography, and Canadian writers and their works series; *ECW's Biographical Guide to Canadian Novelists*; and *George Woodcock's Intro-*

duction to Canadian Fiction. Author biographies, essays and literary criticism, and book reviews are among the database's offerings.

Literary Reference Center

EBSCO's Literary Reference Center (LRC) is a comprehensive full-text database designed primarily to help high school and undergraduate students in English and the humanities with homework and research assignments about literature. The database contains massive amounts of information from reference works, books, literary journals, and other materials, including more than 31,000 plot summaries, synopses, and overviews of literary works; almost 100,000 essays and articles of literary criticism; about 140,000 author biographies; more than 605,000 book reviews; and more than 5,200 author interviews. It contains the entire contents of Salem Press's MagillOnLiterature Plus. Users can retrieve information by browsing a list of authors' names or titles of literary works; they can also use an advanced search engine to access information by numerous categories, including author name, gender, cultural identity, national identity, and the years in which he or she lived, or by literary title, character, locale, genre, and publication date. The Literary Reference Center also features a literary-historical time line, an encyclopedia of literature, and a glossary of literary terms.

MagillOnLiterature Plus

MagillOnLiterature Plus is a comprehensive, integrated literature database produced by Salem Press and available on the EBSCOhost platform. The database contains the full text of essays in Salem's many literature-related reference works, including *Masterplots, Cyclopedia of World Authors, Cyclopedia of Literary Characters, Cyclopedia of Literary Places, Critical Survey of Poetry, Critical Survey of Long Fiction, Critical Survey of Short Fiction, World Philosophers and Their Works, Magill's Literary Annual,* and *Magill's Book Reviews.* Among its contents are articles on more than 35,000 literary works and more than 8,500 poets, writers, dramatists, essayists, and philosophers; more than 1,000 images; and a glossary of more than 1,300 literary terms. The biographical essays include lists of authors' works and secondary bibliographies, and hundreds of overview essays examine and discuss literary genres, time periods, and national literatures.

Rebecca Kuzins; updated by Desiree Dreeuws

GEOGRAPHICAL INDEX

ENGLAND
    Blunden, Edmund, 55
    Brooke, Rupert, 74
    Fuller, Roy, 102
    Gurney, Ivor, 109
    Jones, David, 118
    Logue, Christopher, 123
    Owen, Wilfred, 138
    Rosenberg, Isaac, 176
    Sassoon, Siegfried, 183
    Thomas, Edward, 212

FRANCE
    Apollinaire, Guillaume, 26
    Aragon, Louis, 37
    Reverdy, Pierre, 166

GERMANY
    Brecht, Bertolt, 63

HUNGARY
    Ady, Endre, 8
    Petőfi, Sándor, 147

JAMAICA
    Simpson, Louis, 199

NIGERIA
    Achebe, Chinua, 4

ROMANIA
    Ady, Endre, 8

SPAIN
    Alberti, Rafael, 17

UNITED STATES
    Balaban, John, 48
    Ehrhart, W. D., 83
    Freneau, Philip, 91
    McDonald, Walt, 129
    Seeger, Alan, 194
    Simpson, Louis, 199
    Weigl, Bruce, 219

WALES
    Jones, David, 118

WEST INDIES
    Simpson, Louis, 199

CATEGORY INDEX

AMERICAN COLONIAL POETS
  Freneau, Philip, 91
AMERICAN EARLY NATIONAL POETS
  Freneau, Philip, 91
AVANT-GARDE POETS
  Apollinaire, Guillaume, 26
  Aragon, Louis, 37
  Reverdy, Pierre, 166

CHILDREN'S/YOUNG ADULT POETRY
  Fuller, Roy, 102
  Logue, Christopher, 123
CONCRETE POETRY
  Apollinaire, Guillaume, 26
CUBISM
  Apollinaire, Guillaume, 26
  Reverdy, Pierre, 166

DADAISM
  Aragon, Louis, 37
DEEP IMAGE POETS
  Simpson, Louis, 199
DRAMATIC MONOLOGUES
  Jones, David, 118

ELEGIES
  Blunden, Edmund, 55
  Brecht, Bertolt, 63
EPICS
  Logue, Christopher, 123
  Petőfi, Sándor, 147
EXPERIMENTAL POETS
  Reverdy, Pierre, 166
EXPRESSIONISM
  Brecht, Bertolt, 63

GAY AND LESBIAN CULTURE
  Sassoon, Siegfried, 183
GENERATION OF '27
  Alberti, Rafael, 17
GEORGIAN POETS
  Blunden, Edmund, 55
  Brooke, Rupert, 74
  Sassoon, Siegfried, 183
GOERGIAN POETS
  Rosenberg, Isaac, 176

JEWISH CULTURE
  Rosenberg, Isaac, 176
  Sassoon, Siegfried, 183

LIGHT VERSE
  Logue, Christopher, 123
LOVE POETRY
  Ady, Endre, 8
  Petőfi, Sándor, 147
  Simpson, Louis, 199
LYRIC POETRY
  Ady, Endre, 8
  Alberti, Rafael, 17
  Apollinaire, Guillaume, 26
  Blunden, Edmund, 55
  Petőfi, Sándor, 147

MODERNISM
  Blunden, Edmund, 55
  Brooke, Rupert, 74
  Fuller, Roy, 102
  Jones, David, 118
  Owen, Wilfred, 138
  Rosenberg, Isaac, 176
  Sassoon, Siegfried, 183

NARRATIVE POETRY
    Gurney, Ivor, 109
    McDonald, Walt, 129
    Petőfi, Sándor, 147
NATURE POETRY
    Blunden, Edmund, 55
    Gurney, Ivor, 109
    Thomas, Edward, 212

OCCASIONAL VERSE
    Ehrhart, W. D., 83

PATTERN POETS
    Apollinaire, Guillaume, 26
POLITICAL POETS
    Achebe, Chinua, 4
    Ady, Endre, 8
    Alberti, Rafael, 17
    Aragon, Louis, 37
    Balaban, John, 48
    Brecht, Bertolt, 63
    Ehrhart, W. D., 83
    Freneau, Philip, 91
    Logue, Christopher, 123
    Weigl, Bruce, 219
POSTMODERNISM
    Achebe, Chinua, 4
    Balaban, John, 48
    Fuller, Roy, 102
    McDonald, Walt, 129
PROSE POETRY
    Jones, David, 118
    Reverdy, Pierre, 166

RELIGIOUS POETRY
    Ady, Endre, 8
    Jones, David, 118
    McDonald, Walt, 129
    Sassoon, Siegfried, 183
ROMANTICISM, AMERICAN
    Freneau, Philip, 91

SATIRIC POETRY
    Logue, Christopher, 123
SOCIALIST REALISM
    Aragon, Louis, 37
SONNETS
    Brooke, Rupert, 74
    Fuller, Roy, 102
    Logue, Christopher, 123
    Seeger, Alan, 194
SURREALIST POETS
    Alberti, Rafael, 17
    Apollinaire, Guillaume, 26
    Aragon, Louis, 37
    Reverdy, Pierre, 166
SYMBOLIST POETS
    Apollinaire, Guillaume, 26

TOPOGRAPHICAL POETRY
    Freneau, Philip, 91

VERSE DRAMATIST
    Rosenberg, Isaac, 176

SUBJECT INDEX

A la pintura. See *To Painting*
A minden titkok verseibol. See *Of All Mysteries*
Achebe, Chinua, 4-7
   Christmas in Biafra, 6
   Collected Poems, 6
"Adlestrop" (Thomas), 215
Adventures in the Letter I (Simpson), 204
Ady, Endre, 8-16
   "Man in Inhumanity," 14
   New Verses, 11
   Of All Mysteries, 13
"After Our War" (Balaban), 50
Alberti, Rafael, 17-25
   "Ballad of the Lost Andalusian," 24
   Cal y canto, 20
   Concerning the Angels, 21
   "De los álamos y los sauces," 23
   Entre el clavel y la espada, 23
   Marinero en tierra, 20
   Retornos de lo vivo lejano, 23
   To Painting, 24
   To See You and Not to See You, 21
Alcools (Apollinaire), 32
Anathemata, The (Jones), 121
"Anthem for Doomed Youth" (Owen), 145
Apollinaire, Guillaume, 26-36
   Alcools, 32
   Bestiary, 32
   Calligrammes, 33
   "The New Spirit and the Poets," 26
Aragon, Louis, 37-47
   "Elsa's Eyes," 44
   "Poem to Shout in the Ruins," 42
   "You Who Are the Rose," 45
Archeology of the Circle (Weigl), 223
"Arms and the Boy" (Owen), 144

Arrivistes, The (Simpson), 201
"As the Team's Head-Brass" (Thomas), 214
At the End of the Open Road (Simpson), 203
"At the Great Wall of China" (Blunden), 60
Automatic writing, 41

"Bad Time for Poetry" (Brecht), 69
Balaban, John, 48-54
   "After Our War," 50
   Path, Crooked Path, 52
   "Sitting on Blue Mountain . . . ," 51
   "Words for My Daughter," 52
"Ballad of the Lost Andalusian" (Alberti), 24
Beautiful Wreckage (Ehrhart), 87
Best Hour of the Night, The (Simpson), 206
Bestiaire, Le. See *Bestiary*
Bestiary (Apollinaire), 32
Blunden, Edmund, 55-62
   "At the Great Wall of China," 60
   Poems, 1914-1930, 58
   The Shepherd, and Other Poems of Peace and War, 59
   Undertones of War, 60
"Bolond Istók" (Petőfi), 160
Brecht, Bertolt, 63-73
   "Bad Time for Poetry," 69
   Buckower Elegies, 70
   "In Dark Times," 69
   "Legend of the Origin of the Book Tao-Tê-Ching on Lao-tzû's Road into Exile," 69
   "Of Poor B. B.," 68
   "Remembering Marie A.," 67
   "Song of the Fort Donald Railroad Gang," 67
   Svendborg Poems, 70

Brooke, Rupert, 74-82
   1914, and Other Poems, 79
   "The Old Vicarage, Grantchester," 78
Brutus's Orchard (Fuller), 106
Buckower Elegies (Brecht), 70
Burning the Fence (McDonald), 131

Cal y canto (Alberti), 20
Caliban in Blue, and Other Poems
   (McDonald), 131
Calligrammes (Apollinaire), 33
"Canadians" (Gurney), 113
"Carrefour" (Reverdy), 169
Caviare at the Funeral (Simpson), 205
Chant des morts, Le (Reverdy), 173
Christmas in Biafra (Achebe), 6
Climbing the Divide (McDonald), 135
Clouds (Petőfi), 155
Cold Calls (Logue), 127
Collected Poems (Achebe), 6
Collected Poems, 1936-1961 (Fuller), 106
Concerning the Angels (Alberti), 21

"Dalaim" (Petőfi), 158
"De los álamos y los sauces" (Alberti), 23
"Dead Man's Dump" (Rosenberg), 180
Declension in the Village of Chung Luong
   (Weigl), 224
Distance We Travel, The (Ehrhart), 86
Dream of Governors, A (Simpson), 202
"Dug Out, The" (Sassoon), 190
"Dulce et Decorum Est" (Owen), 143

Ehrhart, W. D., 83-90
   Beautiful Wreckage, 87
   The Distance We Travel, 86
   Empire, 86
   A Generation of Peace, 85
   Mostly Nothing Happens, 87
   Rootless, 86

The Samisdat Poems, 86
Sleeping with the Dead, 88
To Those Who Have Gone Home Tired,
   86
"Elsa's Eyes" (Aragon), 44
Empire (Ehrhart), 86
"Enfin" (Reverdy), 173
Entre el clavel y la espada (Alberti), 23
Epitaphs and Occasions (Fuller), 105
"Erinnerung an die Maria A." *See*
   "Remembering Marie A."
"Et Maintenant" (Reverdy), 174
"Everyone Sang" (Sassoon), 190

Felhok. See Clouds
"First Letter to Calumpang" (Weigl), 223
"For God in My Sorrows" (McDonald), 134
Freneau, Philip, 91-101
   "On the Universality and Other Attributes
   of the God of Nature," 97
From the Joke Shop (Fuller), 107
Fuller, Roy, 102-108
   Brutus's Orchard, 106
   Collected Poems, 1936-1961, 106
   Epitaphs and Occasions, 105
   From the Joke Shop, 107
   "To M. S. Killed in Spain," 104
   "To My Brother," 104

Generation of Peace, A (Ehrhart), 85
"Generations" (Gurney), 111
Good News of Death, and Other Poems
   (Simpson), 201
"Guerre" (Reverdy), 170
Gurney, Ivor, 109-117
   "Canadians," 113
   "Generations," 111
   "To His Love," 112

Hammer of the Village, The (Petőfi), 154

"I Have a Rendezvous with Death" (Seeger), 197
"In Dark Times" (Brecht), 69
In Parenthesis (Jones), 120
In the Room We Share (Simpson), 207

János the Hero (Petőfi), 154
János Vitéz. See *Janos the Hero*
John the Hero. See *Janos the Hero*
Jones, David, 118-122
    The Anathemata, 121
    In Parenthesis, 120
    The Sleeping Lord, and Other Fragments, 121

"Legend of the Origin of the Book Tao-Tê-Ching on Lao-tzû's Road into Exile" (Brecht), 69
"Levél Várady Antalhoz" (Petőfi), 158
"Lines Written in Anticipation . . ." (Sassoon), 190
Logue, Christopher, 123-128
    Cold Calls, 127
    New Numbers, 126
    Selected Poems, 126

McDonald, Walt, 129-137
    Burning the Fence, 131
    Caliban in Blue, and Other Poems, 131
    Climbing the Divide, 135
    "For God in My Sorrows," 134
    A Thousand Miles of Stars, 136
"Main-Morte" (Reverdy), 172
"Man in Inhumanity" (Ady), 14
Marinero en tierra (Alberti), 20
"Mémoire" (Reverdy), 171
Moses (Rosenberg), 179
Mostly Nothing Happens (Ehrhart), 87

"Négy-ökrös szekér, A" (Petőfi), 156
"Nemzeti dal" (Petőfi), 162
New Numbers (Logue), 126
"New Spirit and the Poets, The" (Apollinaire), 26
New Verses (Ady), 11
"Night and Day" (Rosenberg), 178
1914, and Other Poems (Brooke), 79
"No One So Much as You" (Thomas), 216

"Ode in Memory of the American Volunteers Fallen for France" (Seeger), 196
Of All Mysteries (Ady), 13
"Of Poor B. B." (Brecht), 68
"Old Vicarage, Grantchester, The" (Brooke), 78
"On Receiving News of the War" (Rosenberg), 178
"On the Anniversary of Her Grace" (Weigl), 222
"On the Universality and Other Attributes of the God of Nature" (Freneau), 97
Owen, Wilfred, 138-146
    "Anthem for Doomed Youth," 145
    "Arms and the Boy," 144
    "Dulce et Decorum Est," 143
    "Strange Meeting," 143
    "To Poesy," 142
Owner of the House, The (Simpson), 208

Path, Crooked Path (Balaban), 52
People Live Here (Simpson), 206
Petőfi, Sándor, 147-165
    "Bolond Istók," 160
    Clouds, 155
    "Dalaim," 158
    The Hammer of the Village, 154
    János the Hero, 154
    "Levél Várady Antalhoz," 158
    "A Négy-ökrös szekér," 156
    "Nemzeti dal," 162

"Reszket a bokor, mert," 158
"Rózsabokor a domboldalon," 160
"Szeptember végen," 159
"Szeretlek, kedvesem," 160
"Tündérálom," 156
"Poem to Shout in the Ruins" (Aragon), 42
"Poème à crier dans les ruines." *See* "Poem to Shout in the Ruins"
Poems, 1914-1930 (Blunden), 58

"Remembering Marie A." (Brecht), 67
"Repression of War Experience" (Sassoon), 189
"Reszket a bokor, mert" (Petőfi), 158
Retornos de lo vivo lejano (Alberti), 23
Reverdy, Pierre, 166-175
  "Carrefour," 169
  Le Chant des morts, 173
  "Enfin," 173
  "Et Maintenant," 174
  "Guerre," 170
  "Main-Morte," 172
  "Mémoire," 171
Rootless (Ehrhart), 86
Rosenberg, Isaac, 176-182
  "Dead Man's Dump," 180
  Moses, 179
  "Night and Day," 178
  "On Receiving News of the War," 178
  Youth, 178
"Rózsabokor a domboldalon" (Petőfi), 160

Samisdat Poems, The (Ehrhart), 86
Sassoon, Siegfried, 183-193
  "The Dug Out," 190
  "Everyone Sang," 190
  "Lines Written in Anticipation . . . ," 190
  "Repression of War Experience," 189
  Sequences, 191
  "They," 189

"Schlechte Zeit für Lyrik." *See* "Bad Time for Poetry"
Searching for the Ox (Simpson), 205
Seeger, Alan, 194-198
  "I Have a Rendezvous with Death," 197
  "Ode in Memory of the American Volunteers Fallen for France," 196
Selected Poems (Logue), 126
Selected Poems (Simpson), 204
Sequences (Sassoon), 191
Shepherd, and Other Poems of Peace and War, The (Blunden), 59
Simpson, Louis, 199-211
  Adventures in the Letter I, 204
  The Arrivistes, 201
  At the End of the Open Road, 203
  The Best Hour of the Night, 206
  Caviare at the Funeral, 205
  A Dream of Governors, 202
  Good News of Death, and Other Poems, 201
  In the Room We Share, 207
  The Owner of the House, 208
  People Live Here, 206
  Searching for the Ox, 205
  Selected Poems, 204
"Sitting on Blue Mountain . . ." (Balaban), 51
Sleeping Lord, and Other Fragments, The (Jones), 121
Sleeping with the Dead (Ehrhart), 88
Sobre los ángeles. See *Concerning the Angels*
"Song of Napalm" (Weigl), 221
"Song of the Fort Donald Railroad Gang" (Brecht), 67
"Strange Meeting" (Owen), 143
Svendborg Poems (Brecht), 70
"Szeptember végen" (Petőfi), 159
"Szeretlek, kedvesem" (Petőfi), 160

"They" (Sassoon), 189
Thomas, Edward, 212-218
    "Adlestrop," 215
    "As the Team's Head-Brass," 214
    "No One So Much as You," 216
Thousand Miles of Stars, A (McDonald), 136
"Three Memories of Heaven" (Alberti), 21
"To His Love" (Gurney), 112
"To M. S. Killed in Spain" (Fuller), 104
"To My Brother" (Fuller), 104
To Painting (Alberti), 24
"To Poesy" (Owen), 142
To See You and Not to See You (Alberti), 21
To Those Who Have Gone Home Tired (Ehrhart), 86
Triolet, Elsa, 40
"Tündérálom" (Petőfi), 156

Undertones of War (Blunden), 60
Unraveling Strangeness, The (Weigl), 223

Verte y no verte. See *To See You and Not to See You*
Vietnam War
    John Balaban, 48
    W. D. Ehrhart, 83
    Bruce Weigl, 221

Weigl, Bruce, 219-227
    Archeology of the Circle, 223
    Declension in the Village of Chung Luong, 224
    "First Letter to Calumpang," 223
    "On the Anniversary of Her Grace," 222
    "Song of Napalm," 221
    The Unraveling Strangeness, 223
"Words for My Daughter" (Balaban), 52
World War I
    Guillaume Apollinaire, 34
    Edmund Blunden, 57

"Yeux d'Elsa, Les." *See* "Elsa's Eyes"
"You Who Are the Rose" (Aragon), 45
Youth (Rosenberg), 178